An Introduction
to Biblical
Hermeneutics

An Introduction to Biblical Hermeneutics

THE SEARCH FOR MEANING

Walter C. Kaiser, Jr.
and
Moisés Silva

ZondervanPublishingHouse
Academic and Professional Books
Grand Rapids, Michigan

A Division of HarperCollinsPublishers

Requests for information should be addressed to:
Zondervan Publishing House
Academic and Professional Books
Grand Rapids, Michigan 49530

Interior design by James E. Ruark
Cover design by Art Jacobs

Library of Congress Cataloging-in-Publication Data

Kaiser, Walter C.
    An introduction to biblical hermeneutics : the search for meaning / Walter C. Kaiser, Jr., and Moisés Silva.
        p.   cm.
    Includes bibliographical reference (p. xxx-xxx) and index.
    ISBN 0-310-53090-3 (alk. paper)
    1. Bible—Hermeneutics. 2. Hermeneutics—Religious aspects—Christianity. I. Silva, Moisés. II. Title.
BS476.K33   1994   93-33915
220.6'01—dc20   CIP

Printed in the United States of America

94 95 96 97 98 99 / DH / 10 9 8 7 6 5 4 3 2 1

This edition is printed on acid-free paper and meets the American National Standards Institute Z39.48 standard.

To
Dr. Arthur and Alice Holmes,
extraordinary servants of Christ,
with appreciation for academic and
spiritual counsel during college and for lifelong friendship.
Walter C. Kaiser, Jr.

A Tía Fina.
Moisés Silva

Contents

Preface

Just as Bernard Ramm's *Protestant Biblical Interpretation* was written in 1956 for a broad spectrum of Bible readers, so *An Introduction to Biblical Hermeneutics* has sought to engage that same breadth of lay and professional readers by assisting them in understanding the biblical texts. However, the changes in the way texts are understood have been nothing less than catastrophic in the short time since Ramm wrote his volume. Almost every assumption that Ramm made has been challenged and tested by the new winds of modernity and post-modernity. So severe have the currents of thought changed previous patterns of thinking that one might even wonder (though, to our minds, just for a moment) if the reader of this preface is able to understand what we have said so far! The fact is that our day is characterized, as our subtitle notes, by *The Search for Meaning*.

The distinctiveness of this volume, in a field that has suddenly become somewhat crowded with recent entries after an extended period of little publication, can be found in (1) the *uniqueness* of our approach, (2) the way we state the *urgency* of the hour and the need for such a work as we have presented here, and (3) the attention we have given to making this volume *useful* to both the lay reader and, especially in part 4, the more advanced student.

Our approach is so startling that some may even have looked twice when they saw the names Kaiser and Silva together as joint authors, feeling that these two do not seem to fit easily together. But that is why this volume is unique. It is not a case in which two or three authors, having identical or fairly similar viewpoints on issues of interpretation, decide to write a volume that presents a single point of view. Instead, we have dared to write a single textbook on biblical hermeneutics knowing that we each understand the process of interpretation differently in some key areas that represent the most critical points of discussion in interpretation today. In this way, the readers of our text do not get a party line, as it were, but are called upon to come up with their own conclusions after eavesdropping on a vibrant conversation between two writers who dare to agree to disagree (at a few critical points) agreeably. Scholarship—yes, even evangelical scholarship—would be much better off if we had more examples of scholars engaging in such experiments. Let the readers be advised, however: There are more areas that we agree about than disagree, including such fundamental matters as the authority of Scripture and the primacy of authorial meaning. But some of our disagreements focus on the issues that are severe and critical for the future. The distinctive views of each author are especially evident in chapters 8, 11, and 14. It is in this spirit that we invite the readers' participation with us in a warm, but caring conversation.

While our tone is convivial, our readers must not mistake how great the stakes in their conclusions are. Whereas Ramm wrestled with questions such as the way in which naturalistic assumptions affect hermeneutics, our generation has so prized the value of the individual, a person's freedom and initiative, that the primary question is no longer, "Is it true?" but rather, "Does it matter?" Hence the question of relevancy has taken precedence over the question of "What does the text mean?" Indeed, the very meaning of meaning itself is extremely complex and debated vigorously by evangelicals and nonevangelicals alike. Whether any or all of the suggested meanings can be validated and what the criteria for such a validation might be are questions with which we modern readers of the Bible are feeling an increasing discomfort. Meanwhile, a generation waits to hear a word from God. It is almost like the old philosophical conundrum: Did the tree that fell in the forest make any noise if no one heard it fall? In our case the conundrum goes thus: Did God actually disclose and reveal anything to his prophets and apostles if they did not understand some (or many) of the things they wrote and if we, their readers, have so many differences of opinion about what was communicated? That is why this conversation is so urgent and critical. The results of this debate will so shape the next generation of believers that it may easily qualify as the top megatrend in evangelical theology.

But this volume does more than focus on the critical issues. It takes seriously that aspect of the modern clamor for relevancy that we think is legitimate and was part of the divine intention all along. We are concerned to help readers answer the question, "What does it matter?" We believe that the interpretive process is not completed when we have stated what the author was trying to say; instead, we believe that interpretation and exegesis must also decide what is the current relevancy, application, and contemporary significance of this text. Whether all of this is part of the meaning process is the point at which we differ among ourselves—but that issue surely is dwarfed by the greater need to find ways to accomplish it. Therefore, instead of writing a book that merely analyzes the problem, we have decided that we should also offer the best help we are capable of by showing both laypersons and scholars how to derive the contemporary usefulness from the interpretation of various types of biblical texts. Surprisingly enough, the scholar may be at more of a disadvantage when it comes to this step of the meaning process than the layperson who has been asking for this "bottom-line" type of mentality all along!

Finally, we trust that this volume will not detract from your primary focus on the Scriptures themselves. Our desire has been to give you as brief and as straightforward a discussion of the issues and methods as possible and then to leave you alone in the presence of the text of Scripture and the ministry of the Holy Spirit. May this pleasure and joy in the Word and the Sovereign God of the Word be yours in the days to come.

A special word of thanks is due to Leonard G. Goss, imprint editor, for his enthusiasm during the early days of this project; James E. Ruark, managing senior editor, for his patience and assistance in the final production of this volume; and Stanley N. Gundry, editor-in-chief, for his proposing this project in the first place.

Abbreviations

AB	Anchor Bible
AJT	*Asia Journal of Theology*
ATR	*Anglican Theological Review*
AV	Authorized (King James) Version
BAGD	W. Bauer, W. F. Arndt, F. W. Gingrich, and F. W. Danker, *Greek-English Lexicon of the New Testament*
BJRL	*Bulletin of the John Rylands University Library*
CTJ	*Calvin Theological Journal*
CTQ	*Concordia Theological Quarterly*
GiC	*Gospel in Context*
HUCA	*Hebrew Union College Annual*
ICC	International Critical Commentary
IDPSup	*Interpreter's Dictionary of the Bible,* supp. vol.
IJFM	*International Journal of Frontier Missions*
JBC	*Jerome Biblical Commentary,* ed. R. E. Brown et al.
JBL	*Journal of Biblical Literature*
JETS	*Journal of the Evangelical Theological Society*
JR	*Journal of Religion*
JTVI	*Journal of the Transactions of the Victorian Institute*
KJV	King James (Authorized) Version
LB	*Linguistica Biblica*
LCC	Library of Christian Classics
NIV	New International Version
NTS	*New Testament Studies*
SBET	*Scottish Bulletin of Evangelical Theology*
SBLDS	Society of Biblical Literature Dissertation Series
SR	*Studies in Religion/Sciences religieuses*
TJ	*Trinity Journal*
TSK	*Theologische Studien und Kritiken*
VT	*Vetus Testamentum*
WBC	Word Biblical Commentary
WTJ	*Westminster Theological Journal*

PART 1

The Search for Meaning: Initial Directions

The very use of the term *hermeneutics* raises an important question: Why should Bible readers be expected to study principles of interpretation? In spite of what our day-to-day experience may suggest, the process involved in understanding a text is quite complicated. The difficulties surface especially when we try to read a book produced in a different culture or time, as some examples from Shakespeare can make clear. In the case of ancient documents written in other languages, we need to make a special effort to take into account their original setting through a method known as grammatico-historical exegesis. As a whole, the Bible is a fairly clear book to read, and it is helpful to specify in what areas the difficulties arise: language? literary style? application? Moreover, the divine character of Scripture suggests that we need to adopt some special principles that would not be relevant to the study of other writings.

CHAPTER 1

Who Needs Hermeneutics Anyway?

Moisés Silva

The term *hermeneutics* (as well as its more ambiguous and even mysterious cousin, *hermeneutic*) has become increasingly popular in recent decades. As a result, it has been pulled and stretched every which way. With so many writers using the word, it seems to behave as a moving target, and some readers have been known to suffer attacks of anxiety as they seek, in vain, to pin it down and figure out what it means.

Its traditional meaning is relatively simple: the discipline that deals with principles of interpretation. Some writers like to call it the *science* of interpretation; others prefer to speak of the *art* of interpretation (perhaps with the implication, "Either you've got it or you don't!"). Apart from such differences of perspective, the basic concern of hermeneutics is plain enough. It remains to be added, however, that when writers use the word, most frequently what they have in mind is *biblical* interpretation. Even when some other text is being discussed, the Bible likely lurks in the background.

This last observation raises an interesting question. Why should such a discipline be needed at all? We never had to take a class on "How to Interpret the Newspaper." No high school offers a course on "The Hermeneutics of Conversation." For that matter, even with regard to courses on Shakespeare or Homer, which certainly deal with the interpretation of literature, no hermeneutics prerequisite is ever listed. Why then are we told, all of a sudden in our academic training, that we need to become proficient in an exotic-sounding science if we want to understand the Bible?

One possible answer that may occur to us is that the Bible is a divine book, and so we require special training to understand it. But this solution simply will not work. As a Roman Catholic scholar has expressed it: "If anyone is able to speak in an absolutely unambiguous fashion and to make himself understood with irresistible efficacy, such a one is God; therefore, if there is any word that might not require a hermeneutics, it would be the divine word."[1] Protestants, for that matter, have always emphasized the doctrine of the *perspicuity* or clarity of the Scriptures. The Bible itself tells us that the essential prerequisite for understanding the things of God is having the Spirit of God (1 Cor. 2:11), and that the Christian, having received the anointing of the Spirit, does not even need a teacher (1 John 2:27).

It turns out, in fact, that we need hermeneutics not precisely because the Bible is a divine book but because, in addition to being divine, it is a *human* book. Strange though that may sound, such a way of looking at our problem can put us on the right track. Human language, by its very nature, is largely equivocal, that is, capable of being understood in more than one way. If it were not so, we would never doubt what people mean when they speak; if utterances could signify only one thing, we would hardly ever hear disputes about whether Johnny said this or that. In practice, to be sure, the number of words or sentences that create misunderstandings is a very small proportion of the total utterances by a given individual in a given day. What we need to appreciate, however, is that the *potential* for misinterpretation is almost always there.

To put it differently, we do need hermeneutics for texts other than the Bible. Indeed, we need principles of interpretation to understand trivial conversations and even nonlinguistic events—after all, the failure to understand someone's wink of the eye could spell disaster in certain circumstances. But then we are back to our original question. Why were we not required to take hermeneutics in second grade? Why is it that, in spite of that gap in our education, we almost always understand what our neighbor tells us?

The simple answer is that we *have* been taught hermeneutics all our lives, even from the day we were born. It may well be that the most important things we learn are those that we learn unconsciously. In short, as you begin a course in hermeneutics, you may be assured that you already know quite well the most basic principles of interpretation. Every time you read the newspaper or hear a story or analyze an event, you prove yourself to be a master in the art of hermeneutics!

That is perhaps a dangerous thing to say. You may be tempted to close

---

1. Luis Alonso-Schökel, *Hermenéutica de la Palabra* (Madrid: Cristandad, 1986), 1:83.

this "useless" book immediately and return it to the bookstore, hoping to get your money back. Yet the point needs to be made and emphasized. Other than enjoying a right relationship with God, the most fundamental principle of biblical interpretation consists in putting into practice what we do unconsciously every day of our lives. Hermeneutics is not primarily a question of learning difficult techniques. Specialized training has its place, but it is really quite secondary. What matters, we might say, is learning to "transpose" our customary interpretive routines to our reading of the Bible. Yet there precisely is where our problems begin.

For one thing, we must not think that what we do every day is all that simple. Before you could read a magazine, for example, you had to learn English. Do you think that's easy? Ask any foreigner who tried to learn English after adolescence. Remarkably, you went through that difficult and complicated process with outstanding success in the first few years of your life. By the time you were four or five, you—and every other human being not physically impaired—had already mastered hundreds and hundreds of phonological and grammatical rules. True, your vocabulary was rather limited, but learning vocabulary is the easiest part of language acquisition.

In addition, your mind has been receiving, day in and day out, countless numbers of impressions. They are the facts of history—primarily your personal experiences, but supplemented by the experiences of others, including information about the past—with all their associations, whether psychological, social, or whatever. In a way no less astonishing than language acquisition, your brain has carefully organized these millions of impressions, keeping some on the surface, others at a semiconscious level, still others in the equivalent of a trash can.

It is all an essential component of efficient interpretation. To follow up our somewhat fictional illustration: Every time you receive an impression, your mind verifies whether it is a fact already filed away; if not, it relates that new impression to previous ones so you can make sense of it. To use another common analogy, your brain is like a grid that filters all new data. If a previously unnoticed fact does not fit the grid, your brain has only two immediate choices: force it into the grid by distorting the evidence or reject it altogether. The latter is the unconscious equivalent of, "My mind is made up—don't bother me with the facts." There is, however, a third option: admit your ignorance and set the new fact aside until your grid is able to filter it.

We see, then, that our daily practice of interpretation is not so simple as we may have thought. It requires a fairly complex (though usually unconscious) process that focuses on *language* and *history*, using both terms in a fairly broad sense. Obviously, our understanding is curtailed to the extent that the language or the facts being interpreted are unfamiliar to us. If a lawyer uses technical legal language when seeking to strike up a conversation with a stranger in the subway, one can hardly expect much understanding to take place. Similarly, a person who has not kept up with developments in the U.S. government for an extended period of time will not be able to make sense of a newspaper editorial, or even of political cartoons.

The problem becomes more serious if there are significant linguistic and cultural differences between the speaker (or writer) and the hearer (or reader). Suppose that, having only a basic acquaintance with Shakespeare's writings, we decide to tackle *Othello*. From time to time we would come across passages containing words that we have never seen before or that seem to have very unusual meanings. For example:

> If I do prove her haggard,
> Though that her jesses were my dear heart-strings
> I'd whistle her off and let her down the wind
> To prey at fortune. . . . (3.3.260–63)

Even after we find out that *haggard* = "hawk" and that *jesses* = "fastenings," we may find it quite difficult to figure out Othello's meaning, namely, that should his wife be shown to be unfaithful, he would allow his heart to be broken by letting her go.

Consider a more puzzling problem. Earlier in the play the duke of Venice and some senators are discussing recent news regarding a Turkish fleet, but there is considerable discrepancy regarding the number of galleys involved. The duke then says:

> I do not so secure me in the error,
> But the main article I do approve
> In fearful sense. (1.3.10–12)

What may baffle us about a passage such as this one is that all the words are familiar to us—indeed, even the meanings of those words approximate modern usage—yet the total meaning seems to escape us. Unless we are quite familiar with Shakespearean literature, it may take us a while to interpret this statement correctly. In modern prose, "The fact that there is a discrepancy in the accounts gives me no sense of security; it is with alarm that I must give credence to the main point of the story."

The most insidious problems, however, arise when a word or phrase is familiar and the meaning we attach to it makes sense in the context, yet our ignorance about the history of the language misleads us. When Iago reports something that Cassio said in his sleep, Othello calls it monstrous. Iago reminds Othello that it was only a dream, to which the latter responds: "But this denoted a foregone conclusion" (3.3.429). In our day, the expression *a foregone conclusion* means "an inevitable result," and it is possible to make some sense of the passage if we take that to be the meaning here. In Elizabethan times, however, the expression simply meant "a previous experience"; Othello believes that what Cassio said in his sleep reflects something that had indeed taken place.

Those are the kinds of difficulties we encounter when reading a work written in our own language and produced within the general Western culture of which we are a part. When we approach the Bible, however, we see a book written neither in English nor in a modern language closely related to English. Moreover, we are faced with a text that is far removed from us in place and in time. It would indeed be astonishing if the Bible did not appear puzzling at times. We find, then, that with regard to both language and history, the interpretation of the Bible poses a challenge for us. Accordingly, an accurate understanding of Scripture requires what has come to be known as *grammatico-historical exegesis.*[2]

The term *exegesis* (used often by biblical scholars but seldom by specialists in other fields) is a fancy way of referring to interpretation. It implies that the explanation of the text has involved careful, detailed analysis. The description *grammatico-historical* indicates, of course, that this analysis must pay attention both to the language in which the original text was written and to the specific cultural context that gave rise to the text.

We cannot, for example, assume that the linguistic rules of English syntax or the nuances of English words correspond to those of New Testament Greek; otherwise, we run the risk of imposing our ideas on the biblical text. Similarly, if we fail to take note of the distinctive cultural features of Hebrew society or of the historical circumstances behind an Old Testament book, we allow our mental "filter"—that is, our preconceptions—to determine what the biblical passages may or may not mean.

To be sure, the attempt to bring our preconceptions into conformity with the biblical text has created an exceedingly large and complex scholarly discipline. Partly because the distance (both linguistic and historical) separating us from the Bible is so great; partly because the Bible is a rather long document written by many people over a long stretch of time; partly because the Bible has attracted the professional attention of many, many scholars during the last twenty centuries; partly because the Bible touches on the deepest problems faced by people everywhere—for these and other reasons,

---

2. Such terms as *grammatical-historical* and *historical-grammatical* are also used with the same meaning. Note, however, that the expression *historical-critical* has other, more controversial associations. See the discussions on the historical-critical method in chap. 2, p. 32, and chap. 13, pp. 235–37.

no literary document has given rise to a larger body of scholarly writing, involving specialized research of all sorts and generating heated debate.

Nevertheless, we must note again that there is no difference in principle between problems of biblical interpretation and the ones we confront day by day. Most of us do not say that we are practicing grammatico-historical exegesis when we read a letter from a relative, *but that is precisely what we are doing.* The difference is, so to speak, quantitative rather than qualitative. (For the moment, of course, we are focusing only on the human qualities of Scripture. The special questions related to the divine character of the Bible are yet to be dealt with.) In other words, when we read the Bible we come across a much larger number of details about which we are ignorant than is the case when we interpret contemporary English texts.

That way of putting it, by the way, helps us appreciate that the problems of biblical interpretation are usually *our* problems, not the Bible's! While there are indeed some passages in Scripture that, because of their subject matter, are intrinsically difficult to understand, most passages do not at all belong in this category. Fundamentally, the Bible is quite a simple and clear book. We, however, are sinful and ignorant. Whether because of our limitations or our laziness, we often fail to bridge the distance that separates us from the biblical text, and that is what gets us into trouble.

But now, just how difficult is it for most of us to understand the Bible? Very large portions of Scripture consist of straightforward narratives. In these texts, only rarely do we come across a word that really stumps us, or a grammatical oddity that cannot be sorted out. (To put it differently, all the standard translations render these passages in essentially the same way.) Moreover, our information regarding the historical setting is usually quite adequate to make sense of such historical texts. Why, then, so much debate about biblical interpretation?

We may be able to answer that question if we consider a specific and fairly typical example. In Matthew 8:23–27 we read the brief and well-known story of Jesus and his disciples getting into a boat on the Sea of Galilee. While Jesus was sleeping, a sudden storm began to shake the boat. The disciples woke Jesus and asked him to save them. Jesus rebuked them for their little faith and proceeded to calm the waves. Astonished, the disciples said, "What kind of man is this? Even the winds and the waves obey him!"

The question about the meaning of this passage can be considered at various levels. Let us take them one at a time.

1. At the *linguistic* level, we meet no difficulties at all. Every Greek word in this passage is widely and clearly attested. Though translators may differ slightly as to which English words best represent the corresponding

Greek terms, there is no real debate about what those Greek words mean. Similarly, no rare grammatical forms occur.

2. With regard to the *historical* setting (culture, geography, etc.), there is also no dispute. The reference to "the lake" (so NIV; lit., "the sea") is certainly to Lake Gennesaret, or the Sea of Galilee. We are also well informed regarding the sudden storms that arise in that region.

3. The "meaning" of the passage, however, includes more than the bare facts of the story. Usually we are interested in the *teaching* of the passage. Here again, however, the primary thrust of the story is crystal clear. The event demonstrates the great power of Jesus, so that there was no need for the disciples to despair.

4. But what about the *historicity* of the narrative? Many hermeneutical debates focus precisely on this question. In the present case, it arises for two reasons. In the first place, a comparison of this narrative with the parallel passages (Mark 4:35–41; Luke 8:22–25) reveals some interesting differences. Did the event occur at the point in Jesus' ministry where Matthew places it, or was it right after Jesus spoke the parables of the kingdom, as Mark tells us? Were the disciples respectful, as Matthew seems to portray them, or were they more impulsive (cf. Mark 4:38)? In the second place, many moderns reject the possibility of miracles. If supernatural occurrences are out of the question, then certainly this passage will be interpreted in a way different from its apparent meaning.

5. Still another level of meaning arises when we distinguish the historical event itself from the *literary setting* in which we read about the event. This point is made especially clear if we again compare Matthew with the other gospels. For example, the fact that Matthew places the story right after two incidents connected with discipleship (Matt. 8:18–22) may tell us something of importance. When we notice that the story itself is introduced with the statement that "his disciples *followed* him" (words not found in Mark or Luke), we may reasonably infer that one of the reasons Matthew relates the story is to teach us about discipleship, which is an important theme in the whole gospel. (Note, however, that the author's intention is very much part of the first two items above. The distinctions we are drawing here can become somewhat artificial.)

6. In addition to literary context, we need to keep in mind the broader *canonical context,* that is, how does the passage relate to the whole canon (the complete collection) of Scripture? To ask this question is to move toward the concerns of systematic theology. How does our Lord's rebuke of the disciples fit into the general biblical teaching about faith? Does Jesus' power over nature tell us something about his deity? Such queries are certainly part of hermeneutics broadly considered.

7. But we may go even beyond the boundaries of Scripture itself and consider *the history of interpretation*. While it is very important to distinguish the meaning of the biblical text from the opinions of subsequent readers, there is in fact a close connection, since today we stand at the end of a long tradition. It is not really possible to jump over the last twenty centuries as though they had not transpired. Whether we are aware of it or not, the history of interpretation has influenced us directly or indirectly. The more we are aware of this fact, the easier it is to identify and reject those interpretations that we may find unacceptable. What needs pointing out, however, is that all of us quite frequently, though unconsciously, assume that a specific interpretation is the meaning of the text, when in fact we have simply assimilated (through sermons, conversations, etc.) what the history of the church has preserved.

8. Finally, we must consider "what the passage means to me," that is, the *present significance* of the passage.[3] Traditionally, this step has been described as *application* and has been distinguished quite sharply from the *meaning* of the text. In recent decades, however, a number of influential writers—not only in the field of theology but also in philosophy and literary criticism—have protested that the distinction does not hold. It has been argued, for example, that if we do not know how to apply a command of Scripture to our daily lives, then we cannot really claim to know what that passage means.[4] To reject the distinction between meaning and application seems an extreme position, but there is no doubt a measure of truth in it (notice that this eighth category is very similar to the third). Certainly, when most Christians read the Bible they want to know what to do with what they read. We may also consider that the extent to which the Bible affects our lives is at least a measure of how much we have understood it.

What do we learn from these various levels of meaning? For one thing, we begin to appreciate why in one sense the Bible is quite clear, while in another sense its interpretation can become complicated. As far as grammatico-historical exegesis is concerned (primarily levels 1 and 2, but also partially 3 and 5), the story of the stilling of the storm is indeed a simple narrative. In that respect, the story is quite typical of what we find in the Bible as a whole. To be sure, some of the poetic passages of the Old Testament present serious linguistic difficulties; the visions of the book of Revelation are not always plain; we would like to have more historical data relating to the book of Genesis; and so on. It is a little misleading, however, to focus so much on the

3. Sometimes the term *contextualization* is used to describe this point, emphasizing our need to see the relevance of the passage in our own context.
4. See chap. 13, sect. 4 ("The Role of the Reader").

problem passages that we forget how clear most of Scripture is. (We need to keep reminding ourselves of the essential clarity of the biblical message because a textbook on biblical interpretation, by its very nature, focuses on the problems.)

In the second place, the eightfold distinction above may help us understand why many scholars who do not themselves profess the Christian faith (at least not in an evangelical sense) are able to write helpful commentaries and otherwise interpret the Bible. An atheist, for example, may reject the possibility of miracles (and thus completely "misunderstand" level 4) while being able to give a superb exposition of the first two or three levels. In contrast, a Christian of great piety but with little theological maturity may be able to understand the significance of a passage for his or her life (level 8) while having a defective theological knowledge of the nature of faith (level 6).

We should emphasize, however, that the distinctions we have drawn are a little contrived. Most interpreters are seldom conscious of them. Besides, the various levels are so closely intertwined that isolating any one of them is an artificial procedure. For example, it is not uncommon to hear it said that anyone, even an unbeliever, can *interpret* the Bible and that only when he or she proceeds to *apply* it does the question of faith come in. There is a measure of truth in that formulation, but the distinction seems too simple. After all, can anyone interpret the Bible in a completely dispassionate way? Since everyone (even an atheist) has some kind of faith commitment, doesn't that commitment always intrude itself on the exegetical process?

In any case, it should be clear that by categorizing these levels of meaning as we have done, we have almost imperceptibly moved from the human characteristics of Scripture to its divine character. Level 4 on historicity, for example, can hardly be dissociated from a reader's views about biblical inspiration. Level 6 on canonical setting has little weight for someone who is not persuaded of the divine unity of Scripture. Finally, level 8 implies that when we read the Bible we recognize that it is the Word of God addressing us; surely if we have not appropriated God's message, we may consider ourselves hermeneutical failures.

But now, if the Bible is indeed a divine and unique book, should we not expect to use principles of interpretation that apply to it in a special way? By all means. Up to this point we have looked at what is often called *general hermeneutics,* that is, criteria that are relevant for the interpretation of anything. There is also such a thing as *biblical hermeneutics.* While some scholars dispute the need for such a particular discipline, no one who appreciates the special character of Scripture will want to ignore it.

1. In the first place, we must accept the principle that *only the Spirit of God knows the things of God,* as Paul points out in 1 Corinthians 2:11 (part of a

rich portion of Scripture with broad implications). Consequently, only someone who has the Spirit can expect to acquire a truly satisfactory understanding of Scripture. It is fair to note that in that verse the apostle is not addressing directly the question of biblical interpretation.[5] Nevertheless, if we assume that the Bible is where we go to find out about "the things of God," then the relevance of Paul's words for biblical hermeneutics is undeniable.

2. This principle of the need for the indwelling Holy Spirit is emphasized from a different angle in 1 John 2:26–27b. The Christians to whom John is writing are being challenged by false teachers who wish to alter the apostolic message. These Christians, intimidated by the new teaching, have become vulnerable. They need instruction. So John says: "I am writing these things to you about those who are trying to lead you astray. As for you, the anointing you received from him remains in you, and you do not need anyone to teach you." Earlier, in verse 20, he had made clear what he had in mind: "But you have an anointing from the Holy One, and all of you know the truth." We then have a second principle of biblical interpretation: *the essence of God's revelation—the truth—is shared by all who believe. We need no one to supplement, let alone contradict, the message of the gospel.*

3. Indirectly, however, John's words lead us to a third criterion. The fact that Christians know the truth and that they should not let anyone lead them astray from it suggests that *God's message to us is consistent.* To put it differently, we should interpret the various parts of Scripture in a way that accords with its central teachings. Many in our day object to this principle. The fact that God used human authors to give us the Bible, so they argue, means that there must be contradictions in it. But a Word of God corrupted by the ignorance and inconsistencies of human beings would no longer be the Word of God. We may not pit one part of Scripture against another, nor may we interpret a detail of Scripture in a way that undermines its basic message.[6]

4. Finally, *a satisfactory interpretation of the Bible requires a submissive predisposition.* What motivates us to study the Bible? The desire to be erudite? Consider the psalmist's goal: "Give me understanding, and I will keep your law and obey it with all my heart" (Ps. 119:34). Our Lord said to the Jews who were puzzled by his teaching: "If anyone chooses to do God's will, he will find

---

5. It is even possible that apostolic inspiration is the issue here. Cf. Walter C. Kaiser, Jr., "A Neglected Text in Bibliology Discussions: I Corinthians 2:6–16," *WTJ* 43 (1980–81): 301–19.

6. Our recognition that the Bible is human as well as divine does imply that we should appreciate the distinctives of various authors, their different emphases, their unique formulations, and so on. We should not impose an artificial uniformity on the biblical text. How to implement this principle without undermining the unity of Scripture is sometimes difficult. Later chapters in this book address this question.

out whether my teaching comes from God or whether I speak on my own" (John 7:17). The desire to keep God's commandments, the determination to do God's will—this is the great prerequisite for true biblical understanding.

Who needs hermeneutics? We all do. This textbook is merely a guide to help you read the Bible as you read any other book, and at the same time to read it as you read no other book.

The definition of the meaning of a text changed dramatically in 1946 with the announcement that it is a fallacy to depend on what an author meant to say as a guide to determining what a text means. Since that time, three figures have tended to dominate the continuing refinements or protests to this announced fallacy: Hans-Georg Gadamer, Paul Ricoeur, and E. D. Hirsch. Gadamer stressed a "fusion of horizons" (almost in a recasting of the Hegelian dialectic in new terms), Ricoeur envisaged a whole new set of operations when communication is written down, while Hirsch claimed it was impossible to validate meaning if it was not connected with the author's truth-assertions and distinguished from significances of a text.

At present there are four main models for understanding the Bible: the proof-text method, the historical-critical method, the reader-response method, and the syntactical-theological method. The first is often naïve, the second has been judged sterile, the third is often reactionary to the second, and the fourth is holistic in involving both historical and practical applications.

Amid all this dramatic change, we have come to realize that the word "meaning" is currently used to include the referent, the sense, the author's intention, the significance a passage has, its value, and its entailment.

CHAPTER 2

The Meaning of Meaning

Walter C. Kaiser, Jr.

"When I use a word," Humpty Dumpty said in a rather scornful tone, "it means just what I choose it to mean—neither more nor less."

"The question is," said Alice, "whether you *can* make words mean so many different things."

"The question is," said Humpty Dumpty, "which is to be master, that's all."[1]

Alice states a valid principle: words often do possess a wide range of possible meanings, but the meaning they exhibit in a particular context and also share in the public forum cannot be disregarded or arbitrarily used interchangeably. But Alice is not alone in her struggle to interpret and understand what others are saying or writing. Modern scholars and lay readers often feel as confused as Alice did when it comes to figuring out what the meaning of some conversations and books may be. Actually, the problems are even more complicated than poor Alice suspected. In fact, as Lewis Carroll went on to tell us,

Alice was much too puzzled to say anything, so after a minute Humpty Dumpty began again.

---

1. Lewis Carroll, *Through the Looking Glass* (Philadelphia: Winston, 1923; reprint 1957), p. 213.

"Impenetrability! That's what I say!"

"Would you tell me, please," said Alice, "what that means?" . . .

"I meant by 'impenetrability' that we've had enough of that subject, and it would be just as well if you'd mention what you mean to do next, as I suppose you don't mean to stop here all the rest of your life."

"That's a great deal to make one word mean," Alice said, in a thoughtful tone.

"When I make a word do a lot of work like that," said Humpty Dumpty, "I always pay it extra."

"Oh!" said Alice. She was too much puzzled to make any other remark.[2]

Three New Humpty Dumptys

The problem of meaning changed dramatically in 1946. Two literary critics, W. K. Wimsatt and Monroe Beardsley, fired a shot that was eventually heard around the literary world. Wimsatt and Beardsley carefully distinguished three types of internal evidence for meaning, allowing for two types as being proper and useful. However, most of their qualifications and distinctions have now vanished, swallowed up in the popular version of the dogma that whatever an author meant or intended to say by his or her words is irrelevant to our obtaining the meaning of that text! Thus it happened, according to this new concept, that when a literary work was finished and delivered to its readers, it became autonomous from its author so far as its meaning was concerned.

The main fault of previous generations, according to the New Criticism, was the "intentional fallacy," that is, the fallacy of depending on what an author meant to say by his or her own use of the words in the written text as the source of meaning in that text.[3] But even more decisive moments in this century of hermeneutical changes were yet to come.

HANS-GEORG GADAMER

The modern theory of interpretation received another jolt in 1960 when Hans-Georg Gadamer published in Germany his book *Truth and*

2. Ibid., pp. 213–14.
3. W. K. Wimsatt and Monroe Beardsley, "The Intentional Fallacy," *Sewanee Review* 54 (1946): reprinted in William K. Wimsatt, Jr., *The Verbal Icon: Studies in the Meaning of Poetry* (New York: Farrar, Straus, 1958), pp. 3–18.

Method.[4] The title of his book contains the theme of his central thesis: Truth cannot reside in the reader's attempt to get back to the author's meaning, for this ideal cannot be realized because every interpreter has a new and different knowledge of the text in the reader's own historical moment.[5] From this central thesis flowed four affirmations[6] in his method:

1. Prejudice (German, *Vorurteil*) in interpretation cannot be avoided, but is to be encouraged if we are to grasp the whole of a work and not just the parts. This preunderstanding comes from ourselves and not from the text, since the text is indeterminate in meaning.
2. The meaning of a text always goes beyond its author, hence understanding is not a reproductive but a productive activity. The subject matter, not the author, is the determiner of the meaning.
3. The explanation of a passage is neither wholly the result of the interpreter's perspective nor wholly that of the original historical situation of the text. It is instead a "fusion of horizons" (German, *Horizontverschmellzung*). In the process of understanding, the two perspectives are subsumed into a new third alternative.
4. Past meanings cannot be reproduced in the present because the being of the past cannot become being in the present.

PAUL RICOEUR

In *Interpretation Theory,*[7] published in French in 1965, Paul Ricoeur challenged the notion that a text is simply "talk writ down," a dialogue placed on paper. Instead, in his view, writing fundamentally alters the nature of communication and sets up a whole new set of operations, including these four:

1. A text is semantically independent of the intention of its author. The text now means whatever it says, not necessarily what its author had meant.

4. Hans-Georg Gadamer, *Truth and Method: Elements of Philosophical Hermeneutics,* English trans. (New York: Seabury, 1975; reprint, Crossroad, 1982).
5. E. D. Hirsch, Jr., *Validity in Interpretation* (New Haven: Yale University Press, 1967), treats Gadamer's theory of interpretation in appendix 2, pp. 245–64.
6. For the general organization of the points relating to Gadamer and subsequently to Paul Ricoeur and E. D. Hirsch, I am indebted to Sandra M. Schneiders, "From Exegesis to Hermeneutics: The Problems of Contemporary Meaning in Scripture," *Horizons* 8 (1981): 23–39.
7. Paul Ricoeur, *Interpretation Theory: Discourse and the Surplus of Meaning,* English trans. (Fort Worth, Tex.: Texas Christian University Press, 1976).

2. Literary genres do more than classify texts; they actually give a code that shapes the way a reader will interpret that text.

3. Once texts have been written, their meanings are no longer determined by the understanding the original audiences had of those same texts. Each subsequent audience may now read its own situation into the text, for a text, unlike talk, transcends its original circumstances. The new readings are not any less valid. They must not be completely contradictory to the original audience's understanding, but they can be different, richer, or more impoverished.

4. Once a text is written, the sense of what it says is no longer directly related to its referent, that is, what it is about. The new meaning is freed from its situational limits, thereby opening up a whole new world of meaning.

E. D. HIRSCH

The only American to exert a major influence on hermeneutics during the epochal decade of the sixties was E. D. Hirsch, an English professor from the University of Virginia. Hirsch ran counter to the trends established by Wimsatt and Beardsley, Gadamer, and Ricoeur. He affirmed that the meaning of a literary work is determined by the author's intention.[8] Actually he was indebted to Emilio Betti, an Italian historian of law, who had founded an institute for interpretation theory in Rome in 1955. But it was Hirsch who popularized this view and therefore is best known for the following concepts:

1. Verbal meaning is whatever someone (usually the author) has willed to convey by a particular sequence of words and which can be shared by means of linguistic signs.

2. The author's truth-intention provides the only genuinely discriminating norm for ascertaining valid or true interpretations from invalid and false ones.

3. The first objective of hermeneutics is to make clear the text's verbal meaning, not its significance. Meaning is that which is represented by the text and what an author meant to say by the linguistic signs represented. Significance, by contrast, names a relationship between that meaning and a person, concept, situation, or any other possible number of things.

4. The meaning of text cannot change, but significance can and does

8. Hirsch, *Validity in Interpretation; idem, The Aims of Interpretation* (Chicago: University of Chicago Press, 1976).

change. If meaning were not determinate, then there would be no fixed norm by which to judge whether a passage was being interpreted correctly.

These are the major figures in the development of contemporary hermeneutical theory. The impact each has already had on our generation of interpreters—not to mention the future generations of interpreters of all types—has been nothing short of a major revolution in the way we assign meaning to written materials, including the Bible. Hardly any sphere of the interpretive process has escaped major restructuring and rethinking since the decade of the sixties. The life of the interpreter will never be what it was prior to the last half of this century. The effects of this revolution can be illustrated in four models for using the Bible.

Four Models for Understanding the Meaning of the Bible

THE PROOF-TEXT MODEL

The proof-text approach to understanding the Bible's meaning emphasizes the practical and pastoral side of life.[9] Typically a biblical meaning is needed for some real-life purpose, and the interpreter then goes searching for some scriptural texts that support the topical theme or pastoral position desired. The scriptural texts are valued more for their short, epigrammatic use of several key words that coincide with the topic or contemporary subject chosen than for the evidence that they actually bring from their own context. This method, insofar as it ignores context, is completely inadequate. At its worst, it tends to treat the Bible as if it were a magical book or perhaps no more than an anthology of sayings for every occasion. Individual texts, however, belong to larger units and address specific situations, coming out of historical purposes for which they were written and contexts for which they now are relevant.

The proof-text model often relies on a naive reading of the text. It may disregard the purpose for which the text was written, the historical conditioning in which it is set, and the genre conventions that shaped it. Consequently, this method is vulnerable to allegorization, psychologization, spiritualization, and other forms of quick-and-easy adjustments of the

9. For some of the concepts relating to the four models I am indebted to Schneiders, "From Exegesis to Hermeneutics," pp. 23–39.

scriptural words to say what one wishes them to say in the contemporary scene, ignoring their intended purpose and usage as determined by context, grammar, and historical background.

THE HISTORICAL-CRITICAL METHOD

Just as the proof-text method has enjoyed relative hegemony in many evangelical circles in the past, so the historical-critical method has held a similar status among scholarly interpreters of the twentieth century.

This method is more concerned with identifying the literary sources and social settings that gave birth to the smallest pieces of text rather than concentrating on any discussions about how normative these texts are for contemporary readers and for the church. This method has most frequently avoided any discussion of the relation of the text to divine revelation, its function as canon in the church, or its use in the devotional-theological-pastoral enterprise of Christians.

In this method, the theory of meaning and interpretation concludes with what the text meant in a distant time, place, and culture. This is allegedly a matter of disinterested research into the objective facts of grammar, history, and modern critical methodologies. The task of finding out what the text means today for the church and the individual is relegated to theologians and pastors—not to exegetes, critical scholars, and cognate linguists. Moreover, the interpretive task is declared complete after the text has been dissected and left—usually—disjointed in an ancient context with minimal, if any, significance given for its contemporary readers.

But time is proving to be against this truncated model of interpreting the Bible. The meaning of the text has been necessarily stunted from the start because of the method's refusal to offer any assistance as to how the church is to understand these texts. The pastoral and personal problem of application has been left unaddressed. The interpretation process was stopped when it was only partially completed. Moreover, this model emphasized its allegiance more to contemporary theories on the formation of the texts and the alleged Oriental and classical sources that lay behind them than to a consideration of what the text, both in its parts and in its totality, had to say.

THE READER-RESPONSE METHOD

In reaction to the stultifying deadness of the historical-critical method of determining meaning, a third method has grown up around the contributions of Gadamer and Ricoeur. While this view often sees the historical-critical method as one necessary and legitimate step in discerning what a text meant, it emphasizes the necessity of allowing the reader and interpreter to determine what the text now means—mostly in new, different, and partially conflicting meanings.

It was finally time for the church and the individual to receive some help from the exegete. The interpretive process could not be said to have accomplished its goal in any sense until it had involved the text and the original setting, along with the questions, meanings, and responses of the contemporary readers of that text.

Unfortunately, this method has so reacted against the abuses of the historical-critical method that, like many pendulum swings, it has also tended to go too far in the other direction. What has been lost in the shuffle is the primacy of authorial intention and most possibilities for testing the validity of the various suggested interpretations. All meanings now potentially have an equal footing, but few interpreters are now able to say which are normative. The result is that the church has continued to lose any sense of derived authority from the text, since no one can rank, much less determine, which is the correct or preferred meaning from the large number of competing meanings.

THE SYNTACTICAL-THEOLOGICAL METHOD

Old textbooks on hermeneutics tended to name the honored method of the eighteenth- and nineteenth-century interpreters the grammatico-historical method of exegesis. That name, however, has since proved to be somewhat misleading. When Karl A. G. Keil used this term in 1788, his term *grammatico* approximated what we mean by the term *literal,* by which he meant the simple, plain, direct, or ordinary sense. He was not referring simply to the "grammar" that was used. Likewise, the "historical" setting in which the text was penned was just as significant for this view, since it wanted to get as close as possible to the times and the settings in which the original author was speaking.

In order to stress more of the wholeness of a literary work and to emphasize that exegesis has not completed its work when the interpreter has parsed all the words and noted their natural and historical usages, we have labeled this fourth model for interpreting the Bible the syntactical-theological model. This model does the traditional grammatico-historical study of the text, followed by a study of its meaning that shows its theological relevance— both with respect to the rest of Scripture and with respect to its contemporary application. All too often, modern interpreters have failed to observe the syntactic and theological relationships that the words and concepts have in Scripture.

This model of understanding meaning stresses the need for taking whole pericopes or complete units of discussion as the basis for interpreting a text. The key interpretive decisions revolve around how the syntax of phrases, clauses, and sentences contributes to the formation of the several paragraphs that form the total block of text on that subject or unit of thought. Because the Bible purports to be a word from God, the task of locating meaning is not finished until one apprehends the purpose, scope, or reason (indeed, the theology) for which that text was written.

Aspects of Meaning

Before continuing directly our search for the Bible's meaning, we need to look more carefully at the very word *meaning* itself. As we will see, different senses of this word are intimately connected with several other key concepts of hermeneutics, including those of referent, sense, intention, and significance.[10]

MEANING AS THE REFERENT

As the examples from Shakespeare in chapter 1 make clear, it is possible to know the meaning of every word in a text and still be without a clue as to what is being said. In such cases, what is generally missing is a sense of what is being spoken about—the referent. The referent is the object, event, or process in the world to which a word or a whole expression is directed.

Referential questions appear fairly regularly in biblical interpretation, both within the Bible and in the interpretations we make of it. Of course, some readers are content with their own understanding of passages in the Bible. But the interpreter who wants to understand will ask the same referential question that the Ethiopian reader of the Suffering Servant in Isaiah 53 asked the evangelist Philip: "Tell me, please, who is the prophet talking about, himself or someone else?" (Acts 8:34). In other words, to whom do the words refer? To be sure, the Ethiopian could understand the words, but he had no idea what the exact referent was.

Similar questions about the identity of referents arise in various passages. For example, what is Jesus talking about in John 6:53, "Unless you

10. For many parts of the following discussion I am indebted to G. B. Caird, *The Language and Imagery of the Bible* (Philadelphia: Westminster, 1980), chap. 2, "The Meaning of Meaning," pp. 37–61.

eat the flesh of the Son of Man and drink his blood, you have no life in you"? Even though John has not previously recorded the institution of the Lord's Supper, the language here calls for a recognition of that subject. "Flesh" in the Gospels was a reference to Jesus' incarnation, and "blood" referred to his death, that is, to his life given up violently in death. Using the part for the whole, John's hearers were expected to come to a belief in the life and ministry of the incarnated Christ, as well as believing in his death and what it accomplished.

Likewise, the "false apostles" of 2 Corinthians 11:13, who had received a "different spirit," accepted a "different gospel," and preached an "other Jesus" (v. 4), need to be identified in order to understand what Paul was working against in 2 Corinthians 10–13. These "super-apostles" (2 Cor. 11:5) were either Gnostic pneumatics or triumphalistic, miracle-working Hellenistic Jews who wanted to taunt Paul with their own theological creations. But again we must first ask, What is Paul talking about? Who are these super-apostles?

Our appreciation for 2 Thessalonians is greatly enriched when we can identify the referents for the "man of lawlessness" and "the one who holds [lawlessness] back" in 2 Thessalonians 2:3 and 7. Usually the first is equated with the Antichrist of the end time and the latter is seen as the person of the Holy Spirit. But these identifications cannot be made lightly, for the interpretation of this passage is radically affected by the choice of referent that is made.

Similarly, the "one shepherd" of Ezekiel 34:23–24 is critical to understanding the passage. The Good Shepherd of John 10 turns out to be the same one who was contrasted with the evil shepherds (i.e., all leaders, priests, prophets, princes, and the like) who had robbed and preyed on the flock of God in the book of Ezekiel.

Clearly, referent is critical. When we ask, "What do you mean?" we sometimes are trying to find out what the whole discussion is all about or who/what is being talked about.

MEANING AS SENSE

The next most important use of the word *meaning* is its usage as "sense." Meaning as the referent tells what is being spoken about, but meaning as sense tells what is being said about the referent.[11] Once the

11. For a different way of distinguishing the terms *sense* and *reference*, see Moisés Silva, *Biblical Words and Their Meaning: An Introduction to Lexical Semantics* (Grand Rapids: Zondervan, 1983), pp. 102–8.

subject or object of the discourse has been established, we move on to find out what the author attributes to that subject or object.

When we ask for the sense of a word or a passage, we are either searching for a definition or for some type of appositional clause that will show us how the word, or the entire paragraph, is functioning in its context. Meaning as sense is whatever some user has willed to convey by a particular word or series of words in a sentence, paragraph, or a discourse. Beyond the sentence, the *relationship* of propositions within the paragraphs and discourses carry the sense the writer wishes to convey.

As illustration, consider Romans 9:30–10:12. This portion has been subjected to almost every extreme of interpretation, more often than not simply because the interpreter failed, first, to establish the exact referent the passage was addressing and, second, to show what the meaning or sense this passage contributes to that referent or subject. All too frequently one's theological predilections seem to be more formative of what one expects to find in the text than a patient listening to what the text has to say.

If the sense-meaning in this passage is to be heeded, one must understand what four key phrases found in the text mean. Note how some of the phrases are employed in apposition to other terms in the passage and how each of the four phrases, used of the Jewish audience it was addressing, stands in contrast to four corresponding terms used of the Gentiles' method of seeking the same goals as the Jewish community.

> *nomon diakaiosynēs*—Romans 9:31, Israel pursued a "law of
> righteousness"
> *all' hōs ex ergōn*—Romans 9:32, "not by faith, but as [if it
> were possible] from works"
> *zēlon theou . . . ou kat' epignōsin*—Romans 10:2, they are
> "zealous for God . . . not based on
> knowledge"
> *kai tēn idian*—Romans 10:3, they sought to establish "their
> own [righteousness]"

Clearly, the referent of these four phrases was the Jewish population. But what meanings and what sense did the apostle Paul attach to each one? Israel, according to these four expressions, had gone about the whole process of pursuing righteousness (the topic announced in Romans 9:30) totally backward. Paul was urging, in effect: Don't blame the Mosaic law, neither blame God the lawgiver, for what Israel has done here. Israel was guilty of inventing her own law to replace God's law and making a new law out of

God's righteousness. Instead of coming to God by faith, sniffed Paul, Israel insisted on turning righteousness into a works program, as if that were possible! While one must admire Israel's zeal, it was not based on knowledge that came from the Word of God (Rom. 10:4). The result was a homemade righteousness, which was just about as valuable as a wooden nickel.

What could be clearer: The Gentiles obtained the righteousness of God by believing on the One here called the Stone and Rock, our Lord. Thus they were not put to shame. But Israel, who went on a do-it-yourself plan, missed not only the proper approach to receive this grace, but also the end or goal of the law (Rom. 10:5), which was no less than Christ himself and his righteousness. In fact, way back in Moses' day and in the Torah itself, the same righteousness had been described in Leviticus 18:5 *and* Deuteronomy 30:10–14 (the Greek text deliberately used words that joined the two citations rather than contrasting the two). The word that Moses preached was the same word of faith that Paul preached.

The sense remains throughout this whole passage: God's righteousness focused on Christ and came solely by faith, not by works. The person who did these things would live *in the sphere* of them. Thus Romans 10:5 introduced two quotations from Moses, both supporting the consistent sense initiated in the introductory question in 9:30 and sustained in each of the four contrasts exhibited in the propositions of the paragraphs. The *sense* of the use of these words, as they make up the sense of the whole passage, is the second most important meaning to gain once the *referent* has been identified.

MEANING AS INTENTION

In speaking of meaning as intention, we do not profess to get into the mind, psychology, or feelings of the author. We have no way of obtaining or controlling such data. Instead, we are interested only in the *truth*-intention of the author as expressed in the way he put together the individual words, phrases, and sentences in a literary piece to form a meaning.

It must be acknowledged also that it is not always possible to dissociate meaning as sense from meaning as intention. The two are often identical, so the distinctions made here are somewhat arbitrary and merely reflect our penchant for using vocabulary that often overlaps. But some points need to be made under the heading of "meaning as intention," as follows.

The impact left by Wimsatt and Beardsley is that an author's intention does not determine what a literary work means. Instead, what a speaker meant does not necessarily coincide with what the sentence means. Let us complicate matters a bit more for the moment: Teachers have often had the experience of grading a student's paper only to have the student protest that the teacher did not understand what was meant. Typically the teacher will reply, "I can only grade you on what you actually wrote, not on what you meant." In this way, it is thought, the meaning of the text has a meaning independent of its author. But this illustration is effective only to the degree that it comments on the artistic or, in this case, linguistic ability of the student. Authors, like other communicators, often state things poorly with ambiguities or ellipses, assuming that the referent is known without its being stated. But the speaker's intention is never irrelevant, for the only way out of the quagmire created by this objection is to ask the speaker what he or she meant—and if the speaker or writer is no longer available, we must search the context for further clues.

P. D. Juhl illustrates how this might work when a man says, "I like my secretary better than my wife." When we exclaim with raised eyebrows, "You do?" he immediately senses that we have not understood what he intended to communicate. "No, you misunderstand," he protests. "I mean that I like her better than my wife does." It still is not absolutely clear what he is up to, but we are closer now than we were before. The man has even succeeded in influencing the meaning of the previous sentence, even though it was poorly constructed.[12] But these are cases of authorial incompetence. Often it is possible to infer from the context what an author meant, even when he or she has failed to express that intention clearly.

HOW INTENTION AFFECTS MEANING. Intention can affect meaning in several ways. First, the author's intention determines whether the words are to be understood literally or figuratively. Therefore, when the psalmist writes that the trees clapped their hands, it is clear that the joining together of an inanimate subject with a predicate usually attributed to animate beings is enough to give us the clue that the language is figurative.

Second, the author's intention determines the referent a word is to have. Here are some instances where it is sometimes said that an utterance had a meaning *beyond* what the original author intended.[13] For example, if we limit ourselves for the moment only to meaning as referent, the following affirmations seem to contradict our thesis that the author's intention determines meaning: (1) general statements can be applied to any member of a class, (2) general truths can be easily transferred to others, and (3) partial fulfillments within a series of predictions, belonging to a line exhibiting corporate solidarity of all the parts, can also go beyond the immediate and particular to the final manifestation of the prediction.

12. P. D. Juhl, *Interpretation: An Essay in the Philosophy of Literary Criticism* (Princeton, N.J.: Princeton University Press, 1980), pp. 52–65.
13. See the fine discussion in G. B. Caird, *The Language and Imagery of the Bible*, pp. 56–58.

Mark 10:25 illustrates the first objection raised to our principle of authorial intentionality: "It is easier for a camel to go through the eye of a needle than for a rich man to enter the kingdom of God." In the view of some, this utterance goes beyond the author's immediate referent. This statement would apply not only to the rich people of Jesus' time, but to all who were members of that same class of the "rich" in any day. However, since the principle has not changed either in the biblical context or the modern one, the truth-intention remains the same. Rather than breaking our rule, it only helps to further it.

The second objection can be illustrated by Mark 7:6, when Jesus complained, "Isaiah was right when he prophesied about you hypocrites. . . ." We can respond to this objection in similar terms as to the first. Isaiah did not directly address an audience existing seven hundred years after he died, but the truth he affirmed was readily transferred across the centuries because what he said could just as well have been said of Jesus' contemporaries. There is no change in authorial intentionality.

The third category of evidence raised against our thesis of authorial intentionality takes the meaning of the referent to be multiple. That is, it points to a number of persons who fulfilled the prediction and thus beyond the author's immediate intention—just as the prediction about the coming of the "little horn," or antichrist, in Daniel 7:8, 11, 25 is taken by most to be simultaneously a reference to Antiochus Epiphanes IV and to the final manifestation of evil in the last day. But even 1 John 2:18 says that "many antichrists have come," without playing down the fact that "you have heard that the antichrist is [still] coming."

Of course, we agree that one in the line of evil who violently opposed the kingdom of God was and is a legitimate referent in subsequent generations, even though that person may not be the final manifestation of the antichrist of the end time. Nevertheless, it is the author's intended meaning that must be the starting point from which all understanding begins. And in the illustration just considered, even though there are multiple fulfillments throughout history as time advances to the last day, none of these fulfillments constitute double or multiple senses or meanings. They all participate in the one single sense, even though it has had a multiple number of fulfillments over the course of time.

That is the uniqueness of the point being advocated. It is similar to the point made by the Antiochian school of interpretation in the fifth through the seventh centuries A.D. It was a case of multiple fulfillments with a single sense or meaning that incorporated all of them, because of the generic nature of the term used or the collective, singular nature of the term used, or the corporate solidarity that the many referents shared with the representative one who embodied the whole group.

The only place in our Western culture where a similar phenomenon occurs is in the designation of a corporation, such as GMC. GMC stands for "General Motors Corporation," the official name, but if I were to sue the corporation, from a legal standpoint the suit would read *Kaiser v. GMC*. For the purposes of law, both parties would be treated as if they were individuals, even though GMC stands for management, employees, and stockholders, not for just one person. This is an illustration of corporate solidarity, in which the many and the one are treated as *one entity,* even though they are composed of many just as well.

DIVINE INTERVENTION. In the case of Scripture, however, another major intention must be considered: divine intention. We must ask at this point, Is the divine intention in the revealed word *the same as* the human authorial intention, or is it different?

There are cases in Scripture where God's "intentions" clearly differed from those of the humans he was using to assist his purposes. For example, Joseph said to his brothers, "You intended to harm me, but God intended it for good" (Gen. 50:20). Likewise, the Assyrians intended to destroy Israel, but God intended that they only be the rod of discipline in his hands (Isa. 10:5–11). No less oblivious was Cyrus, the Medo-Persian, to the purposes and uses to which God had set him, even though Cyrus "[did] not acknowledge [God]" (Isa. 45:1–4).

But none of these examples is about the *writing* of Scripture. What is being confused here is *purpose*-intention with *truth*-intention. In the case of the writers of Scripture, there was such a divine-human concursus (that is, a "running together" in the realm of thought) that the Spirit of God was able to take the truths of God and teach them in words to the writers of Scripture.

The great teaching passage for this declaration comes from 1 Corinthians 2:6–16.[14] Verse 13 stresses that the writers of the Bible received not words taught by human wisdom but *"words taught* by the Spirit."* That is, the Spirit of God did not mechanically whisper the text into the writer's ears, nor did the authors experience automatic writing. Instead, they experienced a *living assimilation* of the truth, so that what they had experienced in the past by way of culture, vocabulary, hardships, and the like was all taken up and assimilated into the unique product that simultaneously came from the unique personality of the writers. Just as truly, however, it came also from the Holy Spirit! And the Holy Spirit stayed with the writers not just in the conceptual

14. See Walter C. Kaiser, Jr., "A Neglected Text in Bibliology Discussions: 1 Corinthians 2:6–16," *WTJ* 43 (1980–81): 301–19.

or ideational stage, but all the way up through the writing and verbalizing stage of their composition of the text. That is what Paul claimed for himself and his fellow prophets and apostles. It is thus difficult to see how the product of the text can be severed into divine and human components, each reflecting independent intention—one human and the other divine. Therefore, to understand the intention of the human author is to understand the intention of the divine author.

One must quickly add, however, that this is not to say that the divinely intended referents were limited to those that the author saw or meant. It was only necessary that the writer have an adequate understanding of what was intended both in the near and the distant future, even if he lacked a grasp of all the details that were to be embodied in the progress of revelation and of history.

MEANING AS SIGNIFICANCE

In many contexts, the terms *meaning* and *significance* overlap. In their use in textual studies, however, we are well advised to distinguish the two along the lines set out by E. D. Hirsch.

> *Meaning* is that which is represented by a text; it is what the author meant by his use of a particular sign sequence; it is what the signs represent. *Significance,* on the other hand, names a relationship between that meaning and a person, or a conception, or a situation, or indeed anything imaginable.

In another place, Hirsch summarized the distinction this way:

> The important feature of meaning as distinct from significance is that meaning is the determinate representation of a text for an interpreter. . . . Significance is meaning-as-related-to-some-thing-else.[15]

In these terms, meaning is fixed and unchanging; significance is never fixed and always changing. As Hirsch argued, "To banish the original author as the determiner of meaning [is] to reject the only compelling normative principle that could lend validity to an interpretation."[16]

But it would be just as tragic to conclude one's interpretational responsibilities with the task of what a text meant to the author and the original audience without going on to deal with the contemporary significance

---

15. Hirsch, *Validity in Interpretation*, p. 8; *idem, The Aims of Interpretation*, pp. 79–80.
16. Hirsch, *Validity in Interpretation*, pp. 4–5.

of the text. The hermeneutical task *must* continue on to say what the text means to the contemporary reader or listener.

This meaning as significance could also be called the consequent or implicit sense. Along with there being only one, single meaning-as-sense (which is what we are espousing here), there are scores of meanings-as-significance that can and must be named. Some of these latter meanings extend to contemporary persons, events, or issues that go beyond those of the original writers or their audience. Others are new relations that may be legitimately seen between an older textual utterance and the contemporary audience's world. Significance can also relate to certain theological inferences, both contained within the text and coming from outside the text. In fact, the older commentator George Bush presented a good case for the importance of inferences in interpretation:

> If *inferences* are not binding in the interpretation of the divine law, then we would ask for the *express* command which was violated by Nadab and Abihu in offering strange fire [Lev. 10:1–3], and which cost them their lives. Any prohibition in set terms on that subject will be sought for in vain. So again, did not our Saviour tell the Sadducees that they *ought to have inferred* that the doctrine of the resurrection was true, from what God said to Moses at the bush?[17]

The text may also carry a hint of its own significances and inferences within itself, such as in Acts 5:30: "The God of our fathers raised Jesus from the dead—whom you had killed by hanging him on a tree." Why didn't the apostle Peter simply use the verb *crucify* in place of the cumbersome phrase "hanging him on a tree"? No doubt Peter wanted to call to mind the connotations of Deuteronomy 21:22–23 with its references to the accursed status of all who died in this manner. Could not the inference be that the Messiah died under God's "curse" on the sin of Israel and the world as he took our place? The theological implication and significance of the crucifixion as Peter and Luke understood it are thereby brought home for the reader and listener. Rather than classifying this kind of inference as a direct expression of authorial intention, it seems best to consider it an example of "consequent" or "implicit" significances that the text of Scripture encourages us to find as a legitimate part of its total meaning.

It is important, however, to make certain that the consequent or implicit meaning that we attribute to a text is one that accurately reflects the

---

17. George Bush, *Notes, Critical and Practical, on the Book of Leviticus* (New York: Newman and Ivison, 1852), p. 183, emphasis his.

fundamental truth or principle in the text, not a separate and different one. Accordingly, Paul correctly applied (not: allegorized) the principle of not muzzling an ox in Deuteronomy 25:4 to the practical application of paying the Christian pastor or worker. Both the Deuteronomic law and the apostle worked from the same principle, namely, that developing attitudes of graciousness and cheerful giving of one's substance is (in this case) more important than merely being concerned for the livelihood of animals (Deut. 25) or even paying workers what should be paid for their labor (1 Cor. 9:7–12). Not only did Paul say that what was written in Deuteronomy was not written for oxen, but entirely for us; it is also clear that the collection of laws in the section of Deuteronomy from which this one was taken all have as their object the inculcation of a spirit of gentility and generosity about them.[18]

Similarly, Jesus used Hosea 6:6 ("I desire mercy, not sacrifice") to justify his disciples' eating with publicans and sinners (Matt. 9:10–13) and to justify his disciples' action of plucking and eating grain on the Sabbath (Matt. 12:1–7). Surely, the applications differed from one another, but the principle behind both the Old Testament and the New Testament texts remains the same—namely, the attitude of the heart is more important and always takes precedence over a mere external duty.

If those texts illustrate legitimate inferences that carry the meaning over into new areas, but where the significances are of the same order as those contained in the sense that the author meant, what illustration can we give of an inference that is separate and different from the author's sense and therefore to be avoided as being hermeneutically incorrect? One such illustration is Malachi 3:6: "I the LORD do not change." Some have argued this way:

Major premise: God is absolutely unchanging (Mal. 3:6).

Minor premise: What is absolutely unchanging is eternal (known from reason, but not taught here).

Therefore: God is eternal.

But there is no authority in *this* text for claiming that God is eternal. In this case the implication and the application are separate and different from what is taught in the text, and therefore it is not an inference that comes from the principle taught in the text. Eternality is not demonstrable exegetically in this text, since it is talking about the divine attribute of immutability or

---

18. See more detailed argumentation in Walter C. Kaiser, Jr., "Applying the Principles of the Civil Law: Deuteronomy 25:4; I Corinthians 9:8–10," in *The Uses of the Old Testament in the New* (Chicago: Moody Press, 1985), pp. 203–20, esp. pp. 218–19.

unchangeableness. One infers eternality, not on the basis of what this text teaches about God, but instead, from what one knows about God from totally different sources and from one's definition of what it means to be God.

At this point one's theology has overridden one's exegetical skills, and the theology is being imported into the text *ab extra* (or from the outside) and laid as a grid over the text. It is totally different from the statement made in the text. The comparison between "I change not" and "I am eternal" is not a distinction of similar things, but of two different attributes of God.[19] In fact, eternality in this case is probably nothing more than a theological extrapolation. But in that case, it should be so labeled and not directly attributed or connected with the authority of the Scriptures as its source in Malachi 3:6.

There is no doubt that the great contribution of our century to the hermeneutical debate will be our concern for the reader and for the contemporary application and significance that a past meaning has for today. One must be careful, however, to follow the lead of authorial intention and to make clear any connection seen between a principle in a text and modern-day circumstances. Focusing on the significance of a text should never lead to proposing a new meaning of the text that is not actually taught in Scripture. To do otherwise is to risk the loss of authority, for such inferences would have no part in the written nature of the text and thus would not be authoritative for us today.

OTHER MEANINGS OF "MEANING"

Meaning can have additional definitions besides the four preceding ones traced here. Meaning as *value* appears when we say, "The book of Isaiah means more to me than all the other prophetic books." This is an expression of preference and priority. But no claim is made as to the sense, truth claims, or significance of the book of Isaiah.

Meaning as *entailment* is another use of this very wide-ranging word. "This means war," intoned the president of the United States, meaning that one phenomenon has led inexorably to another. Or to use another example, in the life of our Lord, his obedience to the will of the Father relentlessly led him into suffering. "[Jesus] learned obedience from what he suffered" (Heb. 5:8). Note that Jesus did not go to school in order "to learn" obedience, nor did he need to be taught how to obey: rather, he learned what obedience *entailed*. In this case, the meaning of "learning" for the writer of Hebrews

---

19. See C. F. DeVine, "The Consequent Sense," *Catholic Biblical Quarterly* 2 (1940): 151–52. Also Walter C. Kaiser, Jr., "A Response to Author's Intention and Biblical Interpretation," in *Hermeneutics, Inerrancy and the Bible,* ed. Earl D. Radmacher and Robert D. Preus (Grand Rapids: Zondervan, 1984), pp. 443–46.

THE MEANING OF MEANING

carried with it an entailment, much as the interpreter will sometimes see meanings associated with biblical words as legitimate entailments that flow from a valid understanding of the text.

Of course, saying so does not make it so, for each of these instances must be argued for with appropriate evidence. Care must be exercised, however, in the use of entailment lest one fall into the trap of condoning a separate and different inference from what the text actually gives evidence for.

Conclusion

In this chapter we have introduced several revolutionary concepts used in interpreting texts in the twentieth century. While many of these new approaches have been rightfully concerned about understanding the texts more *deeply and creatively,* we may not be any less concerned than before with understanding them *correctly.* For this reason we have attempted to maintain a balance between the two principles of (1) a creative focus on the needs of the reader, and (2) a desire to validate meanings and application of the text as being correct, authoritative, and therefore normative.

As Hirsch has pointed out, the basis for validating the meaning of any passage can only be located in the meaning (i.e., the sense) that the author intended. But the legitimate significance in all contemporary applications of that passage is to be found in the identification of all valid relationships that exist between the intended sense of the author and any suggested contemporary issues, readers, and interpreters. To put it in another way, the authority for the sense of a text is only as solid as our grasp of the truth the author intended to convey.

The act of isolating each of the four meanings from one another is indeed somewhat arbitrary and theoretical. Yet each performs a role, a real function. The problem is that the act of understanding and interpreting calls all of these various functions back together again. Thus the five so-called meanings we have discussed separately for the purpose of analysis must now be restored to one holistic way of looking at the text when we come to interpreting it.

Many issues arising in the study of the Bible relate to linguistic meaning, and the arguments used to support particular views are frequently unsound. We must be careful not to minimize the importance of the original languages of Scripture, since it is easy to read into the text nuances that may be present in the English text but not in the Greek or Hebrew; moreover, there are occasional details of interpretation that can be resolved only by appealing to the original. By contrast, some readers end up exaggerating the importance of the biblical languages as though the English versions were inadequate and therefore unable to convey the proper meaning.

Other possible dangers need attention, such as the tendency of some to assume that the meaning of a word is based on its history; we must especially avoid interpretations that depend heavily on a word's etymology. Again, we often read or hear expositions that combine the various meanings a word may have; instead of identifying the specific function of the word in a particular context, all the meanings are read into the passage. Finally, it is important not to overemphasize subtle distinctions in the vocabulary and grammar, because an author depends on the thrust of the writing as a whole (rather than on faint linguistic differences) to convey the meaning.

CHAPTER 3

Let's Be Logical
USING AND ABUSING LANGUAGE

MOISÉS SILVA

We all like to think of ourselves as rational and astute human beings, especially if we are involved in an argument with somebody. Understandably, whenever we find ourselves losing ground in the dispute, we are ready to use our best weapon—indeed, the ultimate squelch—"You're being illogical!" Along with "That's just your interpretation" and other choice rejoinders, the complaint that our opponent is not logical can be simply a cheap shot.

That is not to deny that sometimes we may have good reason to suspect our opponent's powers of reasoning. It may well be, for example, that when we state, "That's just your interpretation," we have perceived that the other party is merely asserting an opinion and thus has confused the meaning of the text with one of the available interpretive options. It might be more productive (though we can hardly guarantee it!) to specify which other meanings seem reasonable and to point out that we should have persuasive grounds for choosing one over the others.

Similarly, there is greater likelihood of progress in a debate if, instead of throwing out a general allegation about an individual's logical lapse, we make an effort to identify the specific fallacy we have detected. Note the word *effort*. Most of us are lazy thinkers. We may be vaguely aware that an argument is weak, but we are not really prepared to say precisely how. Unfortunately, this problem is not restricted to personal arguments. The same questions arise when we read a biblical commentary, or even when we are pondering by ourselves what the point of a verse might be.

The goal of this chapter is to provide some help in the evaluation of arguments. We will not attempt to give a full treatment, since several excellent textbooks are available.[1] Moreover, our primary concerns do not correspond in every respect with those of the philosophical discipline we call *logic* but focus more narrowly on the use of language. The connections between logic and language are very close indeed, but we are less directly interested in the traditional concerns of philosophy than in the typical problems that arise when students of the Bible seek to figure out the meaning of the text and when they seek to defend their interpretation.

Since a large proportion of exegetical arguments are based on appeals to Greek and Hebrew, we shall need to pay special attention to the proper use of the biblical languages. We may begin by considering two opposite tendencies that often show up in the study of Scripture, namely, the minimizing and the overemphasizing of the original languages.

Don't Minimize the Importance of the Original Languages

For some Christians, hearing references to Greek or Hebrew can prove quite intimidating. The reason may be that they have received poor teaching, such as the view that the King James Version is inspired and is therefore all one needs. This is not a very "logical" position because it raises numerous unanswerable questions. How do we know that the KJV and not another translation is inspired? What did English speakers use before the KJV was produced in the seventeenth century? Does God inspire individual translations into each modern language? Besides, we can demonstrate that those who produced the KJV themselves had to translate from the original languages.

Other believers, realizing that no translation is infallible, have a more reasonable objection. It has to do with the biblical principle that we need no human intermediaries (whether priests or scholars) between ourselves and God. Jesus Christ is the only mediator (1 Tim. 2:5). If I have to depend on a specialist in languages to understand the Bible, don't I compromise this precious truth?

Part of the answer to this concern is to affirm without misgivings that

---

1. For applications of basic logic to the study of the Bible, see especially James W. Sire, *Scripture Twisting: Twenty Ways the Cults Misread the Bible* (Downers Grove, Ill.: InterVarsity, 1980); and D. A. Carson, *Exegetical Fallacies* (Grand Rapids: Baker, 1984).

the English translations available to us are indeed adequate. Even some of the versions that are not of the highest quality present quite clearly the basic message of the gospel and the obedience God requires of us. We should never suggest that a person without a knowledge of Greek and Hebrew or without direct access to a scholar is in jeopardy of missing the essential truths of Scripture.

Let us never forget, however, that whenever we read an English translation, we are in fact recognizing, though indirectly, our dependence on scholarship. *Someone* had to learn the biblical languages and to make great efforts over a long period of time before English readers could make use of a translation they understand. Though the Scriptures affirm that we have direct access to God, the Scriptures also make clear that God has given teachers to his church (e.g., Eph. 4:11). Surely there would be no point in having teachers if Christians never need guidance and instruction in their understanding of God's revelation. Scholars may not impose their views on the church, nor may they act as though they were the great depositories of truth, but the church must not forget how much it has benefited from their labors throughout the centuries.

In any case, it would be a great mistake to deny the importance of paying attention to the original languages. Some years ago, a minister was giving a mid-week Bible study on Ephesians 4. Working from the KJV, he read verse 26, "Be angry and sin not." He then proceeded to affirm that this verse forbids anger in the life of a Christian.

It is understandable why this preacher felt compelled to interpret the verse in this way. After all, other passages in the Bible seem to condemn anger quite vigorously (e.g., Matt. 5:22), so he must have figured that the Ephesians passage could not mean something contrary to the rest of Scripture. His conclusion was that the word *not* applied to both verbs, *sin* and *be angry*. But this interpretation is not really possible. If there is any ambiguity for the modern reader, there is none in the original Greek, where the negative particle (which always affects the word that follows) comes after the verb for "be angry" and before the verb for "sin." Some further reflection on the biblical teaching about anger—including the fact that God himself is sometimes portrayed as being angry (e.g., Rom. 1:18)—makes clear that this human emotion is not necessarily sinful in itself. What the apostle wants us to understand is that, while there may be occasions when anger is appropriate, we cannot allow that anger to turn into an occasion for sin.

Mid-week Bible teachers are not the only ones who occasionally misuse the Bible by failing to take into account the original languages. Scholars too can falter. One rather distinguished writer, who happens to be a proponent of so-called existentialist theology, has argued that the essence of being is a dynamic "letting-be." At a later point in his argument he remarks: "It is significant that the Bible does not begin by merely affirming God's existence but with his act of creation, which is the conferring of existence. His first utterance is: 'Let there be light!' and so begins the history of his letting-be."[2]

What the author of these words fails to tell the reader is that there is nothing in the Hebrew text of Genesis 1:3 that corresponds precisely to the English verb *let*. While Hebrew (as well as many other languages) has a specific verbal form for the third person imperative, English lacks such a form. English does have a second person imperative, such as "Come!" To express the imperative idea in the third person, however, we have to use other means, such as "John must come!" or "Let John come!" In the second example, the verb *let* does not have its usual meaning of "allow," nor does it have any supposed dynamic sense; rather, it functions merely as a helping verb to express the imperatival idea. In short, this theologian's appeal to the *English* rendering of Genesis 1:3 in support of his proposal has very little to commend it. Using the same line of argument, we could point to verse 11 ("Let the land produce vegetation") and conclude that the Bible encourages us to speak about God's letting-produce.

More often than not (as these examples may suggest), some knowledge of the biblical languages proves its value in a negative way, that is, by helping us set aside invalid interpretations. This point becomes particularly significant when we realize that heretical views are often based on a misuse of the text. Some groups, especially the Jehovah's Witnesses, routinely appeal to the fact that in John 1:1c, "And the Word was God," the Greek term for God, *theos*, does not have the definite article, and so, they argue, it means either "a god" or "divine." Even a superficial knowledge of Greek, however, allows the student to note that in many passages that undisputably refer to the only God, the definite article is missing in Greek (even in John 1, see vv. 6 and 18). Students with a more advanced knowledge of the language will know that one of the ways Greek grammar distinguishes between the subject of the sentence (here "the Word," *ho logos*) and the predicate ("God," *theos*) is precisely by retaining the article with the former but omitting it with the latter.

But many features of the biblical languages also have a positive value for interpretation, particularly when the biblical author exploits one of those features for stylistic purposes. In Exodus 16:15, for instance, we are told that the Israelites, upon seeing the manna, asked what it was. Moses responded, "It is the bread the LORD has given you to eat." Now the last phrase may be

2. John Macquarrie, *Principles of Christian Theology*, 2d ed. (New York: Scribners, 1977), pp. 109, 197.

translated literally, "for you for food." It is not a common expression, and an important Jewish scholar has suggested that it may be a subtle allusion to Genesis 1:29, where the same phrase is found.[3] If so, the writer of Exodus may want his readers to view the wilderness experience as a time of testing comparable to the testing of Adam and Eve. This interpretation could be supported contextually from Exodus 16:4 and Deuteronomy 8:2–3.

In the New Testament, no book uses allusions of this sort more frequently than the gospel of John. One interesting possibility is 19:30, which describes Jesus' death with the expression "and gave up his spirit." It has been noted that the verb John uses here for "gave up" (*paredōken,* "handed over, delivered") is not the common word used in this type of context. Since the gospel has numerous references to Jesus' giving of the Holy Spirit to his disciples, some scholars have suggested that the expression here serves to recall that theme. It would be pressing things too much to suggest that the giving of the Spirit actually took place at that moment. More likely, John is reminding his readers that the dreadful event of the crucifixion is not a sign of failure. On the contrary, it is the "lifting up" of Jesus (3:14; 12:32), the time of his glorification, which makes possible the fulfillment of his promise (7:39).

This interpretation of the language of John would not be accepted by all. Indeed, the approach that looks too hard for subtle allusions of this sort often runs the danger of discovering things that are not there in the text. Later in this chapter we shall look at this hazard in more detail. Certainly, we should not place too much weight on such interpretations unless they can be confirmed by the context. Nevertheless, there are plenty of good examples where attention to these stylistic subtleties has helped interpreters shed new light on the text.

The conclusion to be drawn from this section is not that every Christian must attend seminary and become an expert in Greek and Hebrew. What we should keep in mind, however, is that the English versions *by themselves* cannot be the exclusive basis for formulating doctrine. In particular, we must be careful not to adopt *new* ideas if they have not been checked against the original text. Moreover, when there is a difference of opinion among students of the Bible, an attempt should be made to find out whether the Greek or the Hebrew sheds light on the debate. It is also worth pointing out, however, that ministers ought to gain some proficiency in the biblical languages if at all possible. Those who teach their congregations week after week and who must provide leadership in theological questions cannot afford to neglect such an important tool in their ministry.

3. Umberto Cassuto, *A Commentary on the Book of Exodus* (Jerusalem: Magnes, 1967), p. 196.

Don't Exaggerate the Importance of the Biblical Languages

In some respects, it is not possible to overemphasize the value of knowing Greek and Hebrew. Many students of the Bible, however, by shifting the focus of their attention, have indeed overstated the significance of these languages. As we suggested in the previous section, it would be most unfortunate to say that Christians who have access to the Bible only through their modern translations are unable to learn by themselves what God's message of salvation is. Seminary students have been known to give the impression that anyone unacquainted with the original languages must be a second-class Christian. And more than one scholar has seemed to argue, at least indirectly, that the church can say nothing that has not been cleared through the experts.

One common way of overemphasizing the biblical languages is by romanticizing them, by giving the impression that Greek and Hebrew have a unique (and almost divine?) status. For example, in the attempt to show the beauty of Hebrew, some writers look for peculiarities in the grammar that may support their contention. One very frequent illustration given is the fact that Hebrew has no neuter gender, a linguistic feature that is supposed to have some special significance.

While nouns in Greek may belong to one of three genders (masculine, feminine, and neuter), Hebrew nouns can be only masculine or feminine. Now abstract concepts are often expressed in Greek by means of the neuter gender, so some writers have inferred that the two facts are closely related. As one older textbook put it: "The Hebrew thought in pictures, and consequently his nouns are concrete and vivid. There is no such thing as neuter gender, for to the Semite everything is alive."[4]

A moment's reflection, however, should make clear that whether or not the Hebrews thought abstractly has little to do with the structure of their language. In English, for example, there is no gender distinction at all in nouns and adjectives (only in the personal pronouns). Does that fact say anything at all about an English speaker's ability or disposition to think abstractly? It is true that the special interests of a community are sometimes hinted at in its language, particularly the vocabulary. But if we want to know what a group of people really thinks or believes, we should look at the *statements* made, not at the grammatical structure of the language used.

4. Elmer W. K. Mould, *Essentials of Bible History,* rev. ed. (New York: Ronald, 1951), p. 307. These words or comparable statements have been quoted favorably in recent books.

Part of the problem here is that we tend to transfer the qualities of what people say to the medium they use to say it. That is especially true of Greek, a language that has received a great deal of attention. In fact, Greek has been romanticized to extremes. Charles Briggs, a very notable biblical scholar in the last century, put it this way: "The Greek language is the beautiful flower, the elegant jewel, the most finished masterpiece of Indo-Germanic thought." In describing classical Greek, Briggs uses such terms as *complex, artistic, beautiful, finished, strong,* and *vigorous.* He then adds: "Its syntax is organized on the most perfect system. . . . [the Greek language] wrestles with the mind, it parries and thrusts, it conquers as an armed host." Later, when God chose Greek to convey the message of the gospel, this language was "employed by the Spirit of God, and transformed and transfigured, yes, glorified, with a light and sacredness that the classic literature never possessed."[5]

We should keep in mind that this viewpoint was in part influenced by the opinion—very common in the nineteenth century—that the classical languages, Greek and Latin, were inherently superior to others. This opinion, in turn, was related to the emphasis that linguists in that century placed on the comparative and historical study of languages. During the twentieth century, however, scholars have made intensive studies of languages spoken in "primitive" cultures, such as the Indians of North and South America, African tribes, and other groups. The very grammatical features that used to be associated with the alleged superiority of the classical languages (e.g., a complex verbal system) turn out to be present to an even greater degree in the "primitive" ones.

The greatness of Greek civilization is not to be equated with the grammatical system of its language. It is what people did with the language rather than the language itself that deserves admiration. Interestingly, the form of Greek used by the New Testament writers is simpler than that used by the great writers of the earlier, classical period. For example, New Testament Greek contains fewer "irregular" forms, and the word order of the sentences is less involved. One of its most distinctive features, in fact, is that it approximates the language used commonly by the people in their daily conversation.

Such facts do not disprove the beauty of the biblical languages. To some extent, this is a matter of personal taste, and the authors of this textbook happen to believe that Hebrew and Greek are about as beautiful as

5. C. A. Briggs, *General Introduction to the Study of Holy Scripture* (Grand Rapids: Baker, 1970; reprint of 1900 ed.), pp. 64, 65–67, 70–71. Cf. J. Barr's critique in *The Semantics of Biblical Language* (Oxford: Oxford University Press, 1961), pp. 246ff.

they come! Nor do we need to deny that the powerful message of the gospel had a significant impact on Greek, particularly its vocabulary.

In the end, however, we must not confuse the divine message itself with the human means God used to proclaim it. This issue has clear relevance to the topic of biblical interpretation. Some of the fallacies that we shall look at in the rest of this chapter have arisen because of the exaggerated importance attached to human linguistic systems (Hebrew and especially Greek). The biblical authors did not write in a mysterious or coded speech. Under inspiration, they used their daily language in a normal way.

Don't Equate the Meaning of a Word with Its History

Perhaps the most common error one comes across in discussions involving language (and particularly the biblical languages) is the tendency to misuse the study of *etymology,* that is, the origin and development of words. One important reason behind this problem is the inherent interest of the subject. No doubt about it, etymological information can prove to be simply fascinating. I vividly recall from my college days a sermon on the theme of sincerity. To help his audience understand the concept, the speaker appealed to the etymology of the English word *sincere.* It comes, he told us, from the two Latin words *sine cera,* "without wax." The terminology was used to describe statues that, one might say, could be trusted: wax had not been used to cover up defects.

It is important to note that, *as an illustration,* this piece of information was quite effective. The thought was almost captivating, and it helped us see the virtue of sincerity in a new light. The danger, however, lies in the possible inference that the Latin origin of the English word *sincere* actually corresponds to the meaning of the word today. The fact is that, when English speakers use this word, wax and statues are the furthest thing from their mind. For that matter, the meaning "pure" or "unadulterated" for this word is now archaic. When speakers use the word, the meaning they seek to convey is simply "true" or "honest."

But the problems run even deeper. The transference from the physical (literal wax) to the figurative may have been accidental or trivial. Such a shift in meaning would not necessarily prove that anyone understood the virtue of sincerity with reference to the selling of nondefective statues. And even if someone did, why should we adopt that person's understanding of sincerity? Moreover, the Bible was not written in Latin, and so the association with statues could not have been part of the meaning the New Testament authors had in mind.

As if all that were not enough, a brief check of etymological dictionaries of English quickly reveals that there is no certainty whatever that English *sincere* comes from Latin *sine cera!* And some scholars who believe there is such a connection suspect that the real setting was the description, not of statues, but of honey. Etymological reconstructions are often tentative and sometimes purely imaginary. Some thinkers have nevertheless been known to develop great conceptual edifices based on such reconstructions. Very influential, particularly among existentialist philosophers, has been the supposed etymology of the Greek word for "truth," *alētheia.* It is possible that this word was formed by combining the negative particle *a-* with the verb *lanthanō,* "hide," and that possibility is alleged to show that the real significance of truth is "unhiddenness."[6] But this etymology is debatable, and even if it were not, we could not prove that it reflects a philosophical view of truth—much less would it prove that such a view is correct!

One of the unfortunate results of appealing to etymology is that it lends to the argument a scientific tone and makes the speaker's position sound much more authoritative than it really is. Some writers, aware of the tentativeness of their etymological arguments, but unable to resist the temptation of using them anyway, include a "perhaps" or some other qualification, but most readers are unduly influenced by the arguments and end up accepting the conclusion, even though no real evidence has been presented.

The best way to illustrate this point is to make up a few outrageous examples:

> I have mistrusted ranchers ever since I met a few who seemed mentally unbalanced. It is probably not a pure accident that English *ranch* (< *rank* < Old French *reng* < Indo-European *sker*) is etymologically related to *deranged.*

> Christians should be optimists. We should keep in mind that the word *pessimist* comes from the Latin word for "foot," *pes.* Because we stumble with our feet, we find the related verb *peccare,* "sin," and the English cognate *pecadillo.* We may perhaps describe pessimists as people who are in the habit of committing little sins.

> In our religious group we do not believe in having ministers. The word *clergy* (from Indo-European *kel,* "to strike") is related to *calamity* (< Latin, "a severe blow"). Not surprisingly, clergy

6. Macquarrie, *Principles,* pp. 86, 333.

throughout the centuries have abused their power and hurt people.

Dancing is surely forbidden to Christians. Isn't it suggestive that the word *ballet* comes from Greek *ballō,* which is also the origin of *diabolos,* "devil"?[7]

The possibilities are endless! Apart from their outlandish content, the type of argument (i.e., the logic) exemplified in these four observations is exceedingly common. And precisely because this logic is most often used to make points that are not ludicrous and seem otherwise plausible, many people are persuaded by it, even though as a rule no substantive evidence accompanies it.

In biblical commentaries and other serious works, one also comes across etymological comments that usually shed no real light on the meaning of the text. It is common, for example, for writers to comment that the Hebrew word translated "glory," *kabōd,* basically means "weight, heaviness." (Incidentally, the words *basic* and *basically,* when applied to word meaning, are exceedingly ambiguous and are usually—and wrongly—taken to imply something like the "real" or "essential" meaning.) In this case, the connection cannot be doubted, and one can easily see how the notion of "weight" can be related to that of "importance" and thence to the more specific meaning when used in reference to God. While this historical development of the word is accurate and interesting, does it genuinely enhance our understanding of the word (or even the concept behind the word) in passages that speak of God's awesome manifestations? Most doubtful—unless we have good *contextual* reason to think that the biblical author himself was associating this word with the concept of weight.

This problem shows up even more frequently in New Testament studies, since many compound Greek words are relatively "transparent," that is, one can easily see which words have been combined into one. One of the most common examples is the verb *hypomenō* ("be patient"), which is made up of the preposition *hypo,* "under," and the verb *menō,* "remain." Preachers will frequently remark that the Greek word *really means* "to stay under" and then proceed to describe someone carrying a heavy burden for a prolonged period of time.

As an illustration, that imagery may prove useful, but it is highly questionable whether it brings us any closer to the meaning intended by the

---

7. The etymological relationships are taken from Robert Claiborne, *The Roots of English: A Reader's Handbook of Word Origins* (New York: Times Books, 1989), pp. 119, 130–31, 184, 218–19.

biblical author. We need to keep in mind that figurative language quickly loses its freshness, a process that results in many "dead metaphors." Consider the English word *understand*. Would it help a foreign student to be told that this word comes from *stand* and *under* (though most English speakers themselves are normally not conscious of this fact) and that it was originally a figure of speech (though we cannot tell precisely how the new meaning developed)? The figurative etymology of the word is, in fact, quite irrelevant to modern speakers, *since what they mean can be made perfectly clear without a knowledge of the word's origins.*

Of course, one must always keep open the possibility that a biblical writer has deliberately exploited the history (or other associations) of a word. Such a literary technique is more frequently found in poetry than it is in prose. But the only way to determine whether the author has done so is to pay close attention to the context. We cannot presume that an author would necessarily have been aware of a word's etymology. And if he was, we cannot assume, without some evidence, that he intended his readers to grasp the connection. About the only evidence available to us, we must emphasize again, is the context, the thrust of a passage (or even the book) as a whole. With very few exceptions, we will find that the context supports the common usage of a word rather than unfamiliar senses.

Don't Read the Various Meanings of a Word into a Specific Use

Students are often advised to check how a particular word is used throughout the Scriptures. Even Christians who have not learned the biblical languages can use certain concordances (as well as other tools) that are keyed to the Greek and Hebrew terms. In principle, the advice is sound, for such a method helps us to determine the "semantic range" of the word in question; that is, if we are aware of the possible uses of a word, *we are in a better position to decide which specific use* occurs in the passage or passages that we are studying.

The words italicized in the previous paragraph highlight the proper aim of such a word study. In practice, however, students often ignore that very aspect. What happens, instead, is that the whole complex of meanings is injected into one passage. Usually, this takes place in a subtle way. Even a responsible commentator, hoping to shed light on a word, may inform the reader that the word in question is used in a variety of ways in the New Testament. There will follow a list of those uses, including quotations of various passages, with the implication that all of them in some way contribute to the meaning of the word in the verse being analyzed.

From time to time one comes across more glaring misuses of the method. A successful preacher once speaking on Hebrews 12 focused attention on one specific word in that chapter and told his congregation that the word had four meanings. On that basis he had produced a four-point outline that led to four sermonettes with four different texts, even though ostensibly he intended to expound on Hebrews 12.

If we reflect for a few moments on our own language, however, we can appreciate how such an approach succeeds only in distorting meaning. Suppose that an Asian tourist comes across this sentence: "The patient had an acute pain in her knee." This foreigner is not familiar with the word *acute* and asks us what it means, so we respond:

> In geometry, the word is used of angles less than 90 degrees, while in music it may indicate a high-pitched sound. It also is used to describe an accent mark in some languages and scripts. In objects it indicates a sharp point. The word can be used as a synonym for "keen, discerning, shrewd." Things of great importance can be said to be *acute.* In medicine, it may describe a disease that is approaching a crisis. Finally, the word can mean "severe."

Such a disquisition may prove very interesting and informative, but to understand the sentence in question, the foreigner needed merely the last word. The only other meaning that might shed any light on the subject is that of "sharp," since an acute pain is one that is often likened to the sensation of being hurt with a pointed object. Most words in any language have a variety of meanings, but as a rule the context automatically and effectively suppresses all the meanings that are not appropriate, so that the hearers and readers do not even think of them.

The matter gets more complicated when we consider whether certain associations may be present in a particular sentence (cf. above the examples from Exodus 16 and from John 19). It is not always easy to decide this question. If we read in a magazine that "the disagreement among the scholars was acute," we will quickly take the meaning to be "intense, severe," but are we influenced by the frequent combination *acute pain,* so that we deduce, consciously or unconsciously, that the scholars in question were undergoing a painful experience? Is it also possible that, since the people involved are scholars, the meaning "keen, discerning" affects us? Perhaps and perhaps not. It would surely be precarious, however, to come up with interpretations based on what is only a theoretical possibility (unless supported by strong contextual evidence).

While this section has focused on the vocabulary, we should note a related problem when appealing to grammatical facts. In a recent article dealing with the difficult passage on women in 1 Timothy 2, the author has this to say with regard to verse 12 ("I do not permit a woman to teach"):

> In order to gain insight into the meaning of this instruction we may find help in an examination of the verbs in our text. This is the third instance in chapter two of Timothy of a first-person singular verb. 1 Timothy 2:8 began with the first person, "I want the men in every place to pray." The same verb is implied in verse 9 where the author addresses the women—"(I want) women to make themselves attractive." Now in verse 12 we have another first person verb—"I do not permit." In the Greek language there are nine different uses of the present tense. [Here, one of the standard grammars is footnoted.] According to P. B. Payne the first-person present of the verb can be used to indicate temporary restriction. With that sense of the verb a time restriction comes into play. Until women have learned what they need in order to get a full grasp of the true teaching, they are not to teach or have authority over men. There is no reason these women might not later be allowed to teach and have authority (like Phoebe, Prisca, and Junia) if they will learn the true teaching, submitting to Timothy for instruction.[8]

The first part of this paragraph is in fact irrelevant to the author's point. (If anything, it undermines that point, since the verb in verse 8 certainly has no temporal restriction.) From time to time one comes across discussions of biblical texts that appeal to the original languages perhaps only to make an impression; readers need to be discerning whether something substantive is in fact being argued. Our main concern, however, is with the second half of the paragraph, which does contain a substantive argument on the basis of Greek grammar. For our present purposes, we need not determine whether the verb in verse 12 has a temporal restriction; the question, rather, is whether the appeal to the Greek is cogent.

The logic of this author is simply to look for the various attested uses or meanings of the present tense, then choose one that fits that author's understanding of the passage. This approach is not exactly the one that we

8. Gloria Neufeld Redekop, "Let the Women Learn: 1 Timothy 2:8–15 Reconsidered," *SR* 19 (1990): 242.

have already discussed; in the present case the interpreter has not read all of the meanings into one specific occurrence. The problem is similar, however, since the interpreter's decision (as far as we can tell) was merely based on a range of uses and was not controlled by the context. At the very least, we must say that the interpreter *did not offer a contextual reason* for choosing the temporally restricted function of the Greek present tense.

Don't Overemphasize Subtle Points of Grammar and Vocabulary

The view that the biblical languages—Greek in particular—are uniquely rich or precise has led many students to rely heavily on distinctions of various sorts. Very common is the tendency to look for differences among synonyms as a key to the interpretation of passages. It cannot be doubted, for example, that the several Hebrew words used in reference to sin have distinctive meanings (comparable to the differences in such English words as *sin, wickedness, evil, transgression,* etc.). Any careful study of Old Testament texts that contain these words requires some attention to the distinctions, and a slipshod approach to word use is inexcusable.

We can never forget, however, that writers often use a diverse vocabulary for simple reasons of style, such as a desire to avoid repetition. In these cases, we may say that the differences among the words are "neutralized" by the context. Even when an author makes a lexical choice for semantic (rather than stylistic) reasons, it does not follow that our interpretation stands or falls on our ability to determine precisely why one word was chosen rather than another. After all, people normally communicate not by uttering isolated words but by speaking whole sentences.

Important as words are, what really matters, then, is how those words have been combined by the speaker. Since the focus of meaning is therefore the sentence (or even the paragraph), the specific force of any one word depends to a large extent on the broader context. That is not to deny that individual words have a stable range of meanings—after all, without such stability communication would be impossible. It is useful to think of the relationship between word and sentence as a reciprocal one. The word makes a contribution to the meaning of the whole sentence, but the sentence as a whole also contributes to the specific meaning of the word.

We could even say that languages have a built-in system of redundancy. This feature makes it possible for us to understand some sentences even if a sneeze or some other noise keeps us from hearing one or two words.

(Similarly, we do not necessarily fail to grasp the total meaning of a sermon if our mind wanders for a couple of minutes.) Consider how your English vocabulary continues to grow whether or not you look up words in the dictionary. Consciously or unconsciously, you learn the meaning of new words simply by hearing them used in specific sentences, since the sentences as a whole supply that meaning for the hearer.

If that is the way language works, we should infer that subtle lexical distinctions play only a secondary role in interpretation. How many writers are likely to throw all their eggs into one basket and hope that the readers catch the one small distinction that determines the meaning of the whole sentence? One cannot deny, for example, that there are some distinctions between the two Greek verbs for love, *agapaō* and *phileō*. It is less clear, however, whether those distinctions are reflected, say, in the interchange between Jesus and Peter recorded in John 21:15–17. The NIV translators must have thought so, since they translate the former verb (found in Jesus' question) with the words "truly love," while the latter (used by Peter in his response) is translated simply "love." Such a distinction is highly debatable. To mention only one problem, the latter verb is used of the Father's love for the Son in 5:20. But even if the distinction could be sustained, is it reasonable to think that the proper understanding of the passage hangs on our ability to discover such a faint contrast? A solid interpretation should be built on much broader evidence than that.

We may say, generally speaking, that the greater the weight placed on distinctions among synonyms, the more likely it is that such distinctions are being overstated. For example, the Greek verbs *oida* and *ginōskō* can both be translated "know." The most frequently suggested distinction between these verbs is that the latter can more easily be used in contexts that deal with the acquisition of knowledge. Accordingly, *oida* is often found where such acquisition is not in view, but that leaves innumerable contexts where the verbs could be used interchangeably. In spite of that, some scholars proceed to argue that *ginōskō* refers specifically to experiential knowledge, that is, something acquired by experience as opposed to innate or intuitive knowledge. This claim, though plausible, is at best tentative and does not fully take into account the many passages where such a distinction is not present. Those who accept it, however, sometimes go further and suggest that *oida* indicates greater assurance, simply because it is found in some contexts (e.g., Rom. 8:28) that speak of assurance. Others even argue that it reflects divine knowledge.

If there is danger in overstating lexical distinctions, what shall we say about grammatical ones? Think of it this way: when was the last time that you felt you did not understand an English sentence because you could not decide why the speaker chose a simple present tense (e.g., "How do you feel?") rather than a progressive tense ("How are you feeling?")? With rare exceptions, those kinds of decisions are made not on the basis of careful deliberation but more or less automatically. And even when we deliberate about some grammatical choices, that is usually because we are concerned about "proper" English, not because the meaning will be substantially different (e.g., "After he left, the problems began" means the same as the more formal expression, "After he *had left,* the problems began").

When it comes to the Greek New Testament, however, students spend a great deal of effort trying to interpret grammatical subtleties. Consider Hebrews 1:2: "In these last days he has spoken to us by his Son." The last three words translate two Greek words, *en huiō,* literally, "in son." Now it turns out that the use of the definite article in Greek does not correspond exactly with that of English *the.* One of the differences has to do with the omission of the Greek article when we, because of our English habits, expect to see the article. In some instances, the omission may reflect the possibility that the writer's focus is less on the identity of the object than on its quality.

The distinction is barely perceptible (in some passages not at all) and cannot be reproduced in English. When people try to convey the idea, they end up exaggerating (e.g., with such a paraphrase as "in someone who is by nature a son"). One popular expositor waxes mystical: "Again we feel the poverty of English idiom, and must translate, 'His Son,' or 'a Son.' But if we say over and over to ourselves the very words, *God did speak unto us in Son,* our hearts will feel the meaning, though our words cannot translate it."[9] In fact, the presence or absence of the article here does not alter the meaning of the clause. It was a stylistic choice that the original readers of the epistle (and perhaps even the writer!) possibly would not have been able to account for in a satisfactory way.

The most common misuse of grammatical subtlety has to do with the Greek tenses. Part of the reason is that the Greek verbal system includes a tense form that has been labeled *aorist.* Since the term is not used when describing English, it conveys a quasi-esoteric feeling and encourages overinterpretation. Another reason is the fact that Greek verbs exploit "aspectual" distinctions more frequently than English verbs do. The distinction between the English simple past tense ("I ate") and the imperfect ("I was eating") is an aspectual one and corresponds more or less to a similar distinction in Greek. In addition, however, Greek maintains the distinction in

9. William R. Newell, *Hebrews: Verse by Verse* (Chicago: Moody, 1947), p. 3n.

the nonindicative moods, such as the imperative, and that fact creates problems for the English student.

The aorist tense (or better, aspect) was given its name by ancient Greek grammarians who recognized that there was something indefinite about it (the Greek word *aoristos* means "undefined"). Curiously, many New Testament interpreters view it as special in some sense and greatly exaggerate its significance. One of the commentary sets most frequently used by students of the Greek New Testament abounds in this tendency. For example, on Philippians 2:15, "so that you may become blameless," this commentator interprets the aorist verb to mean "may definitely and permanently be." And on Revelation 2:5, "Repent and do the things you did at first," he says that the "two imperatives are ringing, peremptory aorists: 'and repent (completely) and do (decisively) the first works!' as was done in the first love during the days gone by."[10]

In certain cases the choice of aspect (or some other grammatical detail) by a Greek author perhaps contributes somewhat to a meaning that is otherwise clearly expressed in the context. If so, the grammar is at best a secondary support to the interpretation of the passage. However, if a proposed meaning cannot be established apart from an appeal to a grammatical subtlety, chances are that the argument is worthless. The biblical writers were clear and explicit and did not expect their readers to have to decipher complicated linguistic riddles. In any case, lay students of Scripture should not be swayed too easily by an "expert" who tries to persuade them through technical argumentation of this sort.

Summary

Although the principles discussed in this chapter consist of "don'ts," it should be evident that all of them imply positive guidelines. We may summarize these guidelines by rephrasing them:

1. *Do recognize the significance of the biblical languages for proper interpretation.* Attempt to become familiar with Greek and Hebrew. If that is not possible, accustom yourself to the notion that there is a linguistic and cultural distance that separates us from the biblical text. While this distance

10. R. C. H. Lenski, *The Interpretation of St. Paul's Epistles to the Galatians, to the Ephesians, and to the Philippians* (Minneapolis: Augsburg, 1961; orig. 1937), p. 802; *idem, The Interpretation of St. John's Revelation* (Minneapolis: Augsburg, 1961; orig. 1943), p. 88.

should not be exaggerated, beware of reading into the Bible ideas that can be supported only from the English translation.

2. *Do keep in mind that English translations are reliable for most purposes.* While we should be grateful for specialists who can help us with details and ambiguities, it is important to remember that the teaching of Scripture as a whole is readily accessible to all believers.

3. *Do place priority on the attested and contemporary usage of words.* While the origins and development of a word may be interesting, writers depend on the way language is actually used in their time. Normally, proposed meanings are valid only if they can be confirmed by references contemporaneous with the text.

4. *Do focus on specific uses in context.* Being aware of a word's broad range of meaning can be useful as a basis for making a choice, but we must remember that (aside from puns and other types of rare allusions) meanings other than the one specified by the context do not normally occur to the speaker and the audience.

5. *Do emphasize the context.* This is the fundamental principle. It is in fact the guideline that undergirds all of the others. For example, the reason we do not have to be slavishly dependent on scholars is that the broad context of Scripture can be understood without a knowledge of technical details. Before tackling a specific problem in one verse, we ought to read and reread the whole chapter—indeed, the whole book of which it is a part. Surely, constant reading of the Scriptures in their totality is the best prescription for handling the Word aright.

PART 2

Understanding the Text: Meaning in Literary Genres

Narrative is one of the most common genres in the Bible. But unlike prose, which states things directly, narrative depends on the selection of the details, the arrangement of the events, and rhetorical devices to establish the principles it wishes to communicate.

The key elements in a narrative are the scene, the point of view, the dialogue, and the rhetorical devices such as repetition, inclusion, and chiasm. Each element assists the interpreter to more adequately understand what was the meaning and purpose for including each episode narrated in Scripture. Biblical narratives exhibit the elements of structure at four different levels: the verbal level, the level of narrative technique, the level of the narrative world, and the level of conceptual content.

Where the narrative also includes references to historical details of events, persons, or dates in the real world, these details can and must figure in the interpretation of that text to the degree that the author indicated without submitting apologetical concerns and interests for the message of the text.

CHAPTER 4

"I Will Remember the Deeds of the Lord"
THE MEANING OF NARRATIVE

Walter C. Kaiser, Jr.

The most common genre in the Bible is narrative, with well over one-third of the whole Bible in this form. The narrative framework spans the history of God's dealings with humanity from creation to the exile of Judah in the books of Genesis to 2 Kings. In terms of the divisions of the Hebrew canon,[1] narrative is the predominant genre in the Torah (esp. Genesis, Exodus, and Numbers), in all the books of the Earlier Prophets, in some of the Latter Prophets (esp. major sections in Isaiah and Jeremiah, plus parts of Jonah and other books), and also in several books of the Writings (esp. Chronicles, Ezra, Nehemiah, Ruth, Esther, and Daniel). It also dominates the Gospels and Acts. Narrative is clearly the main supporting framework for the Bible.

Narrative in its broadest sense is an account of specific space-time events and participants whose stories are recorded with a beginning, a middle, and an end. Unlike prose, wherein things are stated directly, narrative

1. The Hebrew Canon is divided into three major parts as follows:

Torah: the Pentateuch   *Writings*
Prophets   Poets: Psalms, Job, Proverbs
    Earlier: Joshua, Judges, Samuel,   Five Little Rolls: Ruth, Song of
      Kings   Songs, Ecclesiastes,
    Latter: Isaiah, Jeremiah, Ezekiel,   Lamentations, Esther
      the 12 Minor Prophets   The Histories: Daniel, Ezra,
                      Nehemiah, Chronicles

presents things indirectly. Its style derives from the writer's *selection* (from a usually vast number of possible details), *arrangement* (not necessarily strictly sequential or chronological), and *rhetorical devices*. The last includes pivotal statements taken from the mouths of the narrative's key figures, thereby allowing the author to make the points that reveal the focus and purpose for telling the story.

Readers and interpreters of stories sometimes become so involved in the characters and the plot of the narrative that they forget to consider what the message from God to the contemporary church is. For them, the story becomes an end in itself.

More frequently, however, we find the opposite problem. Readers too often project some moral or spiritual truth over a biblical character or event, paying more attention to the moral lesson they see in the narrative than to the actual story itself. The underlying objection to interpreting the Bible in a moralistic, exemplary fashion for every narrative passage is that it destroys the unity of the message of the Bible. Under this method of handling the text, each narrative tends to be cut off from the redemptive history of Christ and results in a severe fragmentation of the message of the Bible. Rather than considering the whole event, character, and episode for what it contributes to the context in which it is set, a subjective process of analogy too often takes over, along with an individualistic isolation of selected details that happen to fit the fancy of the interpreter's purposes. Such a selection process tends to be arbitrary, subjective, and usually unrelated to the whole context of the narrative, much less to the total message of the Bible.[2]

Such hermeneutical shortchanging of the text cannot carry the authority of the Bible with it. The desire to find what is practical, personal, challenging, and individually applicable is indeed laudatory; methods that essentially allow us to overlook the narrative itself, however, leave much to be desired. The only cure for such abuses is to come to terms with how these narratives are actually being presented and used by the writers of Scripture.

No doubt a large number of Bible readers have personally been fed on the very method of handling narrative texts that we have just criticized. A common defense of such a personalized method of reading the Bible is to say, "But I got such a blessing out of the moral that I saw in the biblical text that I'm sure it must be true!" If the narrative itself did not really express the truth "seen," however, then we have to say, "Good for the blessing—but not so

---

2. For helpful comments on this topic, see Carl G. Kromminga, "Remember Lot's Wife: Preaching Old Testament Narrative Texts," *CTJ* 18 (1983): 33–34; Sidney Greidanus, *Sola Scriptura: Problems and Principles in Preaching Historical Texts* (Toronto: Wedge, 1970), pp. 22–55.

good for the text to which you are attributing it!" Our first job is to listen carefully to the text of Scripture—including each narrative passage.

Literary Devices in Narrative

To help our study of narrative texts and of the meaning they are intended to convey, let us take apart the typical narrative, looking more carefully at its key elements.

THE SCENE

The most important feature of the narrative is the scene. The action of the story is broken up into a sequence of scenes, each scene presenting what took place at one particular place and time. The author uses scenes to focus attention on one particular set of acts or words that he or she wants us to examine.

Each scene usually has no more than two characters. Where a group is present in one of the scenes, it tends to function as one of the characters.

One of the most notable features about biblical narrative is "the pervasive presence of God." Often, God is one of the two characters in these scenes, or the voice of the prophet functions in place of God's presence. Consider such two-character scenes in Genesis as God and Adam (chap. 3), God and Cain (chap. 4), God and Noah (chap. 6), and God and Abraham (chap. 12). God's presence, or even the hint of his presence, often begins to establish the point of view taken by the narrator. Against the backdrop of this explicit or implied presence come the promises, commands, providence, or power of God in these narratives.

The interpreter must identify each of these scenes, much as one would break up a long prose passage into paragraphs. It is helpful to draft a summary statement for each scene, similar to the way we might identify the topic or theme sentence of each paragraph in an essay. This summary statement should focus on the actions, words, or depictions in the scene, keeping in mind the direction the author seems to be following in the whole sequence of scenes. If the author's point in a given narrative is at first unclear, we can profit by focusing for the moment on God's presence, actions, and comments in each scene where they are relevant.

THE POINT OF VIEW

Scenes have a basic pattern, including a series of relationships with a beginning, a middle, and an end. This arrangement we usually designate as the plot of the narrative. Plot traces the movement of the incidents, episodes, or actions of a narrative, usually as they revolve around some type of conflict.

At some point in the narrative, the author brings to a climax the whole series of episodes in the various scenes, thereby supplying the whole point of view for the story. This point of view forms the perspective from which the whole story is told.

The narrative in 1 Kings 17, for example, introduces the reader abruptly to a certain "Elijah, the Tishbite, from the inhabitants of Gilead." We can easily enough identify four individual scenes in this chapter:

1. Elijah in the palace before the Israelite King Ahab (v. 1)
2. Elijah being fed by the ravens at the ravine of Kerith (vv. 2–7)
3. Elijah asking the widow at the town gate of Zarephath, Phoenicia, to feed him, which was followed by the miracle of multiplication of the oil and flour (vv. 8–16)
4. The death of the widow's son in the widow's home and Elijah's restoring him to life with the help of God (vv. 17–24)

But what is the point of view underlying these four scenes? If we cannot answer this question, the scenes for us are just a random collection of stories.

The first time I seriously looked at this passage, I remember rereading it a number of times looking for the point of view and the narrator's purpose in introducing these four episodes. I noted the repetition of the phrase *word of the LORD,* which appears in verses 2, 8, 16, and 24. At first I regarded these merely as formulas of introduction or (in one case) conclusion. However, my view of these formulas changed when I realized that the narrator would also often place the point he wished to make in the form of a quotation or a speech in the mouth of one of the key characters at some climactic stage in the plot. Using this clue, I looked again at verse 24: "Then the woman said to Elijah, 'Now I know that you are a man of God and that the word of the LORD from your mouth is the truth.'"

The narrator's "point of view" in this passage was to show that *God's word was dependable* in each of the circumstances of life depicted in the four scenes. The point of view, therefore, functions in this narrative text exactly as what I have called the pivot point (or fulcrum) functions in didactic or prose texts.[3] This feature, then, guides us in discerning what truth the author intended to convey in choosing and recording these episodes. Focusing on the author's point of view depicted in the larger literary context can keep us from

3. Walter C. Kaiser, Jr., *Toward an Exegetical Theology: Biblical Exegesis for Preaching and Teaching* (Grand Rapids: Baker, 1981), pp. 152–55.

settling merely for surface "lessons" or vague "blessings" as we read the biblical narratives.

DIALOGUE

The third major element of biblical narrative is dialogue. As Robert Alter has noted, "Everything in the world of biblical narrative ultimately gravitates toward dialogue. . . . quantitatively, a remarkably large part of the narrative burden is carried by dialogue, the transactions between characters typically unfolding through the words they exchange, with only the most minimal intervention of the narrator."[4]

The theme of the passage, which the point of view expresses, is generally carried along in its forward movement by dialogue. Alter suggests two helpful rules that alert interpreters to the significance of this movement of dialogue:

> 1. The place where dialogue is first introduced will be an important moment in revealing the character of its speaker—perhaps more in the manner than in the substance of what is said.
> 2. Notice where the narrator has chosen to introduce dialogue instead of narration. The special rhythm of moving back and forth between dialogue and narrative, while centering on some sharp verbal exchange between the characters, will help us to focus on their relation to God and to one another.[5]

Dialogue occasionally appears in the form of stylized speech, where one character repeats a part or the whole of what another character said. In these instances, we should watch carefully for any small differences, slight alterations, reversals of order, elaborations, or deletions. Such variations may well be significant in disclosing character or a different slant to the events being described.

Seldom does a narrator enter the narration directly—for example, in order to give a moral to the story. But the narrator quite frequently gives a summarizing speech at a particularly critical juncture in the narrative in order to (1) speed up the flow of the narrative, (2) avoid excessive repetition, or (3) give some perspective to what has been said.

Dialogue is one of the main ways in which the narrator can present characterization. The narrative that surrounds such dialogue merely tends to

---

4. Robert Alter, *The Art of Biblical Narrative* (New York: Basic Books, 1981), p. 182. This valuable work underlies much of the following section.
5. Ibid., pp. 74–75.

confirm what is said in the dialogue. Hence, it is most important to follow dialogue carefully in order to catch the development of the point being made—often indirectly—by the author.

THE RHETORICAL DEVICES

Biblical narrators commonly relied on certain rhetorical devices that appear also in others kinds of prose and in poetry. Three important ones are repetition, inclusion, and chiasm.

REPETITION. One of the favorite rhetorical devices in Hebrew narrative was repetition. One type of repetition uses the recurrence of words or short phrases; another links together actions, images, motifs, themes, and ideas.

The repetition of words was especially significant. In many cases the author used repeated words or even sentences to express a certain emphasis, meaning, or development of the text. Thus 2 Kings 1:3, 6, and 16 each asks the same question: "Is it because there is no God in Israel [irony] that you are going off to consult Baal-Zebub, the god of Ekron?" in order to drive home the point that the writer wanted to make. A similar repetition through the use of a recurring question appears in a narrative for a dejected and escapist prophet. Twice the narrator records the Lord's question, "What are you doing here, Elijah?" (1 Kings 19:9, 13), where "here" was the cave on Mount Horeb, several hundred miles off base from the assignment God had given.

In yet another example, each of three captains sent to capture Elijah gives the same speech except for the significant variation in the third and final attempt to bring Elijah in before the king. The first two tell Elijah bluntly, "Man of God, the king says, 'Get down at once'" (2 Kings 1:9, 11; my own translation). The third captain, apparently somewhat chastened by the withering experience of his two former colleagues, softens his demand with a respectful, "Man of God, please have respect for my life and the lives of these fifty men, your servants! See, fire has fallen from heaven [a circumlocution for 'God'] and consumed the first two captains and all their men. But now have respect for my life!" (vv. 13–14).

Another type of repetition in Hebrew narrative is "resumptive repetition." In this type, the narrator returns the reader to the original point in the story after developing a related incident. Thus in 1 Samuel 19:12 we read that "Michal let David down through a window, and he fled and escaped." The reader remains with Michal for the moment while David makes good his escape. In verse 18, though, we are brought back to the main point by the narrator's comment that "David had fled and made his escape."[6]

INCLUSION. A second rhetorical device that biblical narrators used is inclusion, which is actually a form of repetition. "Inclusion" refers to a repetition that marks the beginning and the end of a section, thus effectively bracketing or enveloping the marked-off material.

A very good illustration of inclusion can be found in Exodus 6:13 and 26–27. Verse 13 reads, "Now the LORD spoke to Moses and Aaron about the Israelites and Pharaoh king of Egypt, and he commanded them to bring the Israelites out of Egypt." Curiously enough, what follows is a genealogical list of only three of the twelve sons: Reuben, Simeon, and Levi, with a more detailed treatment of Levi—presumably because that list led to Moses and Aaron. Here the genealogy ends just as abruptly as it began. Then the following words in verses 26–27 appear as an inclusion with verse 13: "It was this same Aaron and Moses to whom the LORD said, 'Bring the Israelites out of Egypt by their divisions.' They were the ones who spoke to Pharaoh king of Egypt about bringing the Israelites out of Egypt. It was the same Moses and Aaron."

It so happens that these three sons of Jacob figured in a negative way in previous narrative accounts in Scripture. Reuben slept with his father's concubine (Gen. 35:22; 49:4), and Simeon and Levi massacred the Shechemites after they had urged that all the Shechemite men be circumcised (Gen. 34:25–31). After such incidents, readers might wonder how it would be possible for anyone who came from such origins to be used of God. No wonder the text stresses over and over again in this inclusion, "This is the same Moses and Aaron!" The inclusion thus helps us to focus on the point that the calling and gifts of God for leadership had very little to do with heritage, natural endowments, or human lineage.

CHIASM. A third rhetorical device of biblical narrative is chiasm, a literary device named after the Greek letter chi (χ). It is named for the crossing, or inversion, of related elements within parallel constructions.

Chiasms may involve the inversion of anything from words or clauses in two parallel lines of poetry to a series of dialogues or even of a series of chapters of narration. It is easiest to identify chiasms where the same words, clauses, or phrases are reversed. A clear example is the following, from Isaiah 11:13:

6. Two helpful works on the subject of interpreting biblical narratives are Adele Berlin, *Poetics and Interpretation of Biblical Narrative,* and Burke O. Long, "Framing Repetitions in Biblical Historiography," *JBL* 106 (1987): 385–99.

a	*b*	*c*
Ephraim	shall not be jealous	of Judah
c̗	*b̗*	*a̗*
and Judah	shall not harass	Ephraim

Another type of chiasm goes beyond such parallelism in single verses. It exists also in chapters, sections, and sometimes even whole books of the Bible. Far from being merely a superficial decorative ornament, chiasm is one of the major artistic conventions used for narratives in the Bible. As such, it can be a key in detecting the author's aims, for the main event or principal idea typically appears in the apex—that is, in the middle of the story.[7] A clear illustration of chiasm operating in a section of a biblical book can be seen in the following analysis of Daniel 1–7:

Introduction. Daniel 1

A. Daniel 2   Four Gentile world empires

  B. Daniel 3   Gentile persecution of Israel

    C. Daniel 4   Divine providence over Gentiles

    C' Daniel 5   Divine providence over Gentiles

  B' Daniel 6   Gentile persecution of Israel

A' Daniel 7   Four Gentile world empires

According to this chiastic structure, therefore, the heart of the first seven chapters comes in Daniel 4 and 5. Daniel 4 was God's final word to Nebuchadnezzar, and Daniel 5 was God's final word to Belshazzar; for all intents and purposes, these two kings were the beginning and concluding monarchs of the Babylonian dynasty. As such, they function both as an encouragement and a warning to all the Gentile nations about the plans, purposes, and graces God proffers to all the nations of the world.

It must also be noted that such an analysis does not compromise the unity of the book of Daniel or imply that the first seven chapters were separated from chapters 8–12. Daniel is written in two languages: Aramaic, the lingua franca of the day, was used for Daniel 2–7, and Hebrew was used in the rest of the book. This fact tends to corroborate the line of evidence that comes from the chiastic formulation. In fact, the shift in languages may well be a hermeneutical signal that the primary audience to whom each section is addressed also shifts at precisely those same points.

7. See Y. T. Radday, "Chiasm in Samuel," *LB* 9/10 (1971): 21–31; idem, "Chiasm in Tora," *LB* 19 (1972): 12–23.

Structural Levels in Narrative

THE VERBAL LEVEL

The analysis of structure based on the verbal level focuses particularly on words or phrases that are repeated. S. Bar-Efrat[8] illustrates this form of structuring by the narrative comment appearing six times in Genesis 1: "And there was evening and there was morning, the first [second, etc.] day" (vv. 5, 8, 13, 19, 23, 31). Other examples are the four messengers in Job 1, whose words "I am the only one who has escaped to tell you" (vv. 15, 16, 17, 19) supply a fourfold structure to that text, and the four times Delilah asks Samson for the secret of his strength (Judg. 16:6, 10, 13, 15), which also brings out, and in fact actually provides, the structure of this narrative.

Other stylistic features in addition to repetition include the use of metaphors, similes, and unusual constructions of the grammar or syntax.

THE LEVEL OF NARRATIVE TECHNIQUE

Structure at the narrative technique level is expressed by the alternating patterns of (1) dialogue versus narrator's description; (2) narration versus description; and (3) comment, or even explanation and presentation of scenes, versus summary of the action. The most important, however, is the first.

Narrative technique mainly affects the rate of progress in a narrative and the question of the order of the events. When the author uses scenic presentation, time goes by slowly and we are thereby forced to pay close attention to the details in order to extract the direction or significance of the narrative. But when the narrator switches to summary statements in the narrative, then the velocity of time is accelerated and the point of the narrative may be stated more directly.

Authors may break into their story at any point, doing so in accord with fixed techniques. One such marker of structure is the frequent use of flashbacks to cover the past that is background to the beginning of a narrative. In Hebrew, these flashbacks would be indicated by the use of the perfect form of the verb instead of the normal imperfect.

THE LEVEL OF THE NARRATIVE WORLD

The third structural level focuses on the narrative world, that is, the realm in which the story is set. It deals mainly with the two main components or contents of narratives: characters and events.

8. S. Bar-Efrat, "Some Observations on the Analysis of Structure in Biblical Narrative," *VT* 30 (1980): 157–70.

Characters are developed with respect to their identity, their character- istics, and their functions. Interpreters should notice the *linking* of the various characters as they appear in sequence in a text. Usually the character introduced second in a text becomes the first to appear in the next link as the narrative progresses. Following these links may provide a clue as to what the author wishes us to center our attention on.

The relationships of the events of a story make up the *plot*. Many narratives have a single plot. In the whole book of Esther, for example, Haman's design to exterminate all the Jews in the Medo-Persian empire takes center stage, with Mordecai and Esther's attempts to countermand those actions taking a secondary role. In reality, describing the plot usually boils down to simply paraphrasing the story. Common plot devices include the climax, the second climax, and reversal. Usually plots ascend to the climax and then descend to a peaceful conclusion. Sometimes this pattern is ignored and the narrative immediately ascends to a second climax. Job faced the four messengers, for example, only to be confronted by three "comforters" for a new challenge he had to surmount. In reversal, the action takes a sudden turn in the crucial point. The episode of the sacrifice of Isaac in Genesis 22 illustrates reversal, as does the narrative about Jacob's return to meet his brother Esau after twenty years of service to Laban in Genesis 32–33.

Included in the narrative-world level of analysis of the text are references to the spatial and temporal terms used in the narrative. Often the action of a single story shifts from one place to another, thereby creating distinct structure. Likewise, the story may shift by indicating a change in time or even how long the event took, such as in the narrative of the flood in Genesis 7–8.

THE LEVEL OF CONCEPTUAL CONTENT

The final level giving structure to narratives is that of the conceptual content. This element focuses on *themes,* which are usually expressed in short phrases, or on *ideas,* which come in the form of complete sentences. Themes set forth the central issues of the narrative, while ideas point to the lesson, message, or teaching found in the narrative. Since in the majority of cases both the themes and the ideas of the narrative will be merely implied, not stated explicitly, special care will need to be exercised, along with a lot of self- restraint and self-criticism.

Nehemiah 4–6 can supply us with illustrations of both the themes and ideas of these chapters. Overall, the book might be divided up into the following ideas:

Chaps. 1–7: Principles of effective leadership

Chaps. 8–10: Principles of spiritual renewal

Chaps. 11–13: Principles of dedicated excellence

The themes of chapters 4–6 might well be described in the following manner:

Chap. 4: Opposition to rebuilding

Chap. 5: Oppression of the poor

Chap. 6: Entanglement of the leader

The ideas of this passage are united in their focus on the work of God:

Chap. 4: Obstructing the work of God by open violence

Chap. 5: Obstructing the work of God by internal pressure

Chap. 6: Obstructing the work of God by entrapping leaders

In summary, as Bar-Efrat points out, we can use structural levels to (1) demonstrate the unity of a narrative, (2) determine the boundaries of a story, (3) demonstrate the rhetorical or expressive values found within a text, (4) understand the effect that the author wanted to have on the reader, and (5) notice which elements of the text the author wished to highlight.[9]

Historical Considerations in Narrative

While the literary genre of narrative encompasses much more than historical report, we cannot neglect the matter owing to its extensive use in both testaments. But the question of historicity is extremely complex, especially if one insists on holding onto the nineteenth-century ideal of an accurate, objective, impartial, and noninterpretive history.

Now, we need not use the word *historical* in that way. It will be enough for our purposes if we note whether those persons and events that the writers portray as being part of the space-time continuum actually did live at the times they are alleged to have lived and actually did what is attributed to them. Whether that also falls within the bounds of what has technically been labeled as historical since the nineteenth century is another matter, which we will not take up at this time. Nor is it crucial that we do so in order to interpret the text with any degree of fairness.

9. Ibid., 172.

THE IMPORTANCE OF HISTORICITY

Sidney Greidanus has defined the crucial issue in historicity in a precise fashion:

> Although there is much to be said for the power of story and how it works apart from the question of historicity, it must also be said that treating all biblical narratives like parables is a gross oversimplification, for not all biblical narratives are non-historical. . . . The issue here again is the intent or purpose of the text. If that intent . . . entails relating historical events, then sidestepping that intent in one's interpretation fails to do full justice to that narrative's meaning.[10]

Most modern interpreters would prefer to give all the long, narrative corpus the title of "story," by which *they* mean that it did not contain history, but was only—in the words of Hans Frei—"history-like."[11] Yet a denial of the existence of historical narrative in the biblical text, where the text has claimed such, must be regarded as the equivalent of denying its message. For example, the denial or deletion of the historical referents in the narrative about Jesus' life and ministry were just as destructive of the truth-intentions of the writers as a denial or deletion of all historical contacts in the exodus narrative.

It is true, of course, that the historical allusions are usually not the direct point of the narratives. Nevertheless, they do function as corollaries that validate the teaching and claims made in the text. In many cases, the theology taught in a text rests squarely on the reality of the events occurring as they were depicted there. Should the events prove not to be true, the theology that rests on them would consequently not be true either. For example, the theology that asserts that Jesus "suffered under Pontius Pilate, was crucified, dead and buried; the third day he rose again . . ." is unequivocally linked with history. If Pilate did not exist, and if there was no death, burial, or resurrection of Jesus on the third day, the Apostles' Creed would, in effect, be worthless in that it reflected an unbridled imagination.

By contrast, the message of such passages making historical allusions is not to be found in its apologetics—that is, in the defense of the facticity and reality of what is being alluded to as happening in time and space. The message is still to be found in the teachings of the literary text before us. In most instances, the text has another purpose than merely to teach us that this

---

10. Sidney Greidanus, *The Modern Preacher and the Ancient Text: Interpreting and Preaching Biblical Literature* (Grand Rapids: Eerdmans, 1988), p. 199.

11. Frei used the term for this purpose in his *Eclipse of Biblical Narrative* (New Haven: Yale University Press, 1974), chap. 1.

person or event did or did not happen. Yet the historical referent may not be dispensed with so rapidly or in a cavalier way, as many moderns have unthinkingly presumed—perhaps hoping thereby to avoid the quagmire (and pitifully slim results for a waiting church) from the school of historical criticism.

There are a few historical narratives in which the objective existence of the historical referent is not *hermeneutically* consequential for an adequate understanding of the passage. Greidanus makes this point with regard to the purpose of the books of Job and Jonah.[12] I can agree with him on the book of Job, but I do not think that the purpose of Jonah can be fully grasped without placing it against its historical antecedents.

In the case of Job, no particular historical setting is claimed by the book. It is only when one notices the fact that Job performs his own sacrifices (rather than depending on any Levitical structure) and notices linguistic and cultural features (such as the terms Job uses for buying) that a case can be made for a patriarchal setting during the days of Abraham, Isaac, and Jacob. Yet nothing in the book itself will be seriously affected by that identification or even the lack of it. That identification only serves to enrich our appreciation of the word coloring, the cultural context, and the like.

Jonah is a different story. One must appreciate the brutality of the Assyrians and what their capital city of Nineveh had meant for all who had suffered so mightily under that merciless war machine. Therefore, as in most historical narratives one key component of the story would be lost if the historical referent were dropped, so it is with Jonah. Moreover, abandoning the historical background to the book of Jonah would run counter to the notice given in 2 Kings 14:25, where Jonah, the son of Amittai, the prophet from Gath Hepher, was used by God during the days of Jeroboam II in the northern kingdom to prophesy about the expansion of the boundaries of Israel. In that role Jonah was a happy proclaimer, whereas the role of warning Israel's enemy of the pending disaster risked the enemy's repentance and the unwarranted extension of the mercy of God (unwarranted in the distorted view of the unhappy prophet) to a population Jonah would just as soon have seen liquidated.

All this discussion notwithstanding, interpretation is not to be confused with doing apologetics or the mere extraction of bare facts from the narrative. To participate in this confusion would deny almost everything that has been emphasized in the first two sections of this chapter, and it would subvert the original purpose of the author into substituted purposes that are our own, even if those purposes were regarded as a good cause—the defense

12. Greidanus, *The Modern Preacher and the Ancient Text,* p. 195.

of the faith. Such an apologetic approach to the text would read it as a collection of pieces of evidence, separate and unrelated to one another—an archaeological expedition into the text. That approach gives evidence of very little feeling for the text as literature or for its message, in part or in whole.

TRUTH OR MEANING IN BIBLICAL NARRATIVE

The two contemporary giants in hermeneutics who have written about biblical narrative are Hans Frei and Paul Ricoeur.[13] Frei argued that Christians must stop short of making any claims about the truthfulness of the stories narrated in the Bible. In his influential book *The Eclipse of Biblical Narrative,* he argued instead that it was enough to say that these narratives were meaningful.

The problem began, as far as Frei could determine, when the forces of deism, historical criticism, and Hume's exposition on historical claims converged to saddle biblical interpretation with defending the truthfulness of the historical claims of the Bible. This led to a nettlesome distinction between "meaning" (what the text says) and the text's referents (what it is about). The various attempts to bridge this gulf, warned Frei, have all proved unsuccessful. Frei concluded that the cause of their failure was simply that such realistic narratives do not allow a separation between the meaning and its reference. What the text is about is also found in its literary form, hence it is to be found in its meaning.

Unfortunately, Frei's meaning of what he called realistic narrative is not tied to a discussion of either the author's or even the reader's intentions or responses. His position is that narrative is self-referential and autonomous. Any question about the truth of a biblical narrative for this scholar is an unfortunate category mistake, for what is the point of engaging in rational conversation and apologetical defense of the facts in the narrative since they would only be understood by those who were already believers? Other reasonable persons would be excluded. Therefore, the best solution, Frei said, is to enlarge the boundaries of what we consider "the text itself" to include all Christian readers' experiences of Christianity. "Realistic narratives" do not invite readers to assess the truth of the sentences they use or to appraise their logical coherence. Rather, the narratives are units on their own that cannot be pressed to ask if the Christian picture is more "true" than any other.

Paul Ricoeur agrees with Frei that the meaning of a "history-like" story

13. I was greatly aided in my understanding of these two scholars by Gary Comstock, "Truth or Meaning: Ricoeur versus Frei on Biblical Narrative," *JR* 66 (1986): 117–40.

is its *plot,* the interaction between its characters and their circumstances directed toward an end. But Ricoeur interprets this plot by some type of historical audience—that is, how that textual evidence is construed by some specific audience. While the plot is found "in" the text, Ricoeur adds that the world of the text (its "referent") arises from the fusion of horizons between the text and its reader.[14] However, he too denies that realistic narratives refer to real objects, persons, or events referred to in those texts. Since the world of the text is fictional (in Frei's words, "history-like"), a new world has been created: a possible world.[15]

THE USE OF HISTORY IN HISTORICAL NARRATIVE

To some degree, then, the question of whether the Bible has any examples of history writing is a debate in semantics. If one insists on the rather limited definition of history that prevailed in the nineteenth century— history as "impartial, objective reporting"—then the answer is no. The Bible never claimed to have a disinterested point of view; it is partial to God and his kingdom and has represented itself accordingly.

But if history includes (1) telling what happened, (2) giving the writer's perspective on what happened, and (3) arranging it all into some meaningful pattern so that it conveys a message—then the Bible does include history.[16] The main difference between modern definitions of history and those we are using for biblical materials is that the Bible includes an interpretation of the events and people it describes from a divine perspective. One could call this prophetic history writing, as Greidanus suggests. But we would urge that a chasm not be forged between meaning and referent as Frei and Ricoeur have advised, for that would once again erect Lessing's "ugly ditch" between the events of history and the necessary claims of faith.

The interpretation of narrative must give priority to the literary devices and the literary structure if we are to be successful in interpreting this very profuse genre. But if meaning is also to be held accountable to the criteria of truthfulness and veracity, it will need to be ready to set that text in the primary world of realities in which it purports to have happened. The sad

14. For the term "fusion of horizons," see chap. 2, p. 29.

15. Neither Frei nor Ricoeur has formally developed a general hermeneutic of narrative, but both have contributed to this subject in their writings. For Ricoeur's concepts, see his *Interpretation Theory: Discourse and the Surplus of Meaning* (Fort Worth: Texas Christian University Press, 1976) and *The Conflict of Interpretations: Essays in Hermeneutics* (Evanston, Ill.: Northwestern University Press, 1974). I am again indebted to Comstock for his discussion of Ricoeur in "Truth or Meaning," pp, 131–40.

16. These criteria are suggested in part in Ronald E. Clements, "History and Theology in Biblical Narrative," *Horizons of Biblical Theology* 4–5 (1982–83): 45–60, as called to my attention by Greidanus, *The Modern Preacher,* p. 191, n. 11.

story of most of human endeavor is that when we correct one abuse (in this case, the substitution of apologetics for doing interpretation), the pendulum tends to swing all the way over to the opposite extreme. As a corrective to this overreaction, we propose that interpreters include the historical referents where the text does, for they probably were included by the writer because he felt they had some consequential contribution to make to the meaning process.

One-third of the Old Testament and a surprising amount of the New Testament are in poetic form. While the chief characteristic of Hebrew poetry is parallelism of thoughts—despite some recent dissent of scholars—other characteristics that find greater agreement include a terseness of form and a greater use of rhetorical devices.

All forms of literature use figures of speech, but the poetical books have a much higher frequency ratio. These figures may be grouped according to the principles of comparison, addition, association, contrast, or omission.

The wisdom literature of the Bible includes a host of subgenres such as proverb, riddle, admonition, dialogue, and onomastica. Each subgenre calls for an adjustment in the interpretive strategy.

CHAPTER 5

"My Heart Is Stirred by a Noble Theme"
THE MEANING OF POETRY AND WISDOM

Walter C. Kaiser, Jr.

Although narrative is the most common genre in the Bible, poetry is not far behind. All told, approximately one-third of the Old Testament is written in poetic form, which, if it were all printed together, would make up a volume whose total length would easily exceed that of the New Testament. The New Testament itself also contains a surprising amount of poetic material.

In this chapter we consider first some of the features of this popular biblical genre, including figures of speech that especially characterize poetry. Since all types of biblical literature make some use of figures of speech, however, we take a closer look at these devices in the second section. Finally, we examine in more detail the so-called Wisdom literature. The books of Wisdom—Job, Proverbs, Ecclesiastes, and, for some interpreters, Song of Songs—express the wisdom gained broadly from experience and from reflection on God's ways. Biblical writers used many different forms in conveying this wisdom, which the third section summarizes.

Poetry

The best-known poetry in the Bible is found in the Psalms, followed perhaps by that in Proverbs and other Wisdom books. Even this, however, hardly begins to exhaust the wealth of poetry found in the Old Testament. In fact, only seven books of the Old Testament are without any poetry: Leviticus, Ruth, Ezra, Nehemiah, Esther, Haggai, and Malachi. New Testament poetry includes (1) quotations from ancient poets (Acts 17:28; Titus 1:12; 1 Cor. 15:33); (2) possible first-century Christian hymns (e.g., Phil. 2:5–11; 1 Tim. 3:16; 2 Tim. 2:11–13); (3) passages in the mold of Old Testament poetry, as exemplified in Luke's Magnificat (1:46–55), Benedictus (1:68–79), Gloria in Excelsis (2:14), and Nunc Dimittis (2:29–32); and (4) passages that have the grand and exalted style of poetry, such as Jesus' lament over Jerusalem (Luke 13:34–35), parts of the Upper Room Discourse (e.g., John 14:1–7), and the songs and apocalyptic imagery of Revelation (e.g., 4:8, 11; 5:9–10, 12–13; 7:15–17; 11:17–18; 15:3–4; 18:2, 14–24; 19:6–8). Poetry is thus an extremely important form for the interpreters to understand.

Despite the amount of poetry in the Bible and the wealth of our knowledge of classical poetic form in the Greek and Latin poets, interpreters of the Bible are often unaware of the special hermeneutical demands of poetry. Part of the problem exists within the discipline of Bible interpretation itself, for some of the most important decisions about how we are to treat poetry still have not been successfully resolved by the scholars of this form. This means that we often must take a much more tentative attitude in interpreting biblical poetry.

PARALLELISM

The modern era for the study of poetry in the Old Testament began in 1753, when Robert Lowth published his magisterial work on the subject.[1] Lowth developed the thesis that the chief characteristic of poetry in the Old Testament was what he labeled Hebrew parallelism. "The correspondence of one verse or line with another, I call parallelism. When a proposition is delivered, and a second is subjoined to it, or drawn under it, equivalent, or contrasted with it in sense, or similar to it in the form of grammatical construction, these I call parallel lines; and the words or phrases, answering one to another in the corresponding lines, parallel terms."[2]

Lowth described three basic types of parallelism: synonymous, antithetic, and synthetic. In synonymous parallelism, the second line of the poetic

1. Robert Lowth, *De sacra poesi Hebraeorum praelectiones academicae* (Lectures on the Sacred Poetry of the Hebrews) (Oxford: Clarendon, 1753).

2. Robert Lowth, *Isaiah: A New Translation, with a Preliminary Dissertation and Notes, Critical, Philological, and Explanatory*, 10th ed. (Boston: Peirce, 1834), p. ix.

form repeats the idea of the first line without making any significant addition or subtraction to it. Some examples of this type of poetry are:

> Wisdom calls aloud in the street,
>   She raises her voice in the public squares. (Prov. 1:20)

> Adah and Zillah, listen to me;
>   wives of Lamech, hear my words. (Gen. 4:23)

> My soul praises the Lord
>   and my spirit rejoices in God my Savior. (Luke 1:46b–47a)

In Lowth's antithetic parallelism, the second line of poetry contrasts with, or negates, the thought and meaning of the first line. Proverbs 10–22 is especially noted for its many examples of this type of parallelism. Two examples of this type are the following:

> A wise son brings joy to his father,
>   but a foolish son grief to his mother. (Prov. 10:1)

> The kisses of an enemy may be profuse,
>   but faithful are the wounds of a friend. (Prov. 27:6).

The third form—synthetic parallelism—has been a problem ever since Lowth introduced it. It does not exhibit a rhyming of thought and a paralleling of ideas, as in the other two forms of parallelism. Although poetic lines in synthetic parallelism may be parallel in form, they are not balanced in thought or ideas as the lines in the previous two types are. In the synthetic form, there is neither gradation nor opposition of the words in the parallel lines; the lines are simply parallel in form, seeming to imitate real parallelism without actually doing so. Lowth's first example of synthetic parallelism was the following:

> Praise the LORD from the earth,
>   you great sea creatures and all ocean depths,
> lightning and hail, snow and clouds,
>   stormy winds that do his bidding,
> you mountains and all hills,
>   fruit trees and all cedars,
> wild animals and all cattle,
>   small creatures and flying birds,
> kings of the earth and all nations,
>   you princes and all rulers on earth,
> young men and maidens,
>   old men and children. (Ps. 148:7–12)

Because of problems in characterizing neatly this third category (which even Lowth admitted was troublesome), and because a relatively small percentage of poetry falls into either the synonymous or antithetical types, a growing number of scholars have challenged Lowth's overall thesis. This group, led by James Kugel, argues that the second line of poetry always adds meaning to the first line, in some way developing the thought in the first line. Kugel, however, has reacted so strongly to Lowth's framework that he comes close to denying that the Bible has any poetry at all. Such a position, in our judgment, is overstated.[3]

While we see parallelism as the chief characteristic of biblical poetry, we must admit that many biblical poems exhibit a very weak parallelism or none at all.[4] Moreover, some forms of Hebrew prose exhibit a symmetry that could be classified as parallelism.

Besides parallelism, other features of Hebrew poetry that tend to distinguish it from prose are (1) a relatively greater conciseness or terseness of form and (2) a greater use of certain rhetorical devices. We discuss these features briefly in the sections below.

CONCISENESS OR TERSENESS OF FORM

In contrast with prose, which is typically organized into paragraphs, poetry is divided into strophes, or stanzas. One of the most common features used to mark off the end of a strophe is the presence of a refrain. This feature is witnessed in Ugaritic poetry, and it occurs in some eighteen psalms (Pss. 39, 42–43, 44, 46, 49, 56, 57, 59, 62, 67, 78, 80, 99, 107, 114, 136, 144, 145). For example, the threefold repetition of the refrain in the continuing Psalm 42–43 divides it into three strophes, or stanzas:

> *Why are you downcast, O my soul?*
> *Why so disturbed within me?*
> *Put your hope in God,*

---

3. See James L. Kugel, *The Idea of Biblical Poetry: Parallelism and Its History* (New Haven: Yale University Press, 1981), and, taking a more moderate view, Robert Alter, *The Art of Biblical Poetry* (New York: Basic, 1985). For an evangelical evaluation of many of these same subjects, see these works by Tremper Longman III: *Literary Approaches to Biblical Interpretation* (Grand Rapids: Zondervan, 1987); *How to Read the Psalms* (Downers Grove, Ill.: InterVarsity, 1988); and "Biblical Poetry," in *A Complete Literary Guide to the Bible,* ed. Leland Ryken and Tremper Longman III (Grand Rapids: Zondervan, 1993), pp. 80–91.

4. In Lamentations, for example, 104 out of the 266 lines (39 percent) exhibit no parallelism whatsoever (according to the count in Delbert Hillers, *Lamentations,* AB [Garden City, N.Y.: Doubleday, 1972], p. xxxiv). The facts here are particularly clear-cut, since four out of the five chapters in Lamentations are completely in alphabetic acrostic form, which gives us some of the best control we have on biblical poetic form.

for I will yet praise him,
my Savior and my God. (Pss. 42:5, 11; 43:5)

In addition, it may well turn out that the Hebrew word *selāh* may also mark the end, or some other meaningful point in the strophe. It occurs seventy-one times in thirty-nine psalms as well as in Habakkuk 3:3, 9, 13. Unfortunately, however, no one knows exactly what the meaning of that word is, much less whether it has any poetic function.

Biblical poetry is very elliptic. It frequently drops a noun or the verb out of the second line, thus leaving no parallel grammatical form to balance the line. Even more difficult for interpreters is the decided preference for Hebrew poetry to be written generally without conjunctions (e.g., *and, but, or*) and with few temporal indicators (*when, then, afterward*) or logical connectors (*thus, therefore*). Finally, three common features of Hebrew prose are rare in poetry: the direct-object marker *et,* the relative pronoun *'ašer* ("who," "which," "that"), and the narrative form of the Hebrew verb (which consists of the conjunction "and" plus the imperfect tense).

RHETORICAL DEVICES

Biblical poetry—like poetry everywhere—is rich in the use of imagery and figures of speech, many examples of which we consider in the following section. Here we note three rhetorical devices that particularly characterize Hebrew poetry: chiasm, discussed above in the chapter on narrative, and two other types of parallelism—what we could call emblematic symbolism and climactic (or staircase) parallelism. These devices can serve as clues signaling the presence of poetry and alerting the interpreter to be on the lookout for any special nuances the author intended the text to convey.

EMBLEMATIC SYMBOLISM. In this type of parallelism, one line takes the form of a rather straightforward or factual statement, while the balancing line(s) takes the form of a simile or a metaphor as a figurative illustration of the same statement. Examples of this phenomenon are (with the emblematic symbolism italicized):

Like a gold ring in a pig's snout
    is a beautiful woman who shows no discretion. *(Prov. 11:22)*

Like cold water to a weary soul
    is good news from a distant land. *(Prov. 25:25)*

As a deer pants for streams of water,
    so my soul pants for you, O God. *(Ps. 42:1)*

CLIMACTIC PARALLELISM. In this favorite device (also called "staircase parallellism"), the poet repeats a group of two or three words in two—sometimes three or four—successive lines. The interpreter should take note of the emphasis and the aesthetic beauty of this type of poetry. Here are three examples from the Psalms:

> For surely your enemies, O LORD,
> surely your enemies will perish;
> all evildoers will be scattered. (92:9)

> The seas have lifted up, O LORD,
> the seas have lifted up their voice;
> the seas have lifted up their pounding waves. (93:3)

> Sing to the LORD a new song;
> sing to the LORD, all the earth.
> sing unto the LORD, praise his name (96:1–2a)

Figures of Speech

It is time now to look more systematically at the range of figures of speech that biblical authors employ. These devices appear in poetry, as well as in narrative, prophecy, the letters, and all other genres, as they do in human literature everywhere. Although we know of no totally objective rules for spotting all figures of speech that a biblical author used in conveying his message, still there are certain questions we can ask of a text that can serve as guidelines for determining when an author has departed from the strictly literal sense of the words and phrases used.

1. Is there a mismatch between the subject and the predicate, such as in the statement "God is our Rock," which has an animate subject (God) linked with an inanimate predicate noun (Rock)?
2. Similarly, does the predicate attribute to the subject actions that are not possible in a real world, such as "the mountains clapped their hands"?
3. Is a colorful word immediately followed by a word that defines or restricts it, such as "we are dead" directly followed by the phrase "in our trespasses and sin"? "Dead" here is suddenly transferred from the realm of the grave to the realm of moral conduct.
4. Might there be a reason for a figure of speech at this point in the text in order to give it a more dramatic emphasis, a heightened feeling, or to make it more memorable?

5. Is the feature I have decided to call a figure of speech identifiable in other contexts?

The most thorough handbook on figures of speech is one authored by E. W. Bullinger.[5] In it he cataloged more than two hundred figures of speech and gave some eight thousand illustrations of their use in the Scriptures. In each case, he first defined the figure of speech, then cited examples from the classical world of the Greek and Roman authors, and finally gave scores of examples from the Scriptures themselves. It is a most valuable collection for the interpreter of the Word of God.

Here we mention the most frequently observed types, dividing them into figures of comparison, addition or fullness of expression, relation or association, contrast, and omission.[6]

FIGURES OF COMPARISON

SIMILE. The simplest and most straightforward of all the figures of speech is the simile. A simile is an expressed or formal comparison between two things or two actions in which one is said to be "as," or "like" the other. "As the rain and the snow come down from heaven, and do not return to it without watering the earth . . . so is my word that goes out from my mouth" (Isa. 55:10–11). The simile is designed to illustrate the author's meaning. Since it is an expressed and stated comparison, it is the easiest of all figures of speech to recognize; its function in the text is generally quite clear.

METAPHOR. A more difficult, but much more frequent, figure of speech is the metaphor. Here the comparison is unexpressed or merely implied. In this case, an idea is carried over from one element to another without directly saying that one is "like" or "as" the other. For example, Jesus, in referring to Herod Antipas, said, "Go tell that *fox*" (Luke 13:32). Jesus no doubt passed over the fox's physical features, such as its furriness, and focused on the craftiness that foxes had in common with Herod Antipas. Jesus made this comparison memorable, if not slightly humorous, and now we may find that the imagery of a fox arises whenever we think about Herod Antipas.

Notice that there are three parts in every simile or metaphor: (1) the subject or item being illustrated by the image, (2) the image of the direct or

5. E. W. Bullinger, *Figures of Speech Used in the Bible: Explained and Illustrated* (1898; reprint, Grand Rapids: Baker, 1968). See also George M. Lamsa, *Idioms in the Bible Explained* (New York: Harper & Row, 1985).

6. Cf. A. H. Snyman and J. v. W. Cronje, "Toward a New Classification of the Figures (ΣΧΗΜΑΤΑ) in the Greek New Testament," *NTS* 32 (1986): 113–21. The authors distinguish mainly between grammatical figures and rhetorical figures. Then all figures are grouped according to four principles: repetition, omission, shift in expectancies, and measurement of units.

implied comparison, and (3) the point of the direct or implied comparison and similarity. In some cases, one or more of these may be missing and must therefore be supplied by the interpreter. For example, when Jesus sent out his disciples "like lambs among wolves" he did not directly state (1), which interpreters can readily supply.

It is possible to get overly excited about the possibilities of such comparisons and begin to suggest an unlimited number of direct or indirect ideas. I remember hearing a college student give a most enthusiastic devotional talk on Psalm 104:16, which in the AV says, "The trees of the LORD are full *of sap.*" He proceeded to draw all sorts of "sticky" (but memorable) comparisons between believers and trees that were full of sap. Never mind that the word *sap* was not in the original text (the NIV has, "The trees of the LORD are well watered"); the sap was flowing, and so were the allusions to various points of comparison with believers.

G. B. Caird warned us of this problem.

> When the psalmist tells us that a united family is like oil dripping down Aaron's beard on to the skirts of his robe, he is not trying to persuade us that family unity is messy, greasy, or volatile; he is thinking of the all-pervasive fragrance which so deeply impressed itself on his memory at the anointing of the high priest (Ps 132:2).[7]

PARABLE AND ALLEGORY. When a simile is extended into a story, it becomes a parable. Jesus used this form of comparison most effectively. (See chap. 6, under "He Spoke to Them in Parables.") Likewise, a metaphor can also be extended into a story, thus becoming an *allegory.* One of the most memorable allegories in the biblical text is the one on marital fidelity in Proverbs 5:15–23. The comparison that is drawn there is between the practice of drinking water from one's own well and the need for being faithful in the conjugal responsibilities and privileges of marriage.

FIGURES OF ADDITION OR FULLNESS OF EXPRESSION

PLEONASM. A literary device writers love to use for the sake of emphasizing a point is the figure of speech called a pleonasm. This figure involves a redundancy of expression used in order to obtain a certain effect on the mind of the listener or reader. Thus Genesis 40:23 informs us that "the chief cupbearer, however, did not remember Joseph; he forgot him." The

7. G. B. Caird, *The Language and Imagery of the Bible* (Philadelphia: Westminster, 1980), p. 145.

writer could have ended the sentence after "Joseph." The point was important to him, however, so he added redundantly, "he forgot him."

PARONOMASIA. Another way to capture the attention of the listener or reader is through the figure of speech known as paronomasia. It involves a fullness of expression by repeating words that are similar in sound, but not necessarily similar in sense or meaning in all cases, for often the similar sounding words are used merely to achieve a certain effect. One of the most famous examples of paronomasia is found in the opening chapter of the Bible, *tōhŭ wābōhŭ,* "waste and void" (Gen. 1:2). In the New Testament, there is *panti pantote pasan,* "[in] all things always [having] all [sufficiency]" (2 Cor. 9:8). The effect is about the same as our saying "hurdy-gurdy" or "zoot suit" or the like. It is just plain fun to rhyme the words together, but it is not intended to be construed as having a meaning apart from the other word—as if, in our example, "waste" is a separate idea from "void."

HYPERBOLE. Hyperbole is a conscious exaggeration or a type of overstatement in order to increase the effect of what is being said. The psalmist cried out with deliberate exaggeration in Psalm 6:6, "I am worn out from my groaning; all night long I flood my bed with weeping." (Has any reader ever missed this striking hyperbole?!) In the same way, the interpreter should not take literally some of Jesus' words in the Sermon on the Mount uttered with obvious hyperbole. For example, Jesus taught, "If your right eye causes you to sin, gouge it out and throw it away" (Matt. 5:29). The interpreter should see here a conscious exaggeration on Jesus' part in order to move his audience to be all the more ready to act immediately in removing that which would cause an offense. In Judges 7:12 the Midianites and Amalekites that came up against Israel in the days of Gideon were "thick as locusts" and "their camels could no more be numbered than the sand on the seashore." Such a figure of speech conveys dramatically some sense of the level of frustration and the seeming impossibility of the task that lay ahead of Gideon.

HENDIADYS. Another way to increase the effect of what is being said is with hendiadys—using two words when only one thing is being referred to. In Genesis 19:24 the Hebrew literally says that "it rained down fire and brimstone." The NIV, however, acknowledges the hendiadys, translating "burning sulfur" (or it could also be "brimstone that was on fire"). In the New Testament, John 1:17 may well be another example, where "full of grace and truth" may simply be God's gracious truth.

HENDIATRIS. Related to hendiadys is hendiatris, where three words are used to express a single concept. In John 14:6 Jesus declared, "I am the way, the truth, and the life," probably intending to communicate that he was the one, true, living way to the Father. The same could be said for the ending to the Lord's prayer in Matthew 6:13 which appears only in the late manuscripts, "For yours is the kingdom and the power and the glory forever." This hendiatris intended to indicate that Christ had a glorious, powerful kingdom that would last forever.

Another example comes from Daniel 3:7, where King Nebuchadnezzar of Babylon commanded that at the sound of the instruments, "all the people, the nations, and the languages" (literal translation) should fall down and worship the image he had set up. In that languages do not fall down, much less worship, the figure is a hendiatris in which *the people of every nation and language* were required to bow down in worship of this idol.

FIGURES OF RELATION AND ASSOCIATION

METONYMY. Because figures of speech are based on some type of resemblance or relation that different objects bear to one another, it is possible to express a cause when the effect is intended, or to substitute one noun for another noun closely associated with it. Thus we refer to the military establishment of the United States by the five-sided building that it occupies, the Pentagon. This figure is known as metonymy. Thus Luke 16:29 declares that the rich man's brothers had "Moses and the Prophets," even though both had long since died. Therefore, what was meant was that they had the *books* that Moses and the Prophets of the Old Testament had written. That David's "house," which God promised in 2 Samuel 7:16 would last forever, as would his "throne," did not mean that both the throne and the house can still be seen to this day. David's house was his dynasty and family line; his throne stood for his kingship.

SYNECDOCHE. Closely related to metonymy is the figure of synecdoche, by which the whole could be put for the part, or a part put for the whole. Thus, Luke 2:1 states that "all the world" was to be taxed, when, according to the context, he meant precisely what the NIV translators rendered "the entire Roman world."

Likewise, Matthew 12:40 uses the stereotype formula "three days and three nights," but it does not thereby intend to signify a full seventy-two hours anymore than does 1 Samuel 30:12. In the latter passage, David came upon an Egyptian who had been part of the brigade that had stolen all David's goods and family from Ziklag while he and his six hundred men were away. When David demanded of the Egyptian how much time had elapsed since he had been abandoned by the raiding Amalekites, whom David was pursuing, the answer was "three days and three nights." But then the Egyptian added, "My master abandoned me when I became ill, *and today is the third day*" (v. 13, lit.). Thus all three days and nights were put together because that was the stereotype formula that always went together. Moreover, it was proper, as numerous examples illustrate in the text, to refer to the whole day and night (or year) when only part of it was intended.

A final illustration of synecdoche is Judges 12:7, where the Hebrew text literally translated has the judge Jephthah being buried "in the cities of Gilead." Naturally, Jephthah was not cut apart and buried piecemeal all over Gilead, but the total number of cities or towns were put for a part, and so the NIV correctly renders it, "[he] was buried in a town of Gilead."

FIGURES OF CONTRAST

IRONY. When a writer uses words to convey the opposite of their literal meaning, it is known as irony. It is most frequently used in contexts where one might also find sarcasm or ridicule as well. Thus David's wife Michal scoffed, "How the king of Israel has distinguished himself today, disrobing in the sight of the slave girls of his servant as any vulgar fellow would!" (2 Sam. 6:20). Job exhibits that same penchant for meaning the opposite of what he has just said when he dryly concluded about his so-called three friends who had continued to pummel him with bad applications of theology, "Doubtless you are the people, and wisdom will die with you!" (Job 12:1).

LITOTES. Litotes is a form of understatement that affirms a statement by negating its contrary. Thus, for example, Paul asserted in Acts 21:39, "I am a Jew, from Tarsus in Cilicia, a citizen of *no ordinary city*." Abraham belittled himself, he who was only "dust and ashes" (Gen. 18:27), in order to magnify the greatness of God.

EUPHEMISM. A third form of contrast appears in the substitution of a gentler, more pleasant, and modest expression for a word that is more disagreeable, harsh, and indelicate. This is known as a euphemism. Just as Americans prefer to refer to the "bathroom," rather than using the word *toilet,* so Judges 3:24 and 1 Samuel 24:3 refer to a man "covering his feet" as a euphemism for defecating, because his garments would fall around his feet as he stooped down. Acts 2:39 and Ephesians 2:13 use an ethnic euphemism in their references to "all/those who are afar off/away." Clearly, this is a roundabout way of referring to the Gentiles without having to use the word.

FIGURES OF OMISSION. Often the text omits certain words or expressions, leaving the sense to be supplied by the reader.

ZEUGMA. One very interesting form of this device is zeugma. This form yokes two subjects or objects together with one verb in which the verb actually functions appropriately for only one of the two subjects or objects. Many of these have been clarified by supplied verbs in most modern translations, so they would show up only in literal renderings of the Hebrew or Greek text. My favorite zeugma is found in Genesis 4:20, "Jabal . . . was the father of all who live in tents and cattle" (lit.). In translating ". . . and raise livestock," the NIV shows us more directly (but less colorfully) what the writer thought his audience should understand. Likewise, a statement in 1 Timothy 4:3 fits into this same category, for it decries those who "forbid [people] to marry, [and order them] to abstain from certain foods." The addition of the command *order them* was necessary because of the yoking together of the two concepts when the first verb of forbidding went with only the first idea.

ELLIPSIS. The larger category of such omissions is called ellipsis. In this case, an incomplete statement must be filled out in order to finish the thought. Bullinger devotes the first 130 pages of his 1,100-page *Figures of Speech* to the discussion of ellipsis. There may be ellipses of everything from the subject, the verb, a pronoun, to whole clauses. The last kind is best illustrated in 2 Thessalonians 2:3, where the introductory injunction "Don't let anyone deceive you in any way" is followed by the statement "for [that day will not come] until the rebellion occurs and the man of lawlessness is revealed, the man doomed to destruction" [NIV], with brackets showing the omitted clause supplied. Fortunately, most of these ellipses have already been added in most English translations in order to carry the sense as demanded by the context.

CONCLUSION

The Bible contains many other figures of speech, but we have now surveyed and illustrated some of the main ones. They will always prove to be a rich source of insights, calling our attention to something the writer wants to highlight amid all the data in the text. The interpreter, however, must be especially careful when dealing with figures of comparison (similes, metaphors, parables, and allegories) to resist the temptation to create many more comparisons than the one(s) that the writer has chosen for his direct or implied comparison. Likewise, when figures of relation, contrast, addition, or omission are used, care must be taken to retain as much of the point that is being made as both contextual constraints and range of usage of this particular figure of speech will dictate.

Figures of speech are not as precise in their meanings as prose is. What these figures lack in precision, however, is surely made up for in their increased ability to draw pictures for us and to give a vividness that ordinary prose cannot. In this way, our attention is drawn to certain items that otherwise might have been passed over.

Wisdom Literature

The three or four books of the Bible known as Wisdom literature express the writers' concern that we order our lives according to God's own order in the world. "The whole duty of man," as Ecclesiastes summarizes it, is to "fear God and keep his commandments" (12:13). Those who choose to despise this divine wisdom and discipline are bluntly labeled fools (Prov. 1:7).

In addition to Job, Proverbs, Ecclesiastes, and Song of Songs, Catholic scholarship includes the Apocryphal books Ecclesiasticus (Ben Sirach) and the Wisdom of Solomon among the Wisdom literature. To this list, both Jews and Christians generally add certain psalms that exhibit either the same literary style as the Wisdom books or the same thematic material. These psalms display several features characteristic of Wisdom literature generally:

1. Alphabetic acrostics (successive verses begin with successive letters of the Hebrew alphabet)
2. Numerical sayings ("six things the Lord hates; yea, seven . . .")
3. "Blessed" sayings
4. "Better" sayings ("better the little the righteous have than the wealth of many wicked")
5. Comparisons and admonitions
6. Addresses of father to son
7. The use of proverbs, similes, rhetorical questions, and phrases such as "listen to me"

Usually classified as Wisdom psalms, then, are Psalms 1, 19b, 32, 34, 37, 49, 78, 111, 112, 119, 127, 128, and 133.

If the truth be told, Hebrew Wisdom is not simply one genre but a composite with many subgenres. One is the allegory, which we have considered in the preceding section. Among the subgenres are the proverb, saying, riddle, admonition, dialogue, and onomastica (i.e., lists of names or nouns).

THE PROVERB

Proverbs are brief sayings that are memorable, embody the wisdom of many, possess a fullness of meaning with a wide application, and have a bit of a kick or bite to them to ensure their saltiness and continued usefulness. They are found in practically all parts of the Bible. By their nature and form, proverbs are generalized statements that cover the widest number of instances, but in no case are they to be taken as a set of unbending rules that must be applied in every case without exceptions.

On the contrary, one is able to pit proverb against proverb, both in our culture and often in Scripture. For example, one person advises another concerning the prospects of getting married, "He who hesitates is lost," while some other counselor warns, "Look before you leap." Should the listener hasten his or her pace, then, or proceed carefully?

Likewise Proverbs 26:4–5 advises,

> *Do not answer a fool according to his folly,*
> *or you will be like him yourself.*
> *Answer a fool according to his folly,*
> *or he will be wise in his own eyes.*

Now it is not as if the writer of these proverbs, who probably was Solomon (Prov. 25:1), was ambivalent about whether one should or should not answer a fool; rather, he gave two scenarios in which the wise person could be instructed if he or she applied the truth wisely. In some instances, the wise person would need to conclude that one fool would only entangle the answerer in the mud and the two would soon look like each other. In another case, the wise person might conclude that a word fitly spoken at the right moment might well carry the day and save the fool from destruction.

THE SAYING

Closely related to the proverb is the saying. Sayings typically are statements that note what does or does not take place from time to time. Again, they should not be taken as fixed rules, but only as observations. These sayings may be *didactic* (e.g., Prov. 14:31—"He who oppresses the poor shows contempt for their Maker, but whoever is kind to the needy honors God") or merely *experiential,* describing situations that are apt to come up frequently but that have no fixed rules (e.g., Prov. 17:28—"Even a fool is thought wise if he keeps silent, and discerning if he holds his tongue"). Often these sayings are grouped around one topic, much in the manner that Proverbs 1–9 returns time and again to the two contrasting women Madame Folly and Lady Wisdom.

THE RIDDLE

The riddle is designed to puzzle and to perplex the listener or reader in order initially to obscure and hide some parts of its meaning, thereby testing the acuity and skill of those who attempt to solve it.

The best-known riddle in the Bible does not occur in the Wisdom sections, but in Judges 14:14. Samson tested the Philistines with:

> Out of the eater, something to eat;
> out of the strong, something sweet.

After coaxing Samson's wife (Samson called it "plowing with my heifer" [Judg. 14:18]), the Philistines triumphantly announced:

> What is sweeter than honey?
> What is stronger than a lion?

The Queen of Sheba was one of those who came to Solomon's court "to test" him with riddles and hard questions (1 Kings 10:1). Indeed, "to understand a proverb and an enigma; the sayings and riddles of the wise" (Prov. 1:6, my translation) was one of the purposes for Solomon's writing the book of Proverbs.

There are riddles in the New Testament as well. Revelation 13:18 asks whether anyone has any insight. If so, "let him calculate the number of the beast, for it is man's number. His number is 666."

Some riddles are so difficult that we are not even sure how to translate them at this late date in time. For example, Proverbs 26:10 was rendered by the AV, "The great God that formed all things both rewardeth the fool, and rewardeth transgressors." But the NIV rendered the same verse, "Like an archer who wounds at random is he who hires a fool or any passer-by." These two renderings are worlds apart—and so is the rendering offered in the *New Jewish Publication Society's Tanakh–The Holy Scriptures:* "A master can produce anything, but he who hires a dullard is as one who hires transients." The Hebrew text is susceptible of still more renderings. The verse was designed to puzzle—and puzzle it has!

THE ALLEGORY

An allegory is an extended metaphor—just as the parable is an extended simile. As such, the allegory contains its interpretation within itself. Rather than the imagery and the thing signified being kept separate, as in a simile and a parable, in metaphor and allegory the thing signified is identified with the image itself. Thus, Christians and salt are seen as one for the sake of the metaphor, "You are the salt of the earth" (Matt. 5:13). Jesus and the vine are linked as one for the moment in John 15:1: "I am the true vine, and my Father is the gardener."

A metaphor consisting of only a single word or a sentence is not an allegory. But when it is expanded into a narrative with more details, the figure becomes an allegory. The allegory of the "vine [taken] out of Egypt" in Psalm 80:8–15 clearly refers to what God did for Israel, who in this case is the "vine." But an even better example of the extended metaphor is Proverbs 5:15–23. This allegory encourages sexual intimacy amid marital fidelity with the image of drinking water from one's own cistern or well. The clue that the writer supplies to unlock this allegory comes in verse 18, where he appears to interrupt what would otherwise seem to be a disquisition on saving water; he urges, "Rejoice in the wife of your youth." So intrusive does this statement appear at first that one is tempted to believe the line does not belong there— the subject is water. But when the writer continues, "May her breasts satisfy you always, may you ever be captivated by her love" (v. 19), it is clear that we are dealing with an allegory.

One other striking allegory is found in Ecclesiastes 12:1–7, where the imagery depicts the effects of advancing years on men and women. The teacher in vivid language depicts how the "grinders cease because they are few" (v. 3c, the loss of teeth diminishes the ability to masticate food) and the "sound of grinding fades" (v. 4b, the toothless can handle only soft foods). The "strong men stoop" (v. 3b), owing to the effects of tottering legs and weak knees. "The almond tree blossoms" (v. 5c) as the hair turns white. That "the caperberry is ineffective" (v. 5e, NASB) could refer to the loss of sexual power. The genre of allegory brings a great deal of richness to both wisdom selections and other literary forms in the Bible.

THE ADMONITION

Another type of wisdom subgenre that is so common in the ancient Near East is the admonition. The Egyptians, in particular, developed this form to a high art in the many instructions they gave for the would-be ruler and leader in Egypt.

Admonitions appear in either a positive form (commands) or a negative expression (prohibitions). Normally, a motivational clause is attached to each admonition explaining why the injunction is being issued and noting the results that will follow. For example, Proverbs 23:3 admonishes, "Do not crave [the ruler's] delicacies, for that food is deceptive."

THE DIALOGUE

The book of Job illustrates the most extensive use of dialogue in the Wisdom writings. The dialogue takes place between Job and his three "friends": Eliphaz the Temanite, Bildad the Shuhite, and Zophar the Naamathite. Later, Elihu the Buzite and God enter into the dialogue.

Other portions of Scripture exhibit some weak affinities with the dialogue, such as Proverbs 5:12–14; 7:13–21; 8:4–36. But the form is not as extensive in these texts as it is in Job.

THE ONOMASTICA

Some scholars have theorized that some of the Wisdom materials, such as the poem on wisdom in Job 28 or God's speech to Job in Job 38, along with Psalms 104 and 148, perhaps arose in part from lists on various topics, which were then used by the Wisdom writers in a secondary way to organize their thinking on certain subjects.[8] No one has posited a direct relationship in the use of the lists, but some have suggested that the ordering of the subjects and issues that appear might have been informed by the writers' previous awareness of such lists.

CONCLUSION

The interpreter of Wisdom genres must, as with most genres, first determine to which of the subgenres the text belongs. Each subgenre will call for an adjustment in the interpretive strategy for that text. Perhaps more practical skill is required in determining the exact character and the scope of this type of literature than that of any other biblical form. Of course, one should use the context whenever it is of any help in clarifying the background for any of these differing forms. But where the context is uncertain, common sense and sound judgment are particularly important in analyzing the text at hand.

8. See, for example, Gerhard von Rad, "Job xxxviii and Ancient Egyptian Wisdom," in *Studies in Ancient Israelite Wisdom,* ed. J. L. Crenshaw (1955; reprint, New York: Ktav, 1976), pp. 267–77; James L. Crenshaw, "Wisdom," in *Old Testament Form Criticism,* ed. John H. Hayes (San Antonio, Tex.: Trinity University Press, 1974), pp. 258–59.

The first issue we need to address in the study of the Gospels has to do with their historicity. Although it is not uncommon for scholars to argue that the gospel narratives are unreliable, we cannot really preserve the message of the New Testament if we minimize its historical foundation. Nevertheless, the Gospels were written not merely to communicate factual information, nor were they composed according to the methods and expectations of modern history-writing. The authors were very selective in the material they chose to include and, furthermore, presented it in a way that reflected their own (inspired) interpretation and application of the facts. They wrote as both historians and theologians.

Especially significant for the interpretation of the Gospels is the role played by the parables in Jesus' teaching. Although these stories were intended to instruct the people in very clear and concrete terms, they were also instruments of judgment, for they hardened the hearts of the disobedient. Moreover, a proper understanding of the parables requires that we pay close attention to their historical setting; if we take notice of cultural details, we are more likely to understand their message. Finally, we need to take into account the literary context of the parables, because the gospel writers were interested not only in how a particular parable functioned during Jesus' ministry, but also in how it applied to the Christian church.

The distinctiveness of Jesus' teaching surfaced most clearly when compared with the teaching of the contemporary rabbis. Certainly Jesus' approach was different. More important, however, was the content of his message. One significant element in his teaching was his emphasis on grace, which was sometimes obscured by Jewish teachers of that day. Especially prominent was the theme of fulfillment: Jesus' coming meant the arrival of God's kingdom, with all the blessings associated with it.

CHAPTER 6

"But These Are Written That You May Believe"
THE MEANING OF THE GOSPELS

MOISÉS SILVA

Are the Gospels History or Theology?

As we saw in chapter 1, many questions have been raised about the historical character of biblical narratives. Questions of this sort become crucial particularly when dealing with the Gospels. After all, for the Christian, nothing is so fundamental as the reality of Jesus' life, death, and resurrection.

It is important to remind ourselves that when we talk about the meaning or the interpretation of a passage, any one of several distinct issues may be in view: a syntactic detail, the primary thrust of the passage, its broader significance, and so forth. The issue of historicity would seem to fall outside the category of interpretation, strictly speaking, since the "meaning" of a story is normally not affected by its factual reality. The interpretation of the story of George Washington and the cherry tree, for example, remains the same whether or not that story really happened—namely, people should not lie.

Why, then, does the issue of historicity often come up when dealing with biblical interpretation? Could we not simply say that the story of the stilling of the storm in Matthew 8 may be interpreted correctly without reference to its historical truth? (In chapter 1, compare the discussion of historicity, the fourth level of meaning.) If so, one could argue that, whether or not the incident really happened, Matthew wants to communicate to his

105

readers something about the spiritual power of Jesus and thus encourage them to be faithful disciples. After all, isn't this the way we normally deal with the parables? Most readers recognize that the specific story of the Good Samaritan need not represent a factual event; the truth Jesus taught with that parable stands, irrespective of its historicity. Why not approach the rest of the material in the Gospels the same way?

This way of reading the Gospels and Acts—or at least some of the narrative material in them—is attractive to many people, including a minority of evangelical scholars, because it frees them from having to worry about historical discrepancies. Moreover, those who have given up belief in the supernatural but wish to continue being identified as Christians find here a way out of their dilemma.

Such a "solution," however, is too easy—even imaginary. It faces two major problems—one theological and the other literary. The biblical faith, as is almost universally recognized, has a historical character at its very foundations; in contrast to other religions, this feature is one of its most significant distinctives. Moderns who seek to affirm the *religious* teachings of the Bible while rejecting its *historical* claims are more daring than Houdini. The resulting incoherence is logically unbearable. It would be the equivalent of claiming allegiance to the Declaration of Independence while disavowing, as antiquated, the principle of political freedom.

In addition to this theological obstacle, there is a literary snag. When reading any kind of literature, nothing is more important than doing justice to its character. If we attempt to understand Shakespeare's *Macbeth* as a straightforward historical narrative, we misrepresent its total meaning. We may still be able to interpret many details correctly and even make sense of its "message," but no Shakespearean scholar would put up with the inevitable distortions that would result. This problem is magnified when we make the opposite mistake. If someone like Winston Churchill, when writing his *History of the English Speaking Peoples,* intends to describe a factual event, the historical referent is very much part of his meaning. For the reader to ignore or reject that intent is to make mincemeat of the writing.

In the case of the Gospels, every indication we have is that the writers expected their statements to be taken as historical. Luke in particular, as he begins both his gospel and the book of Acts, makes that purpose quite explicit (see Luke 1:1–4 and Acts 1:1–3), but the other writers give no clue that their intent is significantly different. The very reason we do not feel compelled to interpret the *parables* historically is that they are presented in a somewhat stylized fashion—the reader or hearer is immediately aware that they belong to a different genre (literary type).

No doubt, there is a measure of truth in every lie. The reason many students of the Bible believe they can downplay the historicity of the New Testament narratives is that these narratives do not always conform to the patterns of modern history writing. If we want to do justice to the literary character of the Gospels and Acts, therefore, we must take note not only of their historical character but also of some additional features.

Especially helpful here is the way the gospel of John expresses its aim: "Jesus did many other miraculous signs in the presence of his disciples, which are not recorded in this book. But these are written that you may believe that Jesus is the Christ, the Son of God, and that by believing you may have life in his name" (John 20:31). Admittedly, one would not expect to read a statement of that sort in Churchill's history. The author of the Fourth Gospel had more in mind than the reporting of facts; he wanted to change the lives of his readers.

One must not fall into the trap of making sharp and false distinctions. John hardly minimizes the historical truth of his narrative : "The man who saw it has given testimony, and his testimony is true" (19:35). Nevertheless, it would be wrong-headed to focus so much on the historical question that we fail to appreciate other aspects of the gospel, particularly as they may have affected its composition.

Even a cursory look at the gospel of John makes clear that it is not a history textbook—much less a biography—in the usual sense. Nothing is said about Jesus' birth or childhood. In spite of some chronological references (e.g., to the Passover in 6:4), we read most of the gospel with only a vague notion of its temporal setting. Moreover, the proportions are perplexing: almost one-third of the book (chaps. 13–19) is devoted to the last twenty-four hours of Jesus' life! Especially intriguing is the similarity of style between the narratives and the discourses: in this gospel (but not in the others), Jesus speaks the way John writes.

These and other features help us to understand that the historical trustworthiness of the Gospels is not to be described in terms of modern historiography, which stresses clear and strict chronological sequence, balanced selection of material, verbatim quotations, and so on. In a real sense, the gospel writers are preachers. They select the events of Jesus' life and his teachings, guided not by comprehensiveness but by their purpose in writing. They arrange the material not always on the basis of sequential order but with a view to impress upon the readers certain specific truths.

We get into trouble, therefore, when we approach the text with questions that the gospel writers were not interested in answering. Even Luke, who seems to have been the one most concerned with providing historical details, was not writing an essay intended for an encyclopedia. Surely, he never imagined that, twenty centuries later, searching readers would be analyzing every word he wrote and comparing it with the details of the other Gospels as well as with other documents and archaeological data from the Mediterranean world.

In short, we must read the Gospels and Acts with the expectation that there will be gaps of information and imprecise descriptions that make it difficult—sometimes impossible—to resolve apparent discrepancies. This does not mean for a moment that the biblical writers are not dependable. Lack of absolute precision is of the essence of human language. The degree of precision expected of a speaker or writer depends on the subject matter as well as on the stated (or implied) aims. We do not accuse a public speaker of irresponsibility if, when speaking to a general audience, he or she gives a rough figure for, say, the cost of sending a satellite into space. But if one were preparing a financial report to be audited by Congress, imprecision could land that person in jail.

Think of it this way. If Matthew had given every detail some moderns expect, with the exhaustive precision necessary to answer all potential problems, his narrative would not only have been excruciatingly long— worse, the impact of his message would have been engulfed by the information overload. Given his purpose, however, Matthew has indeed presented the truth in the most persuasive way possible.

It may be helpful to remember that our source of authority is not the bare facts of history but rather the *inspired presentation* of those facts in the Bible. Some scholars, eager to demonstrate the historicity of Jesus and his work, try to get "behind" the Gospels and reach the authentic Jesus. The impression is left that what matters is what Jesus "really" said as opposed to what the Gospels report him as saying. But that conclusion would be a denial of the divine authority that pertains to the Gospels. If Luke, for example, summarizes a discourse by our Lord or paraphrases one of his teachings, it is Luke's account of those words—not the historian's reconstruction of what Jesus "really" said—that is divinely inspired.

Consider the story of the rich young ruler. According to Mark 10:17– 18 and Luke 18:18–19, this ruler called Jesus "good teacher" and asked Jesus what he should do to inherit eternal life. Jesus answered: "Why do you call me good? No one is good—except God alone." When we turn to the gospel of Matthew, however, we find a somewhat different account. Here the ruler addresses Jesus with the simple title "Teacher," then inquires about what *good thing* he should do to inherit eternal life. Jesus' response is, "Why do you ask me about what is good? There is only One who is good" (Matt. 19:16–17).

There have been some attempts to resolve this discrepancy, but if we try to make all three Gospels say the same thing, we may miss a very important point Matthew wants to get across. We may be sure that the early

Christians, when reading or hearing about this story as told by Mark and Luke, must have been puzzled by Jesus' response, which sounds as though he denies being good. Perhaps Matthew anticipates this problem and tells the story in a way that helps the reader understand better the meaning of Jesus' conversation with the ruler.

As the dialogue continues, Jesus points to the Ten Commandments as teaching what the ruler ought to do. The man's response, however, reveals his deepest problem: "Teacher, all these I have kept since I was a boy" (Mark 10:20). Clearly, this man thinks he is guiltless—he is convinced of his own goodness. When he called Jesus "good," the ruler was not recognizing Jesus' unique, divine goodness; he was actually treating Jesus as an equal! He thought, therefore, that he could attain salvation by doing something good. By rephrasing the ruler's question, Matthew helps us to identify his problem immediately. We can then better understand Jesus' further instruction. By asking the ruler to sell all he had and give it to the poor, Jesus was forcing the man to recognize that he was quite wrong in thinking of himself as good; in fact, he was guilty of the greatest sin of all by failing to love God above everything else.

We can see, then, that the changes Matthew introduces are not intended to deceive, nor are they the result of careless error. Rather, he is interpreting, under divine inspiration, the significance of Jesus' encounter with the rich young ruler. Just as every good preacher retells and paraphrases the biblical text to make it clearer and to help the congregation apply it, so do the gospel writers. The difference is that the authors of the Gospels spoke with God's own authority. Indeed, Jesus speaks through these writers no less than he spoke when he lived on the earth.

Most of us tend to treat the Gospels the way we treat windows: we look *through* them at something else. In other words, we are in the habit of reading the Gospels only as a means to reach the historical events to which they point. But these writings are much more than that. They are like stained-glass windows. Not only do they point to and reflect the light that is behind them; they also invite us to look *at* them and enjoy them for what they are.

It is not an accident that God gave us *four* gospels, even though there is much overlap among them. The life and message of Jesus is so rich that we need more than one perspective. You can see why it is so misguided to overlook the differences among the Gospels or try to minimize them. We should rather focus our attention on those distinctives and appreciate what each writer is trying to tell us.

History or theology? That is a false question. The gospel writers are both historians *and* theologians. They recount the facts, but they also interpret them so that we may believe.

He Spoke to Them in Parables

Perhaps the most distinctive feature in Jesus' teaching methods was his use of parables.[1] (See chapter 5, under "Figures of Comparison.") There are some obvious reasons why he might have chosen such a form of instruction. Parables are simple and interesting, so that a general audience could follow the story easily. More important, these stories deal directly with the realities of daily life, so a hearer could quickly "identify" with the contents of the parable and thus appreciate its relevance. Again, parables have the advantage of disarming those who might be offended by their message, since the hearer often has to wait till the very end of the story to figure out its significance (cf. esp. Nathan's parable to King David in 2 Sam. 12:1–10).

There is an important measure of truth in all these explanations, but a serious problem arises. If Jesus' parables are so simple, why has there been so much heated debate about their meaning? The modern scholarly literature on the subject is astounding. While one may be tempted to account for that by blaming the scholars themselves, who cannot leave well enough alone, the truth is that even Jesus' disciples were sometimes perplexed by their master's stories (Mark 4:13). Modern Christians too scratch their heads from time to time, wondering, for example, how Jesus can commend the dishonest behavior of the crafty steward (Luke 16:1–15). And wouldn't it be simply unfair for an employer to pay the same amount to all workers, regardless of how many hours they labored (Matt. 20:1–16)?

In short, we need "hermeneutical skills" to understand the parables no less than we need them for appreciating other parts of Scripture. Moreover, Jesus' use of parables reflects certain theological concerns that cannot be ignored.

THE THEOLOGICAL SIGNIFICANCE OF THE PARABLES

In response to the disciples' question about the parable of the sower, Jesus made a statement that ranks among the most difficult sayings recorded in the Gospels: "The secret of the kingdom of God has been given to you. But to those on the outside everything is said in parables so that 'they may be ever seeing but never perceiving, and ever hearing but never understanding; otherwise they might turn and be forgiven!'" (Mark 4:11–12, quoting Isa. 6:9–10). Jesus appears to be saying that his purpose for telling parables to

---

1. Coming up with a precise definition of *parable* is not easy, since the term could be used very broadly of any kind of comparison. Most Bible readers, however, have a satisfactory working definition of the term as referring to the well-known stories told by Jesus. That is good enough for the purposes of this chapter.

those who do not belong to his group of disciples was the same (retributive) purpose behind the call of Isaiah: to harden the hearers in their unbelief.

Many students of the Bible have found this statement quite incredible. For one thing, it appears to be incompatible with Jesus' desire and mission to seek and save the lost. Besides, some would argue, just as it makes no sense for God to send Isaiah to do and say exactly that which will guarantee failure in his ministry, so one can't imagine that Jesus would deliberately undermine his own preaching of the gospel! Attempts have been made, therefore, to soften or even explain away the apparent meaning of Jesus' words.

It is important to note that, even in the case of God's call to Isaiah, taking those words at face value would *not* imply that the whole of Isaiah's ministry should be characterized in those terms. There were many things the prophet said that had other functions and purposes. Similarly, one should not infer that the words in Mark 4:11–12 describe the *exclusive* reason for Jesus' use of parables. The other possible reasons mentioned at the beginning of this section—simplicity, concreteness, and so on—remain valid if understood in the broader context of Jesus' mission.

What was that mission? When Jesus was but a baby, a godly man named Simeon had declared that the child was "destined to cause the falling and rising of many in Israel" (Luke 2:34). In other words, Christ is both cornerstone (or capstone, Matt. 21:42–44) and a rock of stumbling (Rom. 9:32–33); he is the fragrance of life to those who believe and the smell of death to those who reject him (2 Cor. 2:14–16). At the stage in Jesus' ministry when he told the parable of the sower, people had already been "taking sides." In chapter 3 of Mark, we are told that some Pharisees, enraged at Jesus' healing on the Sabbath, began to plot his death (v. 6). Other teachers of the law accused him of casting out demons by the power of Satan (v. 22). In contrast to these groups who rejected him, Jesus said: "Whoever does God's will is my brother and sister and mother" (v. 35).

In this context, we can see that the parables serve the purpose of discriminating among those who heard Jesus. Certainly, these stories do not "create sin" in the hearts of otherwise innocent people! The parables, rather, when addressed to those who have set themselves against the Lord, become instruments of judgment. Thereby "whoever has will be given more; whoever does not have, even what he has will be taken from him" (Mark 4:25). Any attempt to interpret the parables without taking into account this factor will fail to do justice to Jesus' teaching.

There is another theological point to be made with regard to Jesus' use of parables. According to Matthew 13:35, this method of teaching was a fulfillment of prophecy.[2] The prophecy in view is: "I will open my mouth in parables, I will utter things hidden since the creation of the world" (quoting Ps. 78:2). The main point seems to be that Jesus' parables fulfill God's eternal plan to reveal his truth to his people. Secondarily, however, these words suggest a close relationship between creation and redemption. God's truths are, as it were, "built into" the created order. Jesus does not haphazardly look into nature hoping to find interesting illustrations! As one who is both Creator and Savior, he can simply draw out of the created order those parallels that help us understand his purposes.[3]

THE HISTORICAL SETTING OF THE PARABLES

One prominent scholar has rightly argued that Jesus used the parables as "weapons of warfare" against his opponents.[4] The point here is that the parables must be understood historically, that is, by identifying the specific situations in which they were used.

The parable of the prodigal son in Luke 15, for example, has traditionally been read as an evangelistic passage. Preachers, as a rule, focus on the son's wickedness and repentance and thus exhort their congregations to be converted. This is a completely legitimate use of the parable, but we can gain a deeper insight into its message if we note that Luke tells us specifically what was the historical setting in which Jesus told this story. At the beginning of the chapter he points out: "Now the tax collectors and 'sinners' were all gathering around to hear him. But the Pharisees and the teachers of the law muttered, 'This man welcomes sinners and eats with them'" (vv. 1–2). Jesus then proceeds to address three parables—the lost sheep, the lost coin, and the lost (prodigal) son—to those who were complaining.

While the conversion of the Pharisees and the teachers would naturally have been part of the aim in telling those parables, it is clear that Jesus is using those stories primarily to rebuke them. The man who loses a sheep, even if it is *one in a hundred,* experiences great joy upon finding it; certainly the woman who loses *one of ten* valuable coins will be even more excited if she finds that. Yet the Pharisees complain rather than rejoice when a sinner is "found." The parable of the lost son then functions as a powerful climax. This story is longer, including much more detail, but the point to appreciate is the role of

2. It must be remembered that the word *prophecy* should not be simply identified as prediction. Particularly in the gospel of Matthew, the notion of prophetic fulfillment has a broad scope, which includes not only the coming to pass of a prediction but also such ideas as the granting of a promise and the bringing of God's plans to completion.
3. This idea is briefly suggested by Geerhardus Vos, *Biblical Theology: Old and New Testaments* (Grand Rapids: Eerdmans, 1948), p. 380.
4. Joachim Jeremias, *The Parables of Jesus,* rev. ed. (New York: Scribners, 1963).

the elder son, whose *only* brother—not one in a hundred or even one in ten—had been lost. This elder son represents the grumbling Pharisees, who seem unable to share in the joy of God and the angels in heaven.

Attention to the historical setting also includes sensitivity to the cultural background of the parables. Western readers in the twentieth century have their own set of assumptions, which do not always correspond with those of Jesus' hearers. Inevitably, we tend to lose some of the nuances.[5] For example, the request of the son—"Give me my share of the estate"—would likely have been interpreted as a wish for his father's death. In any case, the incident would create a rift between the son and his family (and even the town as a whole) much more severe than would be the case if the same words were spoken in our society.

Another interesting detail is the fact that the elder brother, in that situation, would have been expected to do all he could to reconcile his brother to the father. Not only does he fail to do that, but he even accepts his own share of the inheritance. In other words, from the very beginning of the story the elder brother is put in a bad light. He actually shares in the sin of his brother, and that gives us a better perspective with which to understand his self-righteous indignation at the end of the story.

Finally, when we read about the father *running* to meet the younger son, we view that merely as an expression of joy. In the Middle East, however, particularly in rural areas, a mature man is expected always to walk slowly and with dignity. It is likely that the father in the parable runs to protect the son from the children in the town, who might decide to meet him with stones. In doing so, however, the father humbles himself and becomes a powerful picture of the God of grace.

While the primary meaning of the parable does not change on the basis of these cultural details, they give us insight into the "overtones" of the story that add greatly to our understanding of Jesus' teaching.

THE LITERARY CONTEXT OF THE PARABLES

The historical setting, however, is not the only issue that requires attention. As we have already seen, the biblical writers were not interested in composing detached, neutral narratives. Rather, they present historical events from a particular angle; in doing so, they interpret the events for us. When we study the parables, therefore, we should be interested not only in their function during the ministry of Jesus but also in the way they are used by the

5. For what follows, see Kenneth F. Bailey, *Poet and Peasant: A Literary Cultural Approach to the Parables of Luke* (Grand Rapids: Eerdmans, 1976), chap. 7.

gospel writers. Under divine inspiration, they bring to bear the teaching of Jesus on the later situation of the Christian churches. A careful study of this feature sheds light on how we may use the parables as well.

Matthew in particular has arranged his material in a thematic way and seems to make a special effort to apply the words of Jesus to the church or churches to which he is writing. It is evident, for example, that Matthew is concerned about the lack of genuine commitment among some Christian groups, and so the theme of true versus false discipleship becomes a major emphasis in his gospel.

Consider the parable of the laborers in the vineyard (Matt. 20:1–16). It is not difficult to understand that parable in the light of its historical context, as discussed in the previous section. This story, too, is a weapon of warfare, whereby Jesus rebukes his opponents for complaining about God's grace to sinners. In the parable, the laborers who come at the end of the day and work for only a brief period in the cool of the evening receive the same pay as those who worked all day and had to endure the heat of the day. Not surprisingly, the latter are offended and complain. But the owner was simply being generous. No doubt he realized that no man can feed a family with a small fraction of a day's wage, and so he is gracious to the group who worked for a short period. This parable, then, strongly resembles the main point of the parable of the prodigal son.

Matthew, however, applies it to the Christian church by the way he places the story in the context of the gospel as a whole. We recall that, at the end of chapter 19, he had related the incident of the rich young ruler, a man who thought he was good enough to inherit the kingdom of heaven. When Jesus made him realize that this was not true, he went away disappointed, and the Lord commented on the impossibility of salvation by human means. At that point, Peter expressed his commitment to discipleship, and Jesus responded that the true disciples will receive many blessings and inherit eternal life. He then ended with the saying, "But many who are first will be last, and many who are last will be first" (v. 30).

By placing the parable of the laborers immediately after that incident and repeating the saying of 19:30 at the end of the parable,[6] Matthew, as it were, tells his Christian readers:

6. It is of course impossible to prove that Jesus himself did not use that saying after the parable, but a careful study of Matthew's method of composition has persuaded most scholars that this is part of the Evangelist's technique. Again, it must not be thought that such a method implies error or dishonesty. Under divine inspiration, Matthew is bringing home to his readers the significance of the parable for them.

Don't feel too comfortable as you read about Jesus' rebuke to the Pharisees. The same problems that Jesus had to face are present in your congregations. There are some of you who do not understand what grace and discipleship are all about. You think that because you call yourselves "Christians," you don't have anything to worry about, and instead you look down on others who don't seem as good as you. Well, remember that some of you who seem to occupy the first seats will end up in the back, and those who are regarded as lowly and undeserving will be given places of honor.

In short, the careful study of the parables involves not only seeing them in the historical context of Jesus' ministry but also understanding how they function in the narrative of each gospel. We should not treat the gospel writers as journalists who should have tried to avoid interpreting the facts they report. Rather, they were inspired theologians and preachers whose own presentation of Jesus' work is an essential key in our appreciation of the biblical text.

He Taught Them with Authority

Although the use of parables was the most distinctive feature in Jesus' method of teaching, it was hardly the only one. One of the most striking descriptions of Jesus' ministry is the comment that "the people were amazed at his teaching, because he taught them as one who had authority, not as the teachers of the law" (Mark 1:22; cf. Matt. 7:28–29). For most readers of the Gospels, this verse seems to speak about the power of Jesus' divine personality. Undoubtedly, this is part of the explanation for the reaction of the audiences. Mark himself at several points draws attention to the awe that the Lord inspired in those who were around him (Mark 4:41; 5:15; 10:32; 16:8), and perhaps the climactic scene in the gospel is the centurion's reaction upon witnessing Jesus' death: "Surely this man was the Son of God!" (15:39).

Nevertheless, it is important to note that, in speaking of Jesus' authority, Mark contrasts the Lord's teaching with that of "the teachers of the law." In other words, it was not so much that Jesus' teaching was more powerful than that of human teachers generally; the contrast is specifically with the Jewish rabbis and scribes, who were mostly associated with the school of the Pharisees. What, then, is the focus of the comparison? Part of the concern may have been simply the style of teaching. Rabbinic literature (although it dates from a later period) gives us some idea of the basic approach used by first-century rabbis. Much of it consists of setting against each other the opinions of leading sages, sometimes without clear resolution. Obviously, Jesus' approach was quite different, and that alone must have made a significant impression on those who heard him.

Not only Jesus' teaching style, however, but the very substance of his message was different. Here again, the value of understanding the historical background becomes clear. Definition often proceeds by negation; that is, we are better able to identify objects if we can distinguish them from other objects with which we are familiar. That is precisely what Mark is doing when he tells us that Jesus did *not* teach like the scribes. To make sense of what Mark means, however, we need to be familiar with the teaching of the scribes.

In recent decades, scholarly research has brought some significant changes to our understanding of Jewish thought in the first century. It is now clear, for example, that we cannot simply dismiss rabbinic theology as a "legalistic system" that totally ignored the doctrine of divine grace.[7] Much of the extant Jewish literature reflects a genuine, if not full, appreciation for that doctrine. We would make a grievous mistake, however, if we concluded that "legalism" was not at all a problem for first-century Judaism. I use quotation marks because the term means different things to different people. The issue here is not whether the Pharisees were "too strict" (as we shall see, they were not sufficiently strict!) or whether they were too preoccupied with matters of law. What, then, was the problem?

Our Lord addressed the central issue most directly in the incident recorded in Mark 7:1–13 (cf. Matt. 15:1–7), which tells us that the Pharisees complained when Jesus' disciples failed to go through the ceremonial rite of purifying their hands before eating. This rite, however, was not a biblical injunction but rather part of "the tradition of the elders" (v. 5; cf. Gal. 1:14). A basic feature of rabbinic thought is the emphasis on the twofold Torah: the written law (i.e., the Hebrew Bible, but especially the five books of Moses) and the oral law (the traditions of the elders). The oral law could be viewed to some extent as an interpretation and application of the written law, yet much of it consisted of debates dealing with technical legal questions, which led to the development of new regulations.

Ironically, many of these regulations had the effect of blunting the force of the biblical commandments. The Pharisees, being very conscious of human weakness, sought to interpret the strong demands of the Torah in a

---

7. Although a number of writers in the first half of the twentieth century were careful to make this point, the most influential work has been E. P. Sanders, *Paul and Palestinian Judaism: A Comparison of Patterns of Religion* (Philadelphia: Fortress, 1977). For more detail on the material that follows, cf. my article "The Place of Historical Reconstruction in New Testament Criticism," in *Hermeneutics, Authority, and Canon*, ed. D. A. Carson and J. W. Woodbridge (Grand Rapids: Zondervan, 1986), pp. 109–33, esp. pp. 117–21.

way that made them, in effect, more "fulfillable." For example, the law required that all debts should be canceled every seventh year (Deut. 15:1–3); human nature being what it is, those with the means to lend money were reluctant to do so, afraid that they might not recover it. As a result, the poor suffered. With a view to solving this problem, a regulation was adopted that interpreted the law as having to do only with personal loans. If the loan was given to the temple, however, so that the priests could administer it to the poor, then the recipient was still obligated to repay it, even on the seventh year. (A comparable regulation, that of the Corban, is mentioned in Mark 7:10–12.) Although such a ruling made a mockery of the law (see esp. the solemn warning in Deut. 15:9–10), the people persuaded themselves that they were now obeying it and thus could, as we might say today, "feel better about themselves."

Jesus, however, had very little patience with this kind of hermeneutics. Quoting Isaiah's condemnation of hypocrisy, he accused the Pharisees of nullifying God's commands by means of human tradition (Mark 7:6–9, 13). In effect, the scribes' teaching undermined the authority of God's Word. This criticism is especially prominent in the Sermon on the Mount, where Jesus introduces several of his teachings with the words, "You have heard that it was said . . . but I tell you" (Matt. 5:21ff.). Curiously, many readers have thought that Jesus is here distancing himself from, or even abolishing, Old Testament commandments. Quite the contrary. He came not to abolish them but to fulfill them (5:17); his own teaching clearly intensified the force of those commandments, over against the rabbinic tendency to relax them. He makes this point quite explicit both at the beginning and at the end of the passage: "For I tell you that unless your righteousness surpasses that of the Pharisees and the teachers of the law, you will certainly not enter the kingdom of heaven" (5:20). "Be perfect, therefore, as your heavenly Father is perfect" (5:48).

That concluding statement makes very plain what the focus of controversy was between Jesus and the rabbis. Over against the rabbinic tendency to relax the divine standard, Jesus' disciples can never be satisfied with less than perfection. This means that Jesus' true disciples are ever conscious of their sin and thus learn to rely not on their own moral strength but on God's grace, praying with the tax collector, "God, have mercy on me, a sinner" (Luke 18:13). If we define "legalism" as a religious outlook that sees people as morally self-reliant, and thus in some way contributing to their own salvation, we will appreciate that all of us—even the most mature Christians—often fall prey to it. We can also see how this human tendency would have been greatly exacerbated by a system of interpretation that in effect lowered the divine requirements and influenced people to feel self-complacent. Whatever one's intentions, such an outlook can only obscure the riches of God's grace.

The Sermon on the Mount, however, draws our attention to another crucial difference between the teaching of Jesus and that of the scribes. In the opinion of some scholars, chapter 5 of Matthew presents Jesus as a new Moses who, from a mountain, delivers the law of the kingdom to his people. Indeed, the Mosaic period is over, and a new era has begun. Without pushing this parallel too far, we must recognize that the Sermon on the Mount reflects an eschatological (i.e., "end-times") point of view. Even the beatitudes that introduce this passage arouse our expectations about the newness of Jesus' work. As we have already seen, in this passage the Lord explicitly describes the purpose of his coming as one of fulfillment (5:17). For that matter, the whole of the gospel of Matthew seems to be structured around this theme, since over and over again the author points out that events in Jesus' life happened in order to fulfill what was prophesied in the Scriptures (1:22; 2:15, 17, 23; 4:14; et al.).

At the beginning of his ministry, Jesus indicated this eschatological nature of his coming with the words, "The time has come. . . . The kingdom of God is near. Repent and believe the good news" (Mark 1:14). Luke, who places much emphasis on this theme, introduces Jesus' public ministry by relating the visit to the synagogue in Nazareth (Luke 4:14–21). There Jesus announced that he had come to fulfill the promise of Isaiah 61:1–2:

> *The Spirit of the Lord is on me,*
> *because he has anointed me*
> *to preach good news to the poor.*
> *He has sent me to proclaim freedom for the prisoners*
> *and recovery of sight for the blind,*
> *to release the oppressed,*
> *to proclaim the year of the Lord's favor. (Luke 4:18–19)*

The presence of the Spirit, whom Jesus had received at his baptism (cf. Luke 3:21–22, in fulfillment of Isa. 42:1), was the clear sign that the last days had indeed arrived. Jesus' miracles, particularly his exorcisms, were in turn the evidence that he was endued by the Holy Spirit: "But if I drive out demons by the Spirit of God, then the kingdom of God has come upon you" (Matt. 12:28).

The gospel of John, more than any other, draws out the significance of this "realized eschatology" for the lives of believers. Alluding to the end-time prophecy of Ezekiel 36:24–27, John reports Jesus' words to Nicodemus, "I tell you the truth, no one can enter the kingdom of God unless he is born of water and the Spirit" (John 3:5). In an important sense, it is as if Jesus' followers have experienced the resurrection, even though the final resurrection is still future: "I tell you the truth, whoever hears my word and believes him who sent me has eternal life and will not be condemned; he has crossed over from death to life. I tell you the truth, a time is coming and has now come when the dead will hear the voice of the Son of God and those who hear will live" (John 5:24–25, but cf. vv. 28–29).

This teaching—that although the final age is not yet fully manifested, believers have already begun to enjoy it—is beautifully expressed in the Upper Room Discourse. In John 14:2, Jesus promises his disciples that he is going to prepare a place for them in his Father's house, where there are many rooms (the Greek word here for "room" is *monē*). This appears to be a promise regarding heaven in the future. However, after he assures them that, upon his departure, the Father will send the Holy Spirit to them, he adds, "If anyone loves me, he will obey my teaching. My Father will love him, and we will come to him and make our home [*monē*] with him" (v. 23). Because he can give his Spirit to us (cf. 7:37–39), we can enjoy his very presence in our lives. The old age under the law of Moses is over; grace and truth now reign over those who place their trust in Jesus.

Truly Jesus "taught them as one who had authority, not as the teachers of the law"!

Conclusion

This chapter has touched on only a few questions that should be considered if we wish to understand the Gospels. Certain technical approaches, such as the study of literary sources, raise other important issues that cannot be ignored in a more advanced examination of these documents. Keep in mind, however, that it is very easy to get lost in the details. Never forget the "big picture." The principles discussed in this chapter will help keep before you a framework within which to read the Gospels responsibly and profitably.

Although the epistles included in the New Testament do not consist of "personal correspondence" in the usual sense, we can easily misunderstand them unless we treat them as real, historical letters (rather than textbooks of theology). In practical terms this means, first, that we should read the New Testament letters as wholes; our tendency to treat them as reference books to be read piecemeal distorts our perception of their message. Second, these writings arise out of concrete historical occasions, which means that we must learn to "read between the lines" so as to understand the text in its original context. Third, we must learn to treat the New Testament letters from a literary point of view, that is, recognizing that they are carefully thought-out documents and may reflect rhetorical methods used in antiquity. Fourth, these writings must be read theologically; while being sensitive to the diversity that they represent, we must seek to appreciate their unifying features, especially the authors' conviction that the last days had arrived with the coming of Christ. Finally, we cannot forget that the epistles of the New Testament are authoritative writings and that therefore their historical character does not undermine their relevance for our lives.

CHAPTER 7

How to Read a Letter
THE MEANING OF THE EPISTLES

MOISÉS SILVA

More than half a century ago, an American philosopher with special interests in the challenges of higher education came to the conclusion that what students needed was help in making sense of books. And what was true of students was just as true of others not enrolled in school. Accordingly, he published a volume entitled *How to Read a Book*.[1] Though some may have wondered how anyone who did not already know how to read a book could read this one, the volume became an instant success.

And not surprisingly. Being able to decipher an alphabet and identify words—and even being able to infer the meaning of sentences and paragraphs—is but a preparatory step to "real" reading. Different kinds of books require different reading strategies, whether or not we are conscious of using such strategies. All of us can improve our skills as we seek to read challenging books more effectively and accurately.

It may be a little surprising, however, to see the title of this chapter. How hard can it be to read personal correspondence? After all, if there is any kind of writing that can be read by just about everyone, even people who have reached only an elementary level of proficiency, it is a letter from a friend. This chapter is needed, however, precisely because most of us don't read 1 Corinthians or James as though they were letters.

---

1. Mortimer J. Adler, *How to Read a Book: The Art of Getting a Liberal Education* (1940; rev. ed., New York: Simon & Schuster, 1972). The current edition does not carry the subtitle.

To say these things, however, is to raise the question of literary genre. Is it really accurate to suggest that Paul's letters, for example, are just like modern personal letters? The fact that sometimes we refer to them as *epistles* (which suggests relatively long and formal documents) is an indication of the difference. Scholars have discussed this issue extensively. In the past some thought that the letters of Paul should be treated like the epistles of such Latin writers as Cicero and Seneca, that is, like carefully crafted documents intended to be read as published works of literature. This viewpoint has been generally abandoned. We have no good reason to think that Paul had any literary pretensions when he wrote these documents.

It is just as clear, however, that they are not simply "personal" letters. Although a few of Paul's letters were written to individuals (1–2 Timothy, Titus, and esp. Philemon), even these go well beyond personal concerns. As for the other letters, personal comments play a minor role, and the overall tone is solemn. Some of them contain involved argumentation and even display the use of rhetorical techniques. Finally, and most fundamentally, they are written with a note of apostolic authority that gives them a unique character.

These qualifications, however, as important as they are, should not be allowed to obscure the most basic fact about these New Testament documents: they were not originally like modern books published for fairly general audiences—thousands of readers that the author has never met; rather they were genuine letters in which the authors, under divine inspiration, gave direct instruction to a specific church or group of churches. (Even those letters that have a more personal character seem to address the church of which the recipient was a leader.) In God's wisdom and providence, Christians everywhere and at all times may profit from these letters as God's Word to them as well. If we wish to use them responsibly, however, we need to respect their character. As noted in the previous chapter, reading a historical account as though it were poetry (or vice versa) does injustice to the writing and leads to misunderstanding. Similarly, reading one of Paul's letters as though it were a technical book of reference or a seminary textbook of theology can take us down the wrong interpretive path.

Reading the New Testament Letters as Wholes

Perhaps the most obvious aspect of reading a letter is the one that we ignore most easily when we read the epistles of the New Testament. All of us, upon receiving a letter from an acquaintance, proceed to read the whole letter at one sitting (often we do not even wait to sit down!). Christians, partly because of the chapter-and-verse divisions in our modern Bibles, seldom take the time to read through a whole epistle. Indeed, we may feel we deserve a pat on the back if we manage to finish an entire chapter.

What would one think of a man who receives a five-page letter from his fiancée on Monday and decides to read only the third page on that day, the last page on Thursday, the first page two weeks later, and so on? We are all aware of the fact that reading a letter in such piece-meal fashion would likely create nothing but confusion. The meaning of a paragraph on the third page may depend heavily on something said at the beginning of the letter—or its real significance may not become apparent until the next page is read. The more cogently the letter was written, the riskier it would be to break it up arbitrarily. Moreover, part of the meaning of a document is the total impact it makes on the reader, and that meaning is often more than the sum of its parts.

Another way of stating these points is to say that specific sections in a New Testament letter *must be read in context.* As we have seen before, contextual interpretation is one of the most basic principles to keep in mind when we seek to understand what people say and write. Ironically, many readers tend to ignore this principle precisely when they need it the most, that is, when they are trying to make sense of a difficult passage.

A good example is Hebrews 6:4–6, which seems to teach that Christians may fall away from the faith and that, if they do so, they cannot possibly be restored. Focusing on those verses in isolation from the rest of the book, readers have come up with a good number of interpretations, all of which can be defended in one way or another: (1) Christians may indeed lose their salvation permanently; (2) Christians may lose their salvation, but restoration is possible; (3) Christians may lose their rewards but not their salvation; (4) the passage describes people who are only professing Christians, not truly regenerate; (5) the passage is purely hypothetical; (6) the passage does not really deal with personal salvation but with broader Jewish Christian matters. And so on.

Since we wish to illustrate only one principle of interpretation, let's not be concerned for the time being about which of these understandings is correct, but only about how we should approach the problem. It is fair to say that most Christians who are troubled by this passage have only a vague idea of what Hebrews is all about, and even those who have tried to read the book with some care usually end up a little confused. Because its subject matter is not familiar to us, we find Hebrews a difficult epistle to understand. As a result, we try to make sense of 6:4–6—a very difficult passage in a difficult book—by ignoring its context, even though this is just the kind of passage that requires special attention to the context!

We ought to read the whole epistle straight through several times, perhaps with different English translations, until we become quite familiar with its contents, the concerns and apparent purposes of the author, the way the argument is developed, and so forth. One important feature we will discover is that 6:4–6 is not the only passage of its kind in the book. In fact, there are four other so-called "warning passages" in Hebrews (2:1–4; 3:7–15 and continuing through chap. 4; 10:26–31; 12:25–29). When we take the argument of the book as a whole, it seems most unlikely that these five warnings could be dealing with different situations. On the contrary, they provide a cumulative effect. The author is deeply concerned about his readers, and he is carefully trying to achieve his one great aim, that is, preventing them from committing some terrible sin that will bring down God's severe judgment.

Having recognized this feature of the letter, we will quickly dismiss some interpretations of 6:4–6. For example, the idea that the passage is talking about the losing of rewards simply does not fit the character of the letter as a whole; it is an interpretation that cannot be supported from the context. Similarly, any view that downplays the personal element is also suspect, since the other warnings (esp. 3:12) make clear that what is at stake is one's individual relationship with God. Again, the view that takes the passage as purely hypothetical makes little sense. What is the point of writing a whole letter, with such emotional and severe warnings, to prevent something that cannot really happen?

Deciding among the remaining options is not easy and requires taking other factors into account. Nevertheless, one can see clearly that the more difficult a passage is, the more attention we need to pay to the context of the whole document.

Reading the New Testament Letters Historically

Every written document should be read "historically"; that is, we ought to take into account that it was written by a particular individual (or group of individuals) in a particular time in history and that it was motivated by some particular occasion. Nevertheless, some types of writing can be understood quite well even when we may know relatively little of their historical setting. Being able to read science textbooks in high school, for example, does not greatly depend on knowing who the authors were or what their historical situation may have been.[2] In other words, textbooks are addressed to very broad audiences, to students all across the country whose personal experiences vary enormously.

In contrast, think of a column in a high school newspaper. In this case we have a writing addressed to a much more homogeneous audience. All the students share many important experiences and a base of common knowledge. They belong to a well-defined geographic region. They all know who the principal and most of the teachers are. More important, they share common perceptions about the school, the people who are part of it, and the challenges it offers. The school newspaper, therefore, will be understood by these students in a way that an outsider cannot grasp as easily—even the parents may struggle with it from time to time! Note also that, in contrast to textbooks, editorials in a student paper have a very short life expectancy. What was a "hot topic" in a particular issue of the paper will possibly have no bearing whatever the following year, or even the following month.

What about the New Testament letters? Biblical scholars often refer to these letters as *occasional* writings. This term does not at all suggest that they are trivial or carelessly written documents. What scholars are seeking to emphasize is that Paul, for example, wrote his letters to meet specific historical needs. It's not as though the apostle, having nothing better to do, thought it might be a good idea to write a theological essay for anyone who might be interested in it! On the contrary. There was always a concrete occasion that motivated him to write these documents. Usually it was a matter of specific churches experiencing problems that had to be solved; in some cases, as with the Galatians, the need was urgent.

Because Paul's letters also deal with principles that have permanent validity, it is easy for us to overlook their occasional character. If we wrest 1 Corinthians out of its historical context, the precise message of this document will escape us. Worse, we could misunderstand or misapply its meaning. Take chapter 7, verse 1: "It is good for a man not to marry" (NIV; lit. "not to touch a woman"). Some have inferred from these words that marriage is a bad thing, to be avoided if at all possible. Such an interpretation, however, is hardly consistent with biblical teaching more generally, or even with Paul's own statements elsewhere (cf. Eph. 5:22–33 and 1 Tim. 3:2; 4:3).

It appears that, among the many issues that divided the Corinthian

2. Even in this case such questions are not completely irrelevant. If an astronomy textbook is four decades old, knowing that fact affects how we read it. If we find out that the author of such a text has a strong ideological motivation (such as the anti-Creationist Carl Sagan, or perhaps someone determined to prove that the world was created in six twenty-four-hour days), we will probably want to take that factor into account as we seek to interpret specific statements in the book.

Christians, one of the most significant had to do with differing ideas about sex and marriage. Some individuals in the church took a very loose view. They thought it was defensible for a Christian to be joined to a prostitute, for example (6:15–16). When one in their midst became intimate with his step-mother, these individuals could not bring themselves to condemn him (5:1–2). Another group in the church, however, perhaps in reaction, went to the other extreme. They believed that even in marriage, sex should be avoided (7:3–5), so they might as well not get married at all. In support of their position, they probably appealed to the fact that Paul himself was single.

One can easily see the difficulty facing Paul. Since this stricter group opposed immorality, he wanted to support them as much as possible. Moreover, there are certain advantages in remaining single, and so he did not want to condemn those who, for the right reasons, had chosen not to marry. Marriage, however, is a divine institution to be upheld, and there are also important practical reasons why most people should marry. So, as he starts his discussion in chapter 7, Paul states what may have been some sort of motto among the stricter group, "It is good for a man not to touch a woman." By doing so, he acknowledges that there is some truth to this group's position, but then he proceeds to qualify that statement and correct the abuses.

If, instead of writing a letter, Paul had composed a treatise on Christian ethics, we might reasonably expect a comprehensive chapter on marriage that gave a more "balanced" presentation. Because Paul wrote 1 Corinthians to address specific historical problems, however, chapter 7 must be understood in the light of those problems. Moreover, we need to keep in mind that, as a result, his instructions in that chapter are only a small part of what the Bible as a whole teaches about marriage.

The following very important question may be raised, however: How can we tell what was the historical context of the New Testament letters? The book of Acts gives us some important information about Paul's ministry and thus provides a basic framework for reading the letters. Unfortunately, many details are missing. Historical documents outside the Bible shed interesting light here and there, but they still leave us with significant gaps. It turns out that, as a rule, we depend on internal evidence, that is, the information that we can get out of the letters themselves. The problem is that this evidence, for the most part, is indirect. Paul does not first describe the situation in Corinth, for example, before he proceeds to deal with that situation. He didn't have to! The Corinthians were fully aware of the problems. We, in contrast, are forced to *infer* what the problems may have been.

In other words, we have to "read between the lines" so as to reconstruct the historical context. For this reason some people may object to our emphasis on historical interpretation. They will argue that this approach injects too much subjectivity into the process, since different scholars will come up with different reconstructions.

This kind of objection is used not only by evangelical Christians who wish to guard the authority and clarity of Scripture. There is also a segment of contemporary scholarship that prefers to treat the New Testament letters strictly as literary objects, that is, more or less divorced from their historical context. One scholar sympathetic to this viewpoint complains that other scholars depend too heavily on "mirror-reading." In his opinion they assume too easily that in the text of Galatians, for example, they can see a reflection of the people who were causing trouble among the churches of Galatia.[3]

In response, we may readily grant that reading between the lines can be a dangerous exercise and that the method has frequently been abused. We must keep in mind, however, that every reading of every text *requires* some measure of reading between the lines. As we saw in chapter 1, understanding is possible only within the framework of assumed knowledge. Paul's brief letter to the Galatians would have become a multivolume encyclopedia if the apostle had spelled out every detail that forms part of the total network of knowledge relevant to his message.

So the question is not *whether* we should read between the lines but *how* we should do it. Certainly, the more an interpretation depends on inferences (as opposed to explicit statements in the text), the less persuasive it is. If a historical reconstruction disturbs (rather than reinforces) the apparent meaning of a passage, we should be skeptical of it. In contrast, if a scholar proposes a reconstruction that arises out of the text itself, and if that reconstruction in turn helps to make sense of difficult statements in the text, we need not reject it on the grounds that it is just a theory.

A good criterion for assessing the validity as well as the value that a theory may have for exegesis is to ask this question: Could the interpretation of a particular passage be supported *even if we did not have the theory?* A good interpretation should not depend so heavily on inferences that it cannot stand on its own without the help of a theoretical construct. A theory about the historical situation may help us to become sensitive to certain features of the text that we might otherwise ignore, but it is the text that must be ultimately determinative.

Let us now go back to 1 Corinthians. Did our theory about the historical situation control our reading of the text, or did the text itself suggest the theory? Note that the issue came up because we were aware of a difficulty in the text. That is, at first blush Paul appears to say something that

3. George Lyons, *Pauline Autobiography: Toward a New Understanding*, SBLDS 73 (Atlanta: Scholars Press, 1985), chap. 2.

is inconsistent with other aspects of his teaching. Second, recall that we have clear information from chapters 5–7 about disputes among the Corinthians regarding sexual behavior. In addition, chapter 7 begins with a reference to a letter that the Corinthians sent to Paul, and clearly it was that letter that raised the issue of marriage. We may say, then, that the basic thrust of our interpretation, while it was suggested by certain historical inferences, depends primarily on the text itself, not on fanciful speculation.

Other aspects of our interpretation may be less certain. For example, we mentioned the theory that the statement "It is good for a man not to touch a woman" may have been a saying used by one of the Corinthian factions. There is no way to prove that theory right or wrong. But notice that the theory is not at all essential for the interpretation. Even if those words were original with Paul, our general reading of the passage can still be easily supported.

A good appreciation for the historical setting of a document can help us not only to deal with difficult verses; it can also enhance our understanding of a letter as a whole. Consider Paul's letter to the Philippians. Most Christians familiar with this book think immediately of Paul's repeated emphasis on the theme of joy as well as the remarkable "Christ-hymn" in 2:6–11. These features, as well as the apostle's obvious warmth for his brothers and sisters in Philippi, have suggested to many readers that this church was a model congregation, perhaps without many problems.

A little reading between the lines, however, suggests a different picture. We do have some external evidence regarding this church, which was located in the province of Macedonia. For example, Acts 16 recounts the founding of the congregation by Paul, Silas, and Timothy. Moreover, 2 Corinthians 8:1–5 makes clear that these believers were very poor and that in spite of their poverty they were unusually generous in supporting Paul's ministry. Paul comments on that very fact in Philippians itself, both at the beginning of the letter (1:5, where the word *partnership* almost surely refers to their financial support) and at the end (4:14–16).

A careful reading of Philippians 4:10–19 gives us the distinct impression that the congregation's financial troubles had become a growing concern. Paul had just received a gift from this church by the hand of their messenger, Epaphroditus (2:25). While the apostle wants to express his deepest thanks for that gift, he clearly wants to avoid the suggestion that material abundance is the key to his happiness (note esp. 4:11 and 17). He ends the passage by assuring them that God will meet their needs (v. 19).

Having noted these details, other features of the letter begin to fall into place in a new way. For example, Paul's strong exhortation not to become anxious (4:6–7) should probably be related to their financial worries.

Moreover, it would seem that the numerous references to joy in the letter indicate, not that the Philippians were a joyful bunch, but exactly the opposite. They had lost their Christian contentment, and Paul must urge them to recover it! A key to that recovery is for them to understand that true joy does not depend on what one has: "I have learned to be content whatever the circumstances" (4:11). We are to rejoice *in the Lord* (3:1; 4:4) because we can do all things through him (4:13).

Even more serious, however, was the presence of dissension within the church. Most Bible readers do not think of the Philippians as having that sort of a problem, but they certainly did. The exhortations to unity and humility in 2:1–4 are there for a reason. Some readers seem to assume that Paul simply thought it would be nice to talk about this subject! The introductory comments (v. 1) are full of emotion and reveal the apostle's deep concern, while the warning against selfishness (v. 4) is closely paralleled to what he had to say to that most divided of the early churches, the Corinthian congregation (see 1 Cor. 10:24). Paul even decides to name names. At the root of the dissension was some serious disagreement between two important members, Euodia and Syntyche (4:2–3).

On the basis of Philippians 2:19–30, moreover, one can reasonably infer what the church said to Paul in the message that accompanied their gift. "We are having serious problems, Paul. We need you here. If you cannot come, please send our dear friend Timothy. You can keep Epaphroditus for assistance." Of course, the Philippians' communication has not survived, so this message is speculative (another instance of historical reconstruction) and certainly not essential in understanding those verses. But the passage, and even Philippians as a whole, takes on a fresh meaning and makes much better sense when we read it in that light.

In any case, it is easy to see how our perception of a letter can be significantly enhanced if we make the effort to identify its historical origins. Again, we should remember that the reason we are able to understand contemporary letters sent to us is that we are fully cognizant of their origin and context (and that the reason we sometimes misunderstand those letters is precisely some gap in our knowledge of the context). Note further that to treat the New Testament letters historically is an important method for applying successfully the first section of this chapter, that is, the need to read letters as whole documents. If we do so, not only will we be able to appreciate the total message of the letters; we will also be in a much better position to solve any specific interpretive problems that we may come across.

Reading the New Testament Letters as Literary Documents

One of the reasons the New Testament letters are sometimes referred to as *epistles* is that they seem more formal in character than one expects from typical personal correspondence. We need to strike a balance here. Since Paul wrote these documents as an apostle, one should indeed expect something more than hurriedly written scribbles. The very fact that he used secretaries suggests special care in his writing.[4]

In recent decades, scholars have begun to give greater recognition to the literary qualities of the New Testament letters. It is apparent, for example, that Paul had some awareness of the techniques taught by teachers of rhetoric in the ancient world. Just how great was his knowledge of these techniques is a matter of debate. Similarly, not all scholars agree whether Paul was making conscious use of these techniques. We may continue to insist that Paul did not view his letters primarily as literary works for general publication. There is much to be learned, however, from current studies about the rhetorical character of the biblical documents.

No letter has received more attention in this respect than Paul's epistle to the Christians in Galatia. That fact alone is suggestive. Given the highly emotional and urgent tone of this letter, one would *not* expect it to be a carefully crafted work. Indeed, Galatians has often been used as evidence that Paul could write in a "rough" style. (One of the best-known examples of this roughness is Galatians 2:4–5, which strictly speaking is an incomplete sentence in the Greek.) At the same time, scholars have recognized that the argument of the letter is disciplined and well-thought-out. But just how literary is this work?

We may begin by noting some fairly obvious items about the structure of Galatians. As he does in his other letters, Paul begins this one with a salutation ("Paul to so-and-so: grace and peace . . .") and ends with a benediction (6:18). Moreover, we can identify a longer section as the *introduction* to the letter (1:1–10) and another one as the *conclusion* (6:11–18). Between these two sections we have the *body* of the letter, which in turn is divided into several sections. The first one (1:11–2:21), in which Paul seems to defend his independent authority, has a historical flavor; the second

---

4. Note esp. Rom. 16:22. It is generally acknowledged that the scribe (or amanuensis) would have been given some discretion in the writing of the letter.

one (3:1–4:31) is more argumentative and doctrinal; the third (5:1–6:10) is primarily hortatory, that is, it is characterized by exhortations.[5]

When we receive a letter from a friend, we do not usually try to come up with an outline. Why should we do it with Paul's letters? Part of the answer is that these letters are a little longer (in the case of Romans and 1–2 Corinthians, *much* longer) than the typical personal letter; keeping in mind where the shifts in topic occur helps orient the reader. But there is a more fundamental issue here. Even a friend's casual letter has a certain structure, whether the writer was conscious of it or not. In some cases, to be sure, the argument may be a little incoherent and one could not come up with an intelligible outline. It is always true, however, that our ability to understand a letter (or any other document) is tied to how accurately we perceive its structure. This process of identification is largely unconscious, but if we receive a longer and more complicated letter, we may start asking ourselves structural kinds of questions ("Is the lawyer talking about something else in this paragraph, or am I missing the connection?"). The more explicit we are about these issues, the more sensitive we become to the information that the context provides.

In addition, this kind of study provides the means of comparing the various letters with one another so that we can identify what is distinctive to each of them. For example, as we study the salutations in Paul's letters, we find that most of them are very brief. Only two of them, those in Romans and Galatians, are expanded to include substantive material. In the case of Galatians, this detail may well be additional evidence of the urgency with which Paul wrote this letter. No sooner has he mentioned his title of apostle than he feels the need to deny one of the accusations that prompted the writing of the letter, so he assures us: "an apostle—sent not from men nor by man, but by Jesus Christ and God the Father."

The second part of the introduction (1:6–10) is even more interesting. At this point in his other letters Paul consistently expresses his thanks (or utters a blessing) to God for the people to whom he is writing. Here, however, instead of beginning with "I thank my God," he exclaims, "I am astonished that you are so quickly deserting the one who called you by the grace of Christ!" Someone familiar with Paul's letters would find this remark completely unexpected, and it is the unexpected that makes the greatest impression on us. More important, for Paul to diverge in this way from his

---

5. This traditional outline of the body of Galatians can be found, with some minor variations, in many commentaries and popular works. As we shall see, however, recent scholars have disputed some important details and even the general approach.

practice tells us a great deal about his mood and motivation in writing Galatians.

So far so good. Very few people would object to this kind of discussion or to the outline on which it is based. But is it possible that Paul made greater use of literary techniques? A long time ago it was noticed that in Galatians 4:4–5 the apostle seems to use a *chiasm,* that is, an ordering of clauses in an A-B-B´-A´ pattern:

> *God sent his Son, born of a woman, {A}*
> *born under the law, {B}*
> *to redeem those under the law {B´}*
> *that we might receive the full right of sons. {A´}*

Taking his cue from this passage—as well as from other evidence that chiasms were used frequently in the ancient world—a New Testament scholar in the 1960s believed he detected other and more sophisticated chiasms in Galatians.[6] Indeed, he proposed that Galatians as a whole was one immense chiasm, composed of secondary chiasms, which in turn were made up of tertiary chiasms, and so on. The notion that Paul, or any other sane person, would invest the time and effort to compose that sort of writing for no apparent benefit (after all, it took twenty centuries for someone to discover it) was too much for contemporary scholars, most of whom have not been persuaded by this theory. The biggest objection to it, however, is that it works only by forcing the evidence. While some of the chiasms proposed by the author are intriguing and may be valid, many others can hardly be considered a natural reading of the text.

More persuasive, though still debatable, is the suggestion that Galatians reflects in its structure the rhetorical principles of ancient Greek and Latin oratory. Particularly influential has been the proposal that Galatians was composed as an "apologetic letter," with the following sections:

Epistolary prescript, 1:1–5
Exordium (introduction of the facts), 1:6–11
Narratio (statement of the facts), 1:12–2:14
Propositio (summary of legal content of *narratio*), 2:15–21
Probatio (proofs or arguments), 3:1–4:31

6. John Bligh, *Galatians in Greek: A Structural Analysis of St. Paul's Epistle to the Galatians, with Notes on the Greek* (Detroit: University of Detroit Press, 1966). Subsequently he wrote a commentary based on those investigations; see his *Galatians: A Discussion of St. Paul's Epistle,* Householder Commentaries 1 (London: St. Paul, 1969).

Exhortatio (exhortations), 5:1–6:10
Epistolary postscript, 6:11–18[7]

Some scholars have disputed the precise identification of Galatians as an apologetic letter, others have objected to various details of the outline. Even this careful outline is not able to account for all the facts (e.g., the exhortations do not fit any known pattern in formal letter writing). More fundamental is the objection that for Paul to follow in such detail the rules of oratory seems inconsistent with his disavowal of eloquent speech (1 Cor. 2:1–5; 2 Cor. 11:6; Col. 2:4).

Whatever the problems, there has been a growing recognition of the need to analyze the letters of the New Testament in the light of ancient rhetorical practices. This development in modern scholarship has had some valuable repercussions, not the least of which is a renewed appreciation for the wholeness and coherence of these documents. An interesting example is Paul's letter to the Philippians. In the past, some scholars have argued that Philippians is really made up of two or three different letters. Recent rhetorical studies, however, have shown that this document is a literary whole and that fragmentation theories cannot account for its structure.

Reading the New Testament Letters Theologically

Even after we have made a special effort to understand the epistles as whole documents, inquiring into their historical context and literary structure, we are left with a crucial task—theological interpretation. In the history of modern biblical scholarship, this task has often been minimized, ignored, or even rejected altogether as something that lies outside the responsibility of the interpreter. In recent decades, however, the validity of theological reflection has become widely recognized. Since the New Testament letters, especially Paul's, address theological issues more directly and extensively than other parts of Scripture, discussions of Pauline theology are now more numerous than grains of sand on the seashore.

To be sure, scholars have diverse ideas about what it means to interpret the Bible theologically. For some, it seems to be an exercise in discovering "contradictions" among the biblical authors (e.g., Paul vs. James) or even between two writings by the same author (e.g., Romans vs. Galatians). At the other extreme, some conservative scholars devote so much

7. Hans Dieter Betz, *Galatians: A Commentary on Paul's Letter to the Churches in Galatia*, Hermeneia (Philadelphia: Fortress, 1979), pp. 14–25.

of their attention to the common features among the writers of Scripture that the biblical message becomes "flattened."

Here, as is so often the case, balance is needed. On the one hand, an evangelical commitment to the divine unity of Scripture certainly implies that we must interpret individual books within the total theological context of the Bible, so that the connection between the parts and the whole becomes as clear as possible. On the other hand, sensitivity to the human and historical character of Scripture will lead us to recognize and even emphasize the distinctiveness of each portion. Indeed, one of the most useful hermeneutical guidelines we can use consists in asking of each writing: "Why did God include *this* book in the canon? What is its distinctive contribution to the whole teaching of Scripture? What is its place in the history of revelation?"

When scholars approach the Bible theologically, a very common topic of discussion is whether they can identify a unifying element in a writer's thought. Accordingly, much ink has been spilled on such subjects as "the center of Pauline theology." Whether or not we can come up with such a center—that is, with a doctrinal nucleus that accounts for everything else Paul teaches—is a question that we need not trouble ourselves with. It is clear, however, that Paul did pay attention to foundational concepts, and if we wish to interpret his writings responsibly, we need to consider how those basic ideas relate to specific passages.

At the time of the Protestant Reformation, theological studies focused on the apostle's teaching about the individual's justification by faith and not by works. Nowadays, however, some argue vigorously that this understanding, motivated by Luther's personal experiences, reflects a distortion of Paul. Such a criticism is surely an extreme overreaction. One can still argue persuasively that the doctrine of justification by faith functions as a kind of conceptual adhesive that helps to make sense of much of Paul's teaching. Nevertheless, there is some truth in every falsehood, and modern scholars make a significant point when they argue that a broader issue, the relationship between Jews and Gentiles, should play a more prominent role in our interpretation of Paul's teaching.

Even the argument of Galatians 3, so crucial for the doctrine of justification, is motivated and undergirded by a bigger, overarching question, namely, Who are the true descendants of Abraham? One could make a case for the view that the very structure of the epistle to the Romans is motivated by the same question. To ask such a question, however, is to reflect on the nature of redemptive history and thus on the way God has fulfilled his promises. As we saw in our discussion of the Gospels, a central aspect of Jesus' teaching was precisely the theme of fulfillment. Because his announcement that the kingdom of God had come implied the arrival of the "last days," we may think of his message as having a basic eschatological character.

Not surprisingly, some scholars have detected a similar emphasis in other parts of the New Testament, especially in Paul's writings.[8] Indeed, it is clear that Paul saw the coming of Christ—in particular, his resurrection and exaltation—as the most important turning point in the history of redemption. The eschatological focus of Paul's teaching is sometimes very explicit, as in 1 Corinthians 10:11, where he says that Christians experience "the fulfillment [lit., the end] of the ages." Even where it is not spelled out, however, this theme seems to provide the framework for Paul's theology in general.

This perspective can be very helpful in correcting our understanding of specific passages. For example, in Romans 1:3–4, where Paul appears to summarize the essence of the gospel he preaches, he describes Christ as one who, on the one hand, "was born out of the seed of David according to the flesh," but on the other hand "was determined Son of God in power according to the Spirit of holiness out of the resurrection of the dead" (lit. trans.). Traditionally, this statement was understood as a reference to the two natures of Christ, with the word *flesh* indicating his human nature and the word *spirit* his divine nature. The resulting idea was that, at the resurrection, Jesus' divinity was demonstrated. This view is partly reflected in the NIV: "who as to his *human nature* was a descendant of David, and who through the Spirit of holiness *was declared* with power to be the Son of God by his resurrection from the dead" (italics added).

Some recent interpreters, however, have argued persuasively that the passage does not refer to the two (coexisting) natures of Christ but rather to the two (successive) stages of his messianic work, that is, his humiliation and his exaltation.[9] Although Christ was eternally divine, the title *Son of God* here probably refers to what He became at the resurrection, namely, the victorious, exalted Messiah (the verb translated "declared" by the NIV has a much stronger force, such as "determine, set, appoint"). Christ's two stages, therefore, reflect two different periods in redemptive history: the present evil age of the flesh and the future glorious age of the Spirit. The close

8. One of the earliest writers to make this point was Geerhardus Vos, *The Pauline Eschatology* (Grand Rapids: Eerdmans, 1930). The most thorough exposition from this perspective is H. Ridderbos, *Paul: An Outline of His Theology* (Grand Rapids: Eerdmans, 1975). For what follows, cf. the useful discussion in Richard B. Gaffin, Jr., *The Centrality of the Resurrection: A Study in Paul's Soteriology* (Grand Rapids: Baker, 1978). Some of the material above comes from Moisés Silva, "Systematic Theology and the Apostle to the Gentiles" (forthcoming in *TJ*).

9. See the extensive discussion in Gaffin, *Centrality*, pp. 98–114, and the literature cited by him.

relationship between the resurrected Christ and the Holy Spirit is emphasized in other passages, such as Romans 8:11; 1 Corinthians 15:44–45; 2 Corinthians 3:17–18.

The marvelous truth encapsulated in Romans 1:3–4 and parallel passages, therefore, is that with Christ's resurrection the future age becomes a reality now, at least in part, for those who are united with Christ in that resurrection. Indeed, in chapter 6 of the same letter, the apostle describes Christians as those who have died with Christ and have also been raised with Him to a new life. Because the Holy Spirit, who is the essence of the age to come, has been given to us as the first installment of our inheritance (cf. Eph. 1:13–14), we have in a very real sense been transported to heaven and sit there with Christ (Eph. 2:6; Col. 3:1–4; cf. Phil. 3:20).

But isn't the "present evil age" (Gal. 1:4) still with us? Doesn't Paul recognize that Christians continue to live "in the flesh" (Gal. 2:20 lit.; NIV, "in the body")? This is precisely where the significance of the Pauline message becomes apparent. In Jewish thought, "this world" was supposed to end with the inauguration of "the age to come." In contrast, according to Paul (and his view is reflected elsewhere in the New Testament), the new age of the Spirit in effect overlaps the old age of the flesh. Theologians often speak of this perspective as an "already-not yet" tension. While Jesus, with his coming, did bring in the kingdom of God and thus has already conquered the forces of the enemy, yet sin and misery continue to be with us until the consummation.

This truth has far-reaching implications for the way we interpret the New Testament. It is clear, for example, that Paul's difficult statements about the Mosaic law must be related to his understanding of flesh and death. Although the apostle clearly understands that law as divinely given and therefore inherently good—implying that it has relevance for the Christian (Rom. 7:12; 1 Cor. 7:19; Gal. 5:14)—yet he affirms that, in the weakness of the flesh, it became an instrument of sin and death (cf. Rom. 7:8–10; 8:3; 1 Cor. 15:56; 2 Cor. 3:6–8). The Mosaic covenant was a temporary arrangement, anticipating the coming of Christ (Gal. 3:23–25).

Again, the doctrine of sanctification is greatly illumined by Paul's eschatological approach. The conflict between the flesh and the Spirit experienced by believers (Gal. 5:16–26) reflects a struggle not precisely between two parts of each individual but rather between two forces of cosmic proportions. However, since we have already died to sin and are not under subjection to the law but alive to God, we are assured that sin will not have dominion over us (Rom. 6:14). In the light of this assurance, moreover, the believer's responsibility to lead an obedient life becomes very clear. If sin has been dethroned, we simply have no excuse when we disobey God. The Spirit of Christ has freed us from sin and death. May we learn to "put to death the misdeeds of the body" as children of God who are led by his Spirit (Rom. 8:13–14).

Reading the New Testament Letters as Authoritative Documents

We must conclude this chapter with a brief but important reminder that the epistles of the New Testament, no less than the rest of Scripture, come to us from God himself and thus bear his authority. As Paul wrote his letters, he did so with the consciousness of speaking the words of God (cf. 1 Thess. 2:13), and he did not hesitate to exercise his apostolic authority when necessary (cf. 2 Thess. 3:6).

This point needs to be made because our emphasis on the letters as historical documents could lead to a downplaying of their significance as Scripture. It is not unusual to hear comments about the *contextualized* character of these books—the implication being that they may have been relevant at one time in a particular historical context, but not now. As with all error, there is a measure of truth in this approach. For example, most Christians today do not believe that it is necessary for women to cover their heads in worship, as 1 Corinthians 11:5 seems to say. The reason normally given is that Paul was probably addressing a cultural practice that is foreign to us. Without question, certain commands and principles in Scripture (not in the letters only!) are difficult to apply in our day; we shall return to this topic in a later chapter.

We must not conclude, however, that this kind of difficulty is typical. Generally speaking, a knowledge of the historical situation helps us to refine our understanding of the commands of Scripture, but it does not remove their validity for us. One must have very persuasive textual reasons to decide that a particular passage in the letters of the New Testament is so historically conditioned that it has no present applicability. After all, the Scripture has been given to us as something "useful for teaching, rebuking, correcting and training in righteousness" (2 Tim. 3:16).

A staggering 27 percent of the Bible deals with predictions about the future, even though the function of foretelling is less prominent as a feature among the prophets than that of forthtelling. This prophecy is not "prewritten history," but it exhibits the characteristics of intelligibility, definiteness, and organic unity.

In spite of the popular aphorism that "the prophets wrote better than they knew," the prophets' self-understanding of their prophecies is exhibited by their awareness of (1) the results of their words, (2) the implictions of their prophecies, (3) the knowledge of things that were humanly impossible to know, and (4) the relation that contemporary events and circumstances had with future events in the same series of happenings.

There are three types of prophecies: conditional, unconditional, and sequential. Each must be interpreted according to its type, or confusion will result.

To express the future, the prophets used terms, events, and persons from the past. They also employed a number of recurring prophetic formulas to mark the presence of a passage about the future. This did not lead to a "double sense" interpretation of prophecy, but to a complex single sense in which the "now" and the "not-yet" were seen as definite pieces of one whole meaning, connected in the interim by a series of multiple fulfillments.

CHAPTER 8

What About the Future?
THE MEANING OF PROPHECY

WALTER C. KAISER, JR.

The topic of prophecy all too frequently produces one of two extremes in readers and interpreters: a wholesale avoidance and an apathy toward the subject, or the creation of a hobbyhorse. Both responses are inadequate and in need of the balance that is presented in the biblical text.

Prophecy is a much larger biblical genre than most people think. All too many connect the word *prophecy* with the idea of futurology. But the bulk of prophecy in both the earlier prophets (Joshua, Judges, Samuel, and Kings), the latter prophets (Isaiah, Jeremiah, Ezekiel, Daniel, and the twelve minor prophets), and the New Testament prophets actually involved God's messengers speaking the word of God to a contemporary culture that needed to be challenged to cease its resistance to the word of God. As such, these prophets were "forth-tellers."

The aspect of prophecy that is more difficult to interpret is that portion that deals with foretelling. The number of predictions about the future in the Bible is so large in both Testaments that it carries with it a silent rebuke for any of us who have been hesitant to enter into their study.

According to the calculations of J. Barton Payne, there are 8,352 verses with predictive material in them out of 31,124 verses in the whole Bible—a staggering 27 percent of the Bible that deals with predictions about the future. Payne calculated that the Old Testament contained 6,641 verses on the future (out of 23,210 total, or 28.6 percent), while the New Testament has 1,711 (out of 7,914 verses, or 21.6 percent). Altogether, these 8,352 verses discuss 737 separate prophetic topics! The only books without any predictive material are Ruth and Song of Songs in the Old Testament and Philemon and 3 John in the New Testament. The other sixty-two books of the Bible are all represented in one or more of the 737 prophetic topics gathered by Payne.[1]

The Old Testament books with the highest percentage of future prophecies are Ezekiel, Jeremiah, and Isaiah, with 65, 60, and 59 percent of their total verses respectively. In the New Testament, the top three are Revelation, Matthew, and Luke, with 63, 26, and 23 percent of their total corpus respectively.

It thus is clear that prophecy about the future cannot be passed off lightly if we are to do justice to the Bible as God wished to compose it. Any declaration of the whole counsel of God needs to interact with these prophetic themes on a fairly wide scale, given the fact that approximately one-fourth of the verses in the Bible are concerned with this topic.

The Characteristics of Biblical Prophecy

Biblical prophecy has its own unique set of distinctive features and characteristics that at once set it off from every other imitation. At the turn of this century, Robert B. Girdlestone addressed this issue, enumerating the following six characteristics:

1. Biblical prophecy plainly foretells things to come without clothing them in ambiguities similar to the oracles of the pagan nations.
2. Biblical prophecy is designed and intended to be a prediction rather than a retrospective declaration, an unwitting prophecy, or a "lucky guess" that just happened to come to pass.
3. It is written, published or proclaimed prior to the event it refers to and is a happening that could not have been foreseen by ordinary human sagacity.
4. It is subsequently fulfilled in accordance with the words of the original prediction.
5. Prophecy does not work out its own fulfillment, but it stands as a witness until the event has taken place.
6. A biblical prophecy is not an isolated prediction, but it can be

---

1. J. Barton Payne. *Encyclopedia of Biblical Prophecy: The Complete Guide to Scriptural Predictions and their Fulfillment* (New York: Harper and Row, 1973), pp. 631–82.

correlated with other prophecies and as such is one of a long series of predictions.[2]

Not all prophecies, of course, fit every one of the six characteristics given here. But where these exceptions exist, they still exhibit the general thrust and spirit of all six descriptions. We examine now in more detail some of the features of biblical prophecy.

INTELLIGIBILITY

A popular slogan calls prophecy "prewritten history." But if that were true in every sense of the word, then prophecy would be as plain and clear as history writing. But prophecy does have an enigmatic aspect to it, even as God acknowledged in his word to Moses in Numbers 12:6–8. In this text, Moses is said to have two distinct advantages over other prophets who followed him. First, God spoke to Moses directly ("mouth to mouth, clearly"), whereas he would speak to the prophets in "dark speeches" (i.e., riddles). Second, God appeared to Moses directly, while he would reveal himself to the prophets in visions and dreams. This surely marks a contrast between the clarity, ease of interpreting, and directness that is to be observed in Moses as the receiver of prophecies and all others in the Bible.

However, this admission must not be pushed to the extreme of saying that nothing can be understood of the prophetic material until God establishes the word of his servant in its fulfillment. Usually the way we get entrapped on this count is to slip the word *fully* into the affirmation, as in: "prophecy is not intended to be fully understood before its fulfillment." As it stands, of course, that is a true statement, but it is redundant. Naturally, the proof is in the pudding, as we say.

There is a sense in which all prophecy was intended to communicate an *adequate* understanding of the future for the first audience to whom it was directed, even if it came in a riddle form, often accompanied by symbols, clothed in a vision, and not being entirely clear. Such observations have led to long discussions and debates over whether prophecies should be understood "literally," "figuratively," or "spiritually."

What is meant by the literal sense? Raymond Brown defined it as "the sense which the human author intended and which his words convey."[3] Although prophecy indeed uses far more figurative language, including

---

2. Robert B. Girdlestone, *The Grammar of Prophecy: Guide to Biblical Prophecy* (repr., Grand Rapids: Kregel, 1955), p. 1.

3. Raymond E. Brown, "The Literal Sense of Scripture," in *JBC*, pp. 606–10.

symbols, figures of speech, allegories, and parables, than does narrative or didactic prose, this is not to say that the words or terms used are any less literal. One must assume the primacy of the grammatical, plain, straightforward, simple sense before one searches for what is "contained in" or "falls within" or "is below" or is "based on" the literal sense.

It is preferable, then, to take prophecy in its natural, straightforward, literal sense. But one must remember that "literal" here simply means that words are to be taken according to their normal grammatical and philological sense; indeed, this is the meaning of the classic grammatico-historical method of interpretation. Although a fair portion of the words are of a figurative type, they are no less meaningful for being figurative, for the author still meant to say something by his use of these words.

The question of the so-called spiritual sense is much more complex. This sense is usually not determined from explicitly stated authorial intentions or from the fact that figurative language is used in these prophecies. Often it is said to be between the lines rather than something identifiable from the grammar of the verse itself. Alternatively, it is first identified in the New Testament and then viewed as a new value given to an older reading, since in the progress of revelation, it is argued, God has the right to introduce such new values for older readings. In that regard, then, usually such new readings for old values are statements that arise from the assumptions one has brought to the passage based upon one's theological frame of reference. (The problem, however, is not to be found in the fact that the interpreter comes with a set of assumptions, or from within one's "hermeneutical spiral" or "circle." We must admit that we all approach the text as the products of our backgrounds, experiences, and previous understandings. Yet we all must test such assumptions against the whole tenor of Scripture and particularly against the evidence from the passage under examination.)

A related question is, Can ancient word values intended by the Old Testament writers to have one set of values be given another new set of values without distorting the general intention of the original statement? One key issue that has divided interpreters into separate schools of thought is the way we interpret "Israel" in the Old Testament text. Since it is clear from Scripture that there is only one "people of God," some have concluded that the word *church* can now be read and substituted for certain key Old Testament prophecies about the future of "Israel." The rationale for this substitution is usually stated as being the progress of revelation and the unity of the people of God mentioned here. But unless this identification can be formally located in the Old Testament text itself, this interpretation would be a case of eisegesis, or reading a meaning (here, gained from the New Testament as a whole) back into an earlier text (here, the Old Testament).

Those wishing to maintain such a "spiritual sense" would perhaps appeal to what has been called the analogy of faith, a method that would apply insights from systematic theology into the practice of doing exegesis. Some have argued against just such a practice, however, wishing to base exegesis as much as possible solely on the conclusions that are supported by the analysis of particular texts.

In response, those defending the use of "analogy of faith" argue that it is appropriate to "read into" the Old Testament, since the author of both Testaments is the same—God—and he is the one who kept adding to his own revelation in the course of giving us the two Testaments. We will deal with this issue further in chapter 11, but for the present let us note that both "progress of revelation" and "analogy of faith" must be defined much more accurately if we are to reflect what the church has meant by these terms. The progress of revelation has an organic aspect in which the identity of the germ contained in the earliest mention of a theme continues in the buildup of that theme as the same seminal idea takes on a more developed form in later revelation. The analogy of faith thus does not establish additional meanings but collects those already present in a rudimentary or seminal form and now expresses these more fully by further exegesis in the progress of revelation.[4]

DEFINITENESS

Our Lord did warn us that, unlike Moses, a certain opaqueness, or enigmatic quality, would be attached to what the other prophets had to say. This is not due to a lack of precision on their part or on the part of the divine Revealer. Rather, it has to do more with things like "prophetic perspective," "corporate solidarity," and a blending of such temporal aspects as the here and now, the "already" with the "not yet" types of disclosures to be found in this kind of literature.

"Prophetic perspective" occurs quite frequently in the Old Testament prophets. It is the phenomenon of blending together both the near and the distant aspects of the prediction in one and the same vision. Thus Joel

4. On this subject, see H. S. Curr, "Progressive Revelation" *JTVI* 83 (1951): 1–23; D. L. Baker, "Progressive Revelation," in *Two Testaments, One Bible* (Downers Grove, Ill.: InterVarsity, 1976), pp. 76–87; James I. Packer, "An Evangelical View of Progressive Revelation," in *Evangelical Roots: A Tribute to Wilbur Smith,* ed. Kenneth S. Kantzer (Nashville: Nelson, 1978), pp. 143–58; Walter C. Kaiser, Jr., "Progressive Revelation," in *Toward Old Testament Ethics* (Grand Rapids: Zondervan, 1983), pp. 60–64. Also note Frederic Gardiner, "The Progressive Character of Revelation," in *The Old and New Testaments in Their Mutual Relations* (New York: Pott, 1885), pp. 28–61.

predicts that as a result of the people's response to the prophet's summons to repent, God would reverse the devastation brought on by the locust plague, the contemporary manifestation of the Day of the Lord, by sending rain showers immediately (Joel 2:23). However, he would also send such a downpour of the Holy Spirit that it would affect everyone (vv. 28–29). This latter aspect was realized only later—in part, at Pentecost (Acts 2:16). Yet, it too awaits a full and final realization at the second coming of Christ (Joel 2:30–31).

Here is one of the aspects of prophecy that adds difficulty to its interpretation. Some have referred to this same phenomenon as prophetic foreshortening. The common illustration is that of two distant mountain peaks that give little hint to the viewer as to how much distance lies between the two. In the same way, interpreters looking across the corridor of time tend to see later events connected with the original context. Old Testament prophets thus tended to see the first coming of our Lord as blending with events connected with his second coming.

Another way to illustrate this blending of the near and the distant aspects of prophecy is to picture the prophet looking through the sights of a gun barrel. The sight on the rifle closest to his eye lines up with the sight out on the end of the barrel; in exactly the same way he is aware of the near fulfillment(s) and the way that they participate in the ultimate fulfillment. However, the interpreter must be careful to note that even though there may be a multiple number of fulfillments, in the prophet's mind they are united together as *one sense* and meaning, since all the fulfillments participate in the organic unity and wholeness to which each member of the future enactments belongs.

This outlook on prophecy is known as inaugurated eschatology. Such an outlook has an "already-fulfilled" and a "not-yet fulfilled" aspect for many of the predictions in both the Old and New Testaments. Accordingly, many antichrists had already come, some were currently on the scene, but the final antichrist would put in his appearance at the end of the age according to several passages, but particularly 1 John 2:18. This compares well with 1 John 4:3: "This is the spirit of the antichrist, which you have heard *is coming* and *even now is already* in the world."

Likewise, Elijah the prophet had ministered and would yet come again, but John the Baptist also had come in the "spirit and power of Elijah" (Luke 1:17). Nevertheless, God would once again send "the prophet Elijah before that great and dreadful day of the LORD comes" (Mal. 4:5). Jesus, of course, confirmed this same understanding when he taught in Matthew 11:14 that "if you are willing to accept it, [John the Baptist] is the Elijah who is to come." Jesus later added in Matthew 17:11, "To be sure, Elijah is coming and will restore all things. But I tell you, Elijah has already come, and they did not recognize him, but have done to him everything they wished." On the face of it, it would appear as if Jesus answered yes and no. John the Baptist was the fulfillment of the promise that Elijah would come before the great Day of the Lord comes, but he came only in the "spirit" and "power" of Elijah. If you are able to receive it, Jesus admonished, there would still be a future coming of an Elijah. Who that would be and in what way it would happen were left unresolved by any further revelation. But it is clear that prophecy had both a "now" and a "not-yet" aspect.

It is little wonder, then, that so many have trouble deciding how definite the prophetic word is when it has such a complex number of fulfillments, even if all of these multiple fulfillments have a single, organically related, and unified meaning. The best way to describe this wholeness is to illustrate it by the messianic line. Each son born in the Abrahamic and Davidic line was a real fulfillment, a down payment on the climactic fulfillment coming at the end of the series, each functioning as God's placeholder and as a tangible evidence in history that God's word about the Messiah's first and second comings was trustworthy. All the while, each son continued to be a pointer to the One who would embody all that any in the series ever was and more. It is here that the concept of corporate solidarity comes into the discussion, for each in the Davidic line was at once part of the *One* (who was to come) and the *many* (in the line of the "Seed").

ORGANIC UNITY

Frequently, the pattern of biblical revelation is to begin by presenting one of the great topics of prophecy in a broad and bold outline, leaving it to subsequent revelations to expand and develop the theme. This interdependence of prophetic discussions within the biblical text becomes most important for the interpreter; we cannot assume that each prediction is a sealed unit to itself. It seldom is!

The prophecies about Christ begin in germ form in Genesis 3:15. But they go on from that point to reappear with Noah (9:26–27), Abraham (12:3; 15:2–8; 18:18), and the rest of the patriarchs and the line of David. Likewise, Balaam's oracle (Num. 24:17–24) contains the prophetic germ of many of the later prophecies against some of the same nations who had taken up their positions against the people of God (e.g., Amos 1–2; Isa. 13–23; Jer. 46–51; and Ezek. 25–32).

Sometimes the same prophet repeated a similar prophecy on the same topic. Thus the prophet Daniel repeated the same subject of the destiny of the four world empires, as opposed to the coming of the kingdom of God with the leadership of the Son of man, in Daniel 7 as he had described earlier in chapter 2. Daniel 2 treats the external aspect of these world powers, while chapter 7 looks at them from their interior aspects. Similarly, the two-horned ram and the shaggy he-goat of Daniel 8 are but a repetition of the second and third world empires of Daniel 2 and 7 (as Daniel is told in 8:20–21).

The Prophets' Self-Understanding of Their Prophecies

One of the most often-repeated answers to the question about the prophets' awareness of what they wrote is that "the prophets wrote better than they knew." Contrary to this repeated aphorism, the prophets understood what it was that they preached and wrote. This is not to say that they were *fully* cognizant of all that they wrote or that they knew what all the ramifications of their writings were. The time and the exact manner in which God would fulfill his promises in the future was often as much unknown to them as it is to us. They did not preach words, however, that had no meaning for them until we modern, New Testament exegetes understood it for the first time. God did not inspire the writers of Scripture at the cost of bypassing their rational faculties. The evidences for the prophets' self-awareness of their messages are fourfold.[5]

The Prophets Were Aware of the Results of Their Prophecies

So cognizant of what was being asked of him was Jonah that he fled in the opposite direction. He did not want his preaching to be the occasion of the repentance of a nation that had had such a bloody and cruel relationship to his own (Jonah 4:3). In like manner, Micaiah ben Imlah knew right well how objectionable his prophecy would be to King Ahab, therefore he gave an ironic, misleading, prophecy at first (1 Kings 22:15b). Moreover, he also knew what would happen to the false prophets in Zedekiah's band (v. 25: they would "hide in an inner room") and what would happen to King Ahab in the battle for which he sought divine guidance before engaging in it (v. 28: he would not return safely).

5. The following discussion draws heavily on a helpful study by Douglas Stuart, "The Old Testament Prophets' Self-Understanding of Their Prophecy," *Themelios* 6 (1980): 9–14.

THE PROPHETS WERE AWARE OF THE IMPLICATIONS OF THEIR PROPHECIES

When the prophet Amos was shown in separate visions that God would send locusts to eat up the second mowing and a fire to consume all, Amos objected and begged God to relent (Amos 7:1–6). How could Amos have prayed as an intercessor if he had had no idea what the two visions meant? In contrast, Jeremiah was forbidden to intervene with God in prayer on behalf of Judah, since things in Judah had gone too far to turn around (Jer. 7:16; 11:14; 14:11). No longer was it a matter of conditional fulfillment if the people did not repent; God's word described what would happen no matter what. And Jeremiah knew it too!

THE PROPHETS WERE TOLD THINGS THAT WERE HUMANLY IMPOSSIBLE TO KNOW

Time after time the prophet Elisha warned the king of Israel to be on his guard in one specific place after another (e.g., 2 Kings 6:9). In fact, Elisha told the Israelite king "the very words" that the Syrian king spoke in his bedroom (v. 12b). Such incidents show clearly what it meant to be a recipient of revelation. Not only were these prophets told secrets from the bedrooms of the enemy, they were transported by way of a vision to see what was going on miles away from them. Thus Ezekiel was shown what was happening in Jerusalem while he was more than 1,200 miles away from home in Babylon (Ezek. 8:3b–11:25). Thus instead of an opacity, the prophets spoke with a keenness, a sense of detail, and an understanding that is unrivaled anywhere.

THE PROPHETS RELATED THEIR PREDICTIONS TO CONTEMPORARY EVENTS
AND CIRCUMSTANCES

A description of the distant future with no ties to the present could hardly be expected to hold the interest of the prophet's audience or have any real personal and practical impact on their lives. That is why prophecies have their roots in the particular contemporaneous events. In some cases God explained first what he was going to do before the prophet passed it on to the audience it was addressed to (Ezek. 14:2–11; Dan. 7:16–28; 12:8–10). The Lord assured Amos that he did "nothing without revealing his counsel to his servants the prophets" (Amos 3:7). Amos's response was: "The LORD God has spoken; who can but prophesy?" (v. 8). There was a divine imperative about prophecy once God had spoken, and that obligation was not fulfilled until the prophet's contemporaries had had a chance to respond to it.

Surely it is clear that the prophets wrote only what was told them by God. In each case, they had an understanding of what they wrote adequate to perceive the implications and results of what they were saying.

Principles for Interpreting Prophecy

Girdlestone warned that "there is no royal road to the scientific study of prophecy."[6] Two prominent reasons for such a conclusion are the enigmatic nature of a large part of the prophetic materials, and the exceedingly large amount of biblical materials that exist on virtually every prophetic topic.

The following guidelines are given to help the interpreter through the more difficult waters of prophecy. In many cases, where special problems do not exist (e.g., because symbols, types, or apocalyptic language does not appear), the interpreter can generally proceed much as one would for other prose passages. But in most prophetic material, one or more of the following four guidelines will need to be heeded.

UNCONDITIONAL PROPHECIES MUST BE DISTINGUISHED FROM CONDITIONAL AND SEQUENTIAL ONES

Prophecies of the Bible may be classified on the basis of their fulfillment: conditional, unconditional, or sequential. All three types appear fairly regularly and are accompanied by indicators in the text that help the reader or interpreter to distinguish between them.

UNCONDITIONAL PROPHECY. The actual list of unconditional prophecies is not long, but they occupy the most pivotal spots in the history of redemption. These promises are unilateral in that they do not depend in any sense for their fulfillment on any mortal's obedience or pledge to maintain them. Typically they are found in a covenantal structure.

The unconditional covenant in Genesis 15, in which God ceremonially passed between the pieces laid out for the covenant ceremony, is significant. In such ceremonies usually the sacrificial animals were cut in half and placed opposite each other to form an aisle so that the ones who were making the covenant could pass through this aisle. Should any persons passing down this aisle fail to keep the oath they had sworn to maintain, their lives would be forfeited, just as the animal's lives that had formed the aisle had been lost (cf. Jer. 34:13).

With this background we can now see why Genesis 15:9–21 is so significant for the Abrahamic covenant. There God, pictured as a smoking torch, passed between the cut-up animals and promised his covenant to

6. Girdlestone, *Grammar of Prophecy*, p. 104.

Abraham, but Abraham himself did not pass through.[7] This is what made the covenant unilateral, one-sided, and therefore unconditional on the part of God.

Other unconditional covenants are: God's covenant with the seasons (Gen. 8:21–22); God's promise of a dynasty, kingdom, and a dominion for David and his descendant(s) (2 Sam. 7:8–16); God's promise of the New Covenant (Jer. 31:31–34); and God's promise of the new heavens and the new earth (Isa. 65:17–19; 66:22–24). These promises pertain to our salvation through the seed of Abraham and David and the New Covenant, along with God's work of maintaining the seasons and restoring the new heavens and new earth.

CONDITIONAL PROPHECY. The majority of prophecies in the Old Testament are conditional. Almost all of these predictions rest on Leviticus 26 or Deuteronomy 28–32. These two texts give a number of specific consequences that will result from either obedience or disobedience to God's word. The sixteen writing prophets of the Old Testament quote from or allude to these two texts hundreds of times.[8]

The most distinctive characteristic of these prophecies is that each one has either an expressed or, more frequently, an implied "if" or "unless" connected to it. Thus, in the case of Jonah there was no explicit promise that if the people repented, they would be spared the calamity that Jonah had threatened would fall on them in forty days. However, only the assumption that Jonah knew that such a reprieve was possible in the event of an unexpected repentance can explain his deep reluctance to proclaim this divine declaration of judgment. If the end was that close, why would Jonah not have enjoyed announcing his enemy's sudden demise? Jonah must have known and counted on the fact that all bets on Nineveh's destruction were off in the event that the people suddenly decided to repent of their sins. So it is with every other declaration of blessing or judgment.

Jeremiah 18:7–10 identifies explicitly the often-implicit conditional by putting it in the form of a general principle:

> If at any time I announce that a nation or kingdom is to be
> uprooted, torn down, and destroyed, and if that nation I warned
> repents of its evil, then I will relent and not inflict on it the

7. Some have vigorously protested against viewing the Abrahamic covenant as unconditional. For a fuller statement of the problem, along with bibliography and a more detailed answer, see Walter C. Kaiser, Jr., *Toward Rediscovering the Old Testament* (Grand Rapids: Zondervan, 1987), pp. 149–55.

8. See, for example, Douglas Stuart, *Hosea–Jonah*, WBC 31 (Waco, Tex.: Word, 1987), pp. xxxii–xlii, which summarizes the citations of these two passages in the first five minor prophets. Stuart found twenty-seven types of curses and ten types of restoration blessings.

disaster I had planned. And if at another time I announce that a nation or a kingdom is to be built up and planted, and if it does evil in my sight and does not obey me, then I will reconsider the good I had intended to do for it.

That principle is at the heart of all conditional prophecies.

Leviticus 26 and Deuteronomy 28–32 list some of the typical kinds of blessing or judgments that will be faced, depending on what the nation's or individual's response is. First Kings 21:20–24 and 27–29 make it clear that what is said of nations, with their alternative prospects, is also true of individuals. When King Ahab repented, God reversed his dire words of doom and declared that the threatened judgment would not come in his day, since he had humbled himself before God's word.

SEQUENTIAL PROPHECY. This third type of prophecy is very much like the "already" and "not-yet" type of inaugurated prophecies that we have discussed above. The predictions contained within them place several events together in one prediction, even though they will be fulfilled in a sequence and a series of acts perhaps stretching over several centuries.

A number of predictions in this category have been used by those who were less than sympathetic with the Bible's own point of view to prove that many of the Bible's predictions never were fulfilled, or at least in the way that the text claimed they would be. Usually this list includes the following:

1. The prophecy of the destruction of Tyre by Nebuchadnezzar (Ezek. 26:7–14; 29:17–20)
2. Elijah's prophecy against King Ahab for his murder of Naboth (1 Kings 21:17–29)
3. Isaiah's prophecy of the destruction of Damascus (Isa. 17:1)

The prophecy of Ezekiel 26:7–14 may be taken as a typical case. It must be noticed that Ezekiel 26:3 specifically says that the Lord would "bring many *nations*" against Tyre. And indeed Nebuchadnezzar, as the king of Babylon, is specified in verse 7 as one of those many nations. What most interpreters fail to notice is that verse 12 has a sudden shift in the number of the pronoun from the singular form in verses 8–11 ("he") to the plural in verse 12 ("they"). When this is put together with the "many nations" of verse 3, it is clear that we are dealing with a sequential prophecy.

History confirms this interpretation. Nebuchadnezzar, after besieging Tyre for thirteen years (about 586–573 B.C.), was only able to drive the city of Tyre off the Canaanite coastline to an offshore island one-half mile out to sea. Even Ezekiel 29:18, the very context that had made the prediction about his role in coming against Tyre, recognized Nebuchadnezzar's frustration at not being able to conquer Tyre. Several hundred years later the Macedonian Alexander the Great came along, and he too was almost frustrated in his attempt to meet this Phoenician Tyrian force in their own element of the sea. However, in accordance with Ezekiel's prophecy in approximately 323 B.C. he scraped up their "stones, timber, and rubble" (26:12) from the old, abandoned on-shore site and literally cast them "into the sea" in order to build a causeway out to the island-city of Tyre, which he easily took. Only this type of handling of the text fits the explanation for "many nations" and illustrates what a sequential prophecy entails. But notice that the text contained the clues for its own proper understanding. Our interpretation was not imposed on the text on the basis of our knowing what the fulfillment would be.[9]

TERMS BORROWED FROM ISRAEL'S PAST HISTORY MAY BE USED TO EXPRESS THE FUTURE

Few features in prophecy are more common than the expression of the future in terms that have been borrowed from Israel's historic past. If the writer and his audience have not experienced the future, how can they meaningfully communicate about it unless they talk about it in analogical terms from the past? Furthermore, if God's methods of operation have a consistency and a pattern about them, borrowing from the past in order to help us conceptualize the future is an eminently logical and natural way of proceeding. Some notable examples of terms used to depict the future are

1. *Creation.* The terms and concepts of Gen. 1–2 reappear in the depiction of the new heavens and the new earth in Isa. 65:17 and 66:22.
2. *Paradise.* The Garden of Eden is used to describe the future paradisiacal conditions of the tree of life with its rivers flowing out of it in Isa. 51:3; Zech. 1:17; and Rev. 2:7.
3. *The Flood.* The days of Noah and the carrying on of life as usual in the threat of disaster in Gen. 6–8 serve as an analogy for what it will be like in the time of the coming of the Son of Man (Matt. 24:37–39). Even the scoffers of that day serve as models for that coming eschatological day (2 Peter 3:3–7).

9. For a discussion of other examples of sequential prophecies, see Walter C. Kaiser, Jr., *Back Toward the Future: Hints for Interpreting Biblical Prophecy* (Grand Rapids: Baker, 1989), pp. 37–40.

4. *The destruction of Sodom and Gomorrah.* What God did to the five cities of the plain in Gen. 18–19 and Deut. 29:23, he will do to the ungodly in a future day according to 2 Peter 2:6; Matt 10:15; 11:24; Rev. 14:10–11; and 19:20.

5. *The Exodus.* Just as God took the nation by the hand once in Pharaoh's day, so he will do so a "second time" at his coming again (Isa. 11:12 and Zech 10:10–11).

6. *The wilderness experience.* The presence of the pillar of cloud and fire, along with streams in the desert, set up additional expectations as to how God will work in that day when he comes again (Isa. 4:5, 35).

7. *Achan's sin and the Valley of Trouble.* What had been nothing but trouble for Israel because Achan had sinned will one day be turned into a "door of hope" (Hos. 2:15).[10]

In addition to these past events serving as models for expressing the future, the text likewise uses historical persons from the past to describe some of the future persons who will come. For example, Elijah, Joshua, Zerubbabel, and David are all "men of a sign" who help us to conceptualize what these future persons who are coming in their place will be like (Matt. 11:14; Hag. 2; Zech. 3–4, 6; and 2 Sam. 7, 1 Chron. 17; Pss. 89 and 132).

A good illustration of this use of the past to depict the future can be seen in Haggai 2:20–22. It reads:

> Tell Zerubbabel governor of Judah that I will shake the heavens and the earth, I will overturn royal thrones and shatter the power of foreign kingdoms. I will overthrow chariots and their riders; horses and their riders will fall, each by the sword of his brother.

At least three major historical allusions may be heard in this text about what God did in the past as a basis for understanding what he will do in the future: (1) just as he "overthrew" Sodom and Gomorrah (Deut. 29:23), so he will "overthrow" those sitting on royal thrones "on that day" (Hag. 2:23); (2) just as the "horse and rider went down" in the Red Sea (Exod. 15:1, 5), so Messiah's opponents will be conquered "on that day"; and (3) similar to Gideon's marvelous conquest, wherein every man put his own brother to death by the sword in the camp of the enemy (Judg. 7:22), so will God's victory be won "on that day." In this manner we can understand to some

---

10. For a fuller discussion of this use of the past to describe the future, see Girdlestone, *Grammar of Prophecy*, pp. 66–75. Also see Kaiser, *Back Toward the Future*, pp. 51–60.

degree what none of us has ever experienced as yet, since the event has not yet happened.

RECURRING PROPHETIC FORMULAS MARK THE PRESENCE OF PROPHETIC PASSAGES

In cases where the interpreter is not certain that the passage is to be understood as a prophecy, it is helpful to refer to a master list of expressions used commonly in prophecy. Most of these expressions have appeared so frequently that they have become technical terms for the concepts they represent.[11]

The following list is representative of these formulas:

1. *In the latter days* or *in the last days.* This expression refers to the period of time introduced in connection with the complex of events that surround the second coming of our Lord. Early examples of its use appear in Jacob's blessing on his sons (Gen. 49:1) and Balaam's predictions (Num. 24:14). In the prophet's use of the term, it refers to the time of restitution (Isa. 2:2; Jer. 49:39; Mic. 4:1; Hos. 3:5). In John 6:39, 40, 44, 54 the expression *last day* is used of the time of the resurrection of believers.

2. *The day of the Lord.* This is not any twenty-four hour period but the grouping of events that precedes and includes the second advent of Christ, during which time God moves in judgment and salvation. Harbingers of this day have been seen all through prophetic history, but the day still remains "near" and ready to be revealed. The classic description of that day is found in Amos 5:18. The earliest reference may be Exod. 32:34, "the day when I visit." It appears frequently in the prophets (e.g., Joel 1:15; 2:1; 3:14; Isa. 13:6; Ezek. 30:3; Zeph. 1:7, 14). Sometimes it is simply referred to as "that day" (as in Amos 8:3, 9, 13; 9:11).

3. *The Lord comes.* The book of Jude (v. 14) says that all the way back in the prepatriarchal age, Enoch looked for the Lord's coming again. This second advent is spoken of as an epiphany or parousia, a manifestation of the Lord. Christ will return to earth to punish (Isa. 26:21), to save (Isa. 40:10), to come to his temple (Mal. 3:1), and to visit Zion (Isa. 59:20). This he will do "suddenly" (Rev. 3:11; 22:7, 20), comparable to a flash of lightning or the unexpectedness of a thief (1 Thess. 5:2; 2 Peter 3:10; Rev. 3:3; 16:15). Believers thus

---

11. The main content of this section comes from Girdlestone, *Grammar of Prophecy,* chap. 8, "Recurrent Prophetic Formulae."

need to be ready and to watch constantly (Luke 12:39; 21:34; 1 Thess. 5:4).

4. *Restore the fortunes of my people* or *return the captivity.* God will liberate his people Israel from all over the world a second time just as he released them from the Egyptian captivity. Usually this event is placed very near to his coming again. Jeremiah and Ezekiel use this expression repeatedly (e.g., Jer. 30:3; Ezek. 39:25). The same formula can be used in connection with God's restoration of foreign nations as well, namely Moab, Ammon, and Egypt (Jer. 48:47; 49:6; Ezek. 29:14).

5. *The remnant shall return.* Similar to the preceding formula, this one also predicts restoration of Israel back to its native land of Canaan. It appears first in Gen. 45:7 but is used repeatedly in the prophets (Isa. 6:13; 10:21, 22; and books like Joel, Amos, Micah, Zephaniah, Jeremiah, and Ezekiel). In the New Testament, Paul takes up the idea in Rom. 9:27 and 11:5. God has always had his faithful few, who formed the remnant.

6. *The dwelling* (or *tabernacle*) *of God is with men.* The promise theme of the Bible uses this concept as one part of its famous tripartite formula, repeated almost fifty times throughout both Testaments. God promised that he would dwell among the people of Israel (1 Kings 8:27), but in that final day he would personally come to be in the midst of the nation (Ezek. 37:27, 28). The same truth is taught in Zech. 2:10, 11; 8:3; as well as in Rev. 21:3. Just as the word became flesh and tabernacled among us in the first advent (John 1:14), so Christ would come once again to walk and talk in our midst; only then he will rule and reign as well.

7. *The kingdom of God.* Moses' song at the Exodus promised that "the LORD will reign for ever and for ever" (Exod. 15:18). God is recognized as king in 1 Sam. 12:12, but the concept of Messiah having a kingdom builds from the promise made to David in 2 Sam. 7:16 and the prophetic vision of Messiah ruling as a king over the earth in the Royal Psalms and pictures of the same in passages such as Isa. 9:6–7; 24:23; Mic. 4:7; Obad. 21; Dan 7:14 gives this kingdom and dominion to the Son of Man. This theme becomes one of the keynotes of our Lord's ministry in the Gospels and the Pauline Epistles.

These and many other such expressions play an important role in alerting the interpreter to the presence of prophetic materials. Almost always they signal the fact that the setting for the final or ultimate fulfillment of texts that use these expressions is the time of the second coming of our Lord. Watch for their appearance and check to see whether their usage in each context has this technical significance.

CERTAIN PROPHETIC TERMS ARE RICH WITH ALLUSIONS

The language of prophecy often has a vivid texture and history to it. The actions and descriptions it uses are often typical, symbolic, and full of allusions to what happened in the past.

Some of these terms will help the interpreter to gain some perspective on biblical literature. Six of the most common are the following:[12]

1. *Earth.* Often one of the most difficult decisions for the interpreter is whether to translate *'ereṣ* "land" or "earth." Isa. 24 is a good test case. This prophecy probably points to a worldwide context, given its use of *heaven* as a counterpoint in v. 21. Thus, we may formulate this rule: where earth is used in distinction to heaven, it is used in its wider sense; but where it is set over against the Gentiles, it denotes "land."

2. *Sea.* The sea may refer to more than a large body of water. It may stand for a multitude of people, as it does in Dan. 7:2–3, out of which the four world empires arise.

3. *Sand of the sea* and the *stars of heaven.* Here too, both forms of thought may stand for a large number of people or the unmeasurable population of Israel (Gen. 22:17; Hos. 1:10; 1 Kings 4:20; Gen. 15:5; Heb. 11:12).

4. *Day of clouds and darkness; blood and fire and billows of smoke; the sun will be turned into darkness and the moon into blood.* Usually these phrases represent national and worldwide calamities. They are symbols of great suffering and destruction permitted by God in connection with his judging humankind at his second coming. Their roots are located in destructions of the past, such as that of the Flood and the destruction of Sodom and Gomorrah. See such texts as Joel 2:10, 30–31; 3:15; Isa. 13:10; 34:4; Ezek. 32:7; 34:12; Matt. 24:29; Rev. 6:12.

5. *The North.* Sometimes the North stands for Assyria, at other times for Babylon or Medo-Persia. This is because all the conquerors against Israel from the East had to swing out of the North, since the desert prevented a direct westward incursion. Later the North

12. Ibid., chap. 7, pp. 48–53.

refers to the Syrian and Seleucid monarchs who held sway over Syria and Palestine (Dan. 11:6–40). In Ezek. 38–39, the king of the North is identified with Gog, Rosh, Meshech, and Tubal, identities some have said are powers resident in the former Soviet Union. The same themes that are in Ezek. 38–39 appear again in Rev. 19:17, 18; 20:8.

6. *Marriage of the Lamb.* This marks the accomplishment of the projected union of Christ with his church at the conclusion of history (Rev. 19:7–9; 21:2, 9).

Prophecy often uses a great deal of symbolic imagery, especially in the sections called apocalyptic. Apocalyptic literature appears in Daniel 7–12, the entire book of Zechariah, Matthew 24–25, 2 Thessalonians, and the book of Revelation. Here revelation is conveyed by angels, visions, and dreams, along with other supernatural means. Mixed in with these messages are seas and bowls of blood, froglike spirits, and other symbols. These symbols may be classified into three groups:

1. Symbols that are explained in the same context (e.g., Dan. 2:37–44; 8:20–21; Rev. 1:20; 4:5)
2. Symbols that are paralleled by Old Testament imagery (e.g., the tree of life from Gen. 2:9; 3:24 is used in Rev. 2:7; 22:2)
3. Symbols that are unexplained in the context or in the Old Testament (e.g., the "white stone" of Rev. 2:17; the "pillar" in Rev. 3:12), for which we are dependent of local customs or the immediate contextual usage.[13]

The Alleged Double Sense of Prophecy

One of the most frequently made assertions about prophecy is that there is what some call a "double sense" of prophecy. Usually what is meant by this term is that a prophetic passage has two different senses, each separate from the other in the contexts of both Testaments. This term does not include those types of prophecies where the earlier fulfillments contain the germ or the seeds of the ultimate fulfillment (i.e., the inaugurated eschatology described above with its "already" but "not-yet" type of realization pattern).

Support for such a concept of a double sense comes from the fact that New Testament writers seem to exhibit unusual latitude in the way that they

13. See numerous other examples in Kaiser, *Back Toward the Future,* pp. 41–49.

employ certain passages from the Old Testament. If the New Testament writers were able to use these older texts in a way that appears to be somewhat, or even entirely, different from their original purpose, then this must be a divine indication that there is a double sense and meaning, at least to texts dealing with prophecies and types.

This argument, however, fails to note that some of these New Testament passages are merely using the familiar language of the Old Testament. Other arguments have failed to understand fairly what the point of agreement was between the Old and New Testaments.

Others have urged that some prophetic passages should be given a double sense because the same prophecies refer to different events, the one near and the other remote, or the one temporal and the other spiritual, or even eternal, in its referent. But that is where the confusion enters. These examples are not properly instances of double sense, for a prophecy may indeed relate to more than one thing (e.g., to both temporal and spiritual things) but still have only one sense. This is true for the prophecy of inaugurated eschatology.

Weighty objections can be raised, however, against the idea of a true double sense of prophecy. For example, if Scripture can have different meanings, only one of which can be detected directly from the passage in either Testament, then we cannot be certain what the text really meant to teach. Again, this theory of double senses destroys the value of prophecies, for it either complicates their meaning, so as to leave in doubt what the proper fulfillment is, or it avoids this peril by making the prophecies so general that they are incapable of any specific fulfillment. Another objection arises when it is said that the second and different sense is derived from the new meaning that was first seen in the New Testament for this Old Testament text. But that possibility dissolves the force of any apologetic value that claims that the Old Testament anticipated what happened in the New.

The solution to these matters can be found mainly in two affirmations: (1) A distinctive characteristic of prophecy is that it often looks forward "not simply to a single event or person, but to a series in the same line of progressive development, having . . . always the same sense, but with a manifold application";[14] and (2) in the combination of type and prophecy, what is said of the type in the Old Testament can be prophetically applied to its antitype in the New Testament.

In these concessions, it can be seen that there is a certain amount of

14. Frederic Gardiner, "The Alleged 'Double Sense' of Scripture," in *The Old and New Testaments in Their Mutual Relations* (New York: James Pott, 1885), p. 271. I am indebted for the main shape of my thought in this section to Gardiner.

truth to the claim for double sense. Many prophecies have a manifold number of applications or fulfillments as the means for ensuring that that word is kept alive while we await the climactic fulfillment, but they all share one and the same sense. The only point that is denied here is that prophecies can have one sense in the natural, or original, meaning of the utterance, but another that emerges later and relates to a different matter supposedly concealed in the very same words.

Therefore, while we deny the presence of "multiple sense," "double sense," or the like, we affirm that there is "multiple fulfillment." Misunderstanding arises when we fail to distinguish double sense from multiple fulfillment. I prefer the label applied by Willis J. Beecher. He referred to multiple fulfillments as "generic prohecy," which he defined as "one which regards an event as occurring in a series of parts, separated by intervals, and expresses itself in language that may apply indifferently to the nearest part, or to the remoter parts, or to the whole—in other words, a prediction which, in applying to the whole of a complex event, also applies to some of the parts."[15] This definition is one of the best available to deal with the very aspects that are raised here.

The key to all this is an idea derived from our ancient heritage that has been newly rediscovered in this century (from the Antiochian school of interpretation, with its view of *theōria,* from the fifth to seventh centuries A.D.).[16] That crucial idea is that there are three aspects to prophecy, not two. These three parts are

1. *The predicted word* that preceded the event toward which it pointed;
2. *The historic means* by which God kept that predicted word alive for each succeeding generation, by giving what amounts to down payments that connected the first announcement of the word with its climactic fulfillment; and
3. *The ultimate fulfillment* of that word in the New Testament era of the First Advent, or in the days of the Second Advent.

Each fulfillment is thus at once a partial realization of what had been promised and a continuation of the word pointing to the future climactic fulfillment.

---

15. Willis J. Beecher, *The Prophets and the Promise* (New York: Thomas Y. Crowell, 1905), p. 130.
16. See further on *theōria* and the Antiochian school in chap. 12, p. 223.

PART 3

Responding to the Text: Meaning and Application

The devotional method of studying the Bible is rooted in a strong desire to apply the Bible to one's everyday life. It correctly presumes that the words of Scripture are clear enough to be understood in their basic message, but it does not demand that all Scripture be equally clear and perspicuous. The reader is dependent on the Holy Spirit for the work of illuminating those Scriptures used in a devotional study. Especially included in the illuminating work of the Holy Spirit are the issues of application, the ministry of encouraging the downcast, and the task of convicting all of the presence of sin as readers are exposed to the Scriptures.

Central to the devotional method is the act of meditating on the Word of God. Meditation does not have as its goal self-abnegation, as it usually does in oriental religions and some of the contemporary cults. Instead, biblical meditation seeks to establish communion with and the worship of the living God by involving the entirety of one's person—body, soul, and mind. It uses the Scriptures as the place where meditation is centered.

CHAPTER 9

"As the Deer Pants for Streams of Water"
THE DEVOTIONAL USE OF THE BIBLE

WALTER C. KAISER, JR.

The art and discipline of using the Bible in one's devotional life is fast becoming a lost habit of the heart, mind, and soul. For those who still do attempt to maintain a regular daily devotional practice, it frequently may involve reading a half page of heavily illustrated comments in a devotional guide printed on very small pages, easily digested in a matter of minutes, and ostensibly centered on a verse, clause, or phrase of Scripture. Unfortunately, the biblical portions, meager as they are, are frequently detached from their scriptural contexts and often reflect little or no connection with the purpose that they originally held in their canonical settings.

If this problem is more acute in recent years than before, it certainly is not a new issue for the body of Christ. Near the beginning of this century, Wilbert W. White, founder of a seminary in New York, spotted this same weakness in the Bible reading and study habits of that day. In an attempt to meet that need, he developed what has become known as the inductive method of Bible study. Dr. White's principal goal was to train readers of the Bible in developing for themselves a way that they could independently gather from the text of Scripture original ideas that would help them to grow in the grace and knowledge of our Lord Jesus Christ. Moreover, it was his hope that those who had discovered this new method of systematically and inductively gathering from the text of Scripture its teachings would go out and teach others also, thereby causing the benefits of this new devotional use of the Bible to expand.

In time, this inductive method became quite famous, so that today there are a host of users of this approach, many of whom perhaps have not so much as heard of Wilbert White. Without it being called the inductive method today, it is especially noticeable in the parachurch ministries of the last four or five decades and in several Bible study guides, especially those that have been aimed at the campus ministries in the Western world. This method has honed the special patience of the reader, who carefully sits with a text and steadily observes it until the text has mastered the observer, rather than the observer mastering the text. Whether a strict inductive method is followed or not, believers ought to give serious attention to their devotional use of the Scripture.

Definition

The devotional method of studying the Bible is rooted in a strong desire to find in the scriptural texts solid applications to one's everyday life. Such study is not motivated by intellectual, historical, or critical curiosities; instead, it involves a strong commitment to seeing changes in one's own attitudes, values, and actions.

The terms *devotion* and *devotional method* are linked with the verb *to devote,* which in *Webster's Dictionary* is defined as a solemn act of dedication involving the giving of one's self wholly, as the focus of one's attention is centered completely on the other. Thus the major goal in the exercise of the devotional reading of Scripture is not the mastery of God but God's mastery of the reader, through the ministry of the Holy Spirit, as each reader uses the Word of God as a challenge to making progress in Christian growth and fruit.

One volume that has had an enormous amount of influence in the very area being discussed is one by Merrill C. Tenney, the late dean and professor of New Testament at Wheaton Graduate School of Theology: *Galatians: Charter of Christian Liberty.* In this wonderful anthology of the different ways one may approach the study of the biblical text, Tenney defined the devotional study of the Bible as "not so much a technique as a spirit; it is the spirit of eagerness which seeks the mind of God; it is the spirit of humility which listens to the voice of God; it is the spirit of adventure which pursues earnestly the will of God; it is the spirit of adoration which rests in the presence of God."[1]

1. Merrill C. Tenney, *Galatians: Charter of Christian Liberty* (Grand Rapids: Eerdmans, 1950), pp. 207–8.

The Bible itself urges believers to enter into the regular discipline of approaching the Word of God in order that each person might be daily refreshed by the instruction, encouragement, rebuke, and guidance that is to be found in that Word. Perhaps the best-known text encouraging this kind of exposure to the Word of God is the word the Lord gave to Joshua as he took over the reins of leadership: "Do not let this Book of the Law depart from your mouth; meditate on it day and night, so that you might be careful to do everything written in it. Then you will be prosperous and successful" (Josh. 1:8). This text practically defines the devotional approach in its entirety. Devotional study must be regular ("day and night"), reflective ("meditate on it"), retentive ("be careful to do everything written in it"), and regulated ("do not let this Book of the Law depart from your mouth").

The Scripture was not intended to be the special province of scholars and professional clergy; it was directed to the people themselves. Indeed, one of the central issues in the Reformation itself was the issue of the clarity of the Scriptures and their availability to all readers.

The Clarity of the Scriptures

If all believers are encouraged to use the Bible devotionally, there must be a presumption that the words of Scripture are perspicuous, or clear, enough that all can understand what they say without needing the counsel of a scholar at their elbow to instruct them. Is this a reasonable presumption? Can we ensure such readers that they will not fall into error when they wander off into the full canon of Scripture, reading the text for themselves and according to their own insights and understandings?

No one was more forceful in taking a stand that the Bible is plain in its meaning, and that it should therefore be accessible to all, than Martin Luther. His most vigorous affirmation of this principle can be found in his book *On the Bondage of the Will*, written in response to a work entitled *On the Freedom of the Will* by the highly respected scholar Erasmus. According to Erasmus:

> There are some things which God has willed that we should contemplate, as we venerate himself, in mystic silence; and, moreover, there are many passages in the sacred volumes about which many commentators have made guesses, but no one has finally cleared up their obscurity: as the distinction between the divine persons, the conjunction of the divine and human nature in Christ, the unforgivable sin; *yet there are other things which God has willed to be most plainly evident,* and such are the precepts for the good life. This is the Word of God, which is

not to be bought in the highest heaven, not in distant lands overseas, but it is close at hand, in our mouth and in our heart. These truths must be learned by all, but the rest are more properly committed to God, and it is more religious to worship them, being unknown, than to discuss them, being insoluble.[2]

Though Luther at first seemed to disagree violently with Erasmus, implying that everything in Scripture was plain and equally available, he eventually settled down and allowed that there were certain kinds of obscurities in Scripture. "I admit, of course, that there are many texts in the Scriptures that are obscure and abstruse, not because of the majesty of their subject matter [as Erasmus had argued], but because of our ignorance of their vocabulary and grammar; but these texts in no way hinder a knowledge of the subject matter of Scripture."[3]

In the end, the argument between Luther and Erasmus was not over the application of learning and scholarship, or even over whether the texts of Scripture were sufficiently clear so that the main message of the Bible could be understood by the average reader. At the bottom of all this debate was this question: To what degree was the average reader, indeed the whole church, obliged to submit to tradition and the official pronouncements of the pope for the proper exposition of Scripture? To this question, the Reformers shouted a loud, "None, for the essential meaning of the message of the Bible!" There was no need of anyone's history of tradition to interpret the Scriptures; the Bible was sufficiently perspicuous without it.

What, then, was meant when the Scriptures were declared to be clear and perspicuous for all? Simply this: the Bible was understood to be clear and perspicuous on all things that were necessary for our salvation and growth in Christ. It was not a claim either that everything in the Bible was equally plain or that there were no mysteries or areas that would not defy one generation of Bible readers or another. If readers would exert the effort one generally put into understanding a literary work, it was asserted that they would gain an understanding that would be adequate and sufficient to guide them into a saving relationship and a life of obedience with their Lord.

This definition on the clarity of Scripture was represented in many Protestant works shortly after the Reformation. The best known is paragraph 7 on the doctrine of Scripture in the Westminster Confession of Faith (1647).

2. E. G. Rupp et al., eds., *Luther and Erasmus: Free Will and Salvation,* LCC 17 (Philadelphia: Westminster, 1969), pp. 39–40 (my emphasis).
3. Ibid., pp. 110–11.

All things in Scripture are not alike plain in themselves, nor alike clear unto all; *yet those things which are necessary to be known, believed, and observed for salvation,* are so clearly propounded, and opened in some place of Scripture or other, that not only the learned, but the unlearned, in a due use of the ordinary means, may attain unto a sufficient understanding of them (my emphasis).

More is indeed at stake here than the mere understanding of the words in and of themselves. Even when ordinary laypersons are able to gain an adequate and sufficient understanding of what is being said in the Bible, there is the other dimension of the reception and application of these matters to one's own life and heart. Does this not have an effect on the issue of the clarity of Scripture?

The Illuminating Work of the Holy Spirit

One of the key texts that must be considered here is the pivotal statement of the apostle Paul in 1 Corinthians 2:14: "The man without the Spirit does not accept the things that come from the Spirit of God, for they are foolishness to him, and he cannot understand them, because they are spiritually discerned." While working on my doctoral program, a most unusual experience took place in one of the seminars I attended that graphically sealed this text on my heart and mind.

A distinguished professor, recently retired from Yale University, was offering a special seminar entitled "Origins of Christianity" at the university I was attending on the East Coast. One day the class sidetracked the professor into discussing his understanding on the meaning of Romans 1–5. With unusual eloquence and masterful exegesis, he walked through these chapters with a precise deftness, affirming that everyone in the class had sinned and therefore had come short of the glory of God. But for those who would believe in God's sacrifice of his Son for their sins, they would not just be made righteous; no, they would be declared righteous by a God who justified sinners, much as a judge did who dismissed a case that had failed to prove its defendant guilty. Rarely have I ever heard such a bold and fair treatment of this text of Paul.

After two hours, however, the spell was suddenly broken when one of the Jewish students in the class who, along with many others had sat uncomfortably through this long and, to them, seemingly parochial tirade, blurted out (amid all the nervous smoking that was going on in the seminar by now), "Do I get the impression that the professor of this class believes this stuff?"

Immediately the professor responded in a scoffing tone, "Who said anything about believing it? I am just arguing that this is what Paul said. I'm sick and tired of hearing the younger neoorthodox scholars say, 'This is what this or that text means to *me*.' I was trained under the old liberal theology; we learned what *Paul* said. We just don't happen to believe what Paul said!"

I then began to perceive what Paul was driving at in 1 Corinthians 2:14. This professor did not "welcome" (as *dechetai* could be translated) the things that he knew well enough to teach, practically without a flaw, for almost two hours. It thus is clear that the ministry and work of the Holy Spirit, in illuminating the hearts and minds of those who hear spiritual truths, is not to be treated lightly in this whole area of biblical interpretation, especially in the area of the application of those things that are taught in the Bible.

Some have felt that there might be two separate types of logic in the world: one for the believer and the other for the unbeliever. But Paul makes it clear in Romans 1–2 that those who are unconverted understand the essential truth about God well enough to condemn themselves, since they have not acted on what they did know about God. And 1 Corinthians 2:14 adds the thought that, without the indwelling ministry and illuminating work of the Holy Spirit, such persons will neither welcome nor embrace the realities found in the biblical text. Thus, one of the unique roles of the Holy Spirit is to convict, convince, and arouse sluggish hearts by applying the truths perceived in the text of Scripture to the lives of individuals. As a further aid to placing oneself in a position where the ministry of the Holy Spirit can work more effectively, Scripture calls upon the reader to ponder and meditate carefully on what is being said in the biblical text.

The Act of Meditating on Scripture

The art and practice of meditating on the Scriptures plays an important role in one's devotional use of the Bible. Meditation is presented in Scripture as an act of worship, one that involves communion with God. Instead of its being an avenue of escape, wherein the individual is swallowed up, absorbed, or mingled with the divine in some sort of unspecified mystical process, as it so frequently is taught in many Eastern religions or some of the modern Western cults, meditation in Scripture can be carefully defined as to its objects, its methods of practice, and its results.

We can get a good idea of the meaning of meditation by examining the contexts where the concept and words of meditation are found. Especially prominent is Psalm 77, with references to meditation in three of its verses. The psalm falls into two parts: verses 1–9 express Asaph's sorrow and distress; verses 10–20 report how he rose above these problems. In the time of his distress, and through sleepless nights, he mused or meditated on the Lord (v. 3). In his disquietude, the psalmist recalled happier days in the past (v. 5), and in the long night hours his heart mused (or meditated, v. 6) on what he had learned of God from his Word during the good times of life. Would God cast him off forever? he wondered. But then in verse 10 he suddenly recalled God's former deeds. At that point he decided that he would "meditate on all [God's] works and consider [or ponder, meditate on] all [God's] mighty deeds" (v. 12). Thus, the psalmist's deep despondency gave way to God's deliverance when he focused on meditating on the works of God. This is exactly the desired outcome of all devotional reading of the text of Scripture.

Meditation is a function of the heart, that is, of the whole person. Such meditation is stressed in Psalm 19:14; 49:3; Proverbs 15:28; and Isaiah 33:18. The goal of meditation, according to Psalm 49:3, is understanding, not, as is so frequently stressed in Oriental religions and some of the cults of our day, self-abnegation. In order to meditate, one must not try to be emptied of oneself, so that allegedly the divine can flow through one's being almost in a pantheistic way. Rather, one is to bring one's whole person—body, soul, and mind—to focus on God, his works, and especially his Word, which tells about both his person and his work.

Based on the sheer number of references, it would appear that the meditation encouraged by Scripture finds its basic focus on the Word of God. As we have noted, Joshua 1:8 commands meditation on the book of the law all through the day and the night. The Psalter itself begins with a blessing for the person who delights in the law of the Lord and who meditates on that law day and night (Ps. 1:1–2). Repeatedly, Psalm 119 urges its readers to "meditate on [God's] precepts" (vv. 15, 78), his decrees (vv. 23, 48), his law (v. 97), his statutes (v. 99), and his promises (v. 148). The mind of the meditator is not to be blank and empty; it is to be filled with Scripture, the Word of God. Accordingly, when the law of God is in one's heart, that person's feet do not slip, because "the mouth of the righteous man utters [or ponders] wisdom" (Ps. 37:30–31). That is what it means to meditate on the Word of God as it is read devotionally. The result is that the Word of God remains constantly in the heart of believers in every situation that they find themselves in: when they sit down in their houses, get up to walk, lie down in the evening, or get up in the morning (Deut. 6:6–9; Prov. 3:22–24; 6:22).

Conclusion

No one method of studying the Bible can claim exclusive rights over all other methods. In fact, Howard Vos identified some seventeen different approaches to studying the Bible in his book *Effective Bible Study*.[4] True, some of his seventeen methods involved more than one approach; however, the point is that one may undertake one's devotional study of the text using approaches such as the biographical method, the topical method, the doctrinal method, the inductive method, or the analytical method. No one method is a magical wand that removes the need for using one's mind or for accepting the hard discipline that is needed in all these methods.

In fact, it would be well for readers of Scripture to vary their devotional use of Scripture from time to time. One should never be so bound that there is no room for freedom of experimentation and enlarging the sphere of one's investigation. The only caution needed is that one should always be careful to let the text first say what it wants to say before we attempt to apply that text into our contemporary situations. It will always be helpful if we use a pen or pencil to pull together what it is that we think we are seeing in the text. A notebook recording our observations will complete the tools required, especially if we are going to draw together the various pieces into some organization that gives us larger overviews of what we are looking at.

Finally, one of the best ways to continually mull over a text is to select one or more verses from the passage we are reflecting on and to commit it to memory. There in the memory it can be stored for further moments of thought and reflection to be called upon for application in the various vicissitudes of life.

4. Howard Vos, *Effective Bible Study*, 2d ed. (Grand Rapids: Zondervan, 1956).

The interpreter must bridge the gap between the cultural elements that are present in the text of Scripture and those in our own times. One proposal to bridge this gap is called ethnohermeneutics, which recognizes three horizons in cross-cultural interpretation: the culture of the Bible, the culture of the interpreter, and the culture of the receptor. Care must be exercised not to let the second and third horizons dictate the message of the first horizon.

The early church fathers used the terms "condescension," "accommodation," and "acculturation" to deal with cultural matters in the text. In their view, the cultural aspects of the Scriptures were meant to make the truth more accessible and to assist us in applying the text to our own day.

When interpreting cultural aspects of Scripture, three options are available. We may (1) retain the theology taught along with the cultural-historical expression of that principle, or (2) retain the theology of a passage, but replace the expression of the behavior, or (3) replace both the principle and the practice. Five guidelines for doing this are (1) to observe the reason given in the text for a cultural element, (2) to modify the cultural form but retain the content, (3) to avoid all practices integral to pagan culture, (4) to retain practices grounded in the nature of God, and (5) to adjust when the circumstances alter the application of a law or principle. But above all, be hesitant and humble in all cases where we are uncertain.

CHAPTER 10

Obeying the Word
THE CULTURAL USE OF THE BIBLE

WALTER C. KAISER, JR.

The revelation of God in Scripture was originally written in Hebrew, Aramaic, and Greek by writers who represented a variety of cultures that differed often in dramatic ways from those of the cultures into which the Bible has been translated. These differences may not always be appreciated for what they are until we begin to translate the Bible into another language.

In his book *Customs, Culture, and Christianity*, Eugene A. Nida relates how so-called literal translations of the Bible can produce misleading connotations in another culture. For example, the Kpelle of Liberia view the placing of palm branches in Jesus' path during the triumphal entry into Jerusalem as an insult, for their culture requires that all leaves be cleared from the path of any dignitary. Likewise, the Zanaki of Tanganyika regard Jesus' knocking at the door (Rev. 3:20) as strange, since in their culture men stand at the door and call out if they wish admittance; only thieves knock to see if anyone is home before they rob the house.[1]

What is true in the area of Bible translation is also true in the area of interpretation as well. The interpreter must bridge the gulf of explaining the cultural elements that are present in the text of Scripture, acknowledge his or her own cultural baggage as an interpreter, and then transcend both in order to communicate the original message of Scripture into the culture of the

1. Eugene A. Nida, *Customs, Culture and Christianity* (London: Tyndale, 1954), pp. 220, 218.

173

contemporary audience. All of this demands some understanding of what culture is all about.

The Definition of Culture

Culture is not all that easy to define. In its broadest sense, it usually means the patterned way people do things together. Thus it implies some degree of homogeneity over a certain span of time. As Eugene Nida defined it, "Culture is all learned behavior which is socially acquired, that is, the material and nonmaterial traits which are passed on from one generation to another."[2] Thus *culture* designates the unique ways a given group of people view and do things in a particular period of time, including their values, manners, morals, expressions, and accomplishments.

While there are certain basic needs common to most groups of people, it is surprising how cultures vary and differ from each other. In the area of foods, for example, non-Westerners are often horrified to think that Westerners eat fermented milk (cheese), while some Westerners are scandalized when they realize that Koreans eat pickled cabbage, Eskimos eat pungent walrus meat, and the Chinese eat fermented duck eggs. One man's meat, as they say, is another man's poison—but that's culture for you.

God's revelation of his Word came in terms of the culture of its writers and first audiences. Therefore, if we are to use that word effectively today, we must be able to enter into a cross-cultural communication of the Bible with the people to whom we wish to unfold that message of the gospel. The Bible writers used the cultural material that was available to them, whether merely in the incidental employment of terms that had had a history of previous associations or in the direct use of a term that was meaningful in that culture. Thus the problem would arise, for that term was not the way people in later cultures would have put the matter. Indeed, the Old Testament refers to the sea monster of Leviathan and even to seven-headed dragons! If our culture no longer finds these figures meaningful or part of our ordinary discourse, then the problem is ours as interpreters and not that of the Bible.

The very fact that the Bible was written in a particular time to a particular people by a particular writer for a particular situation was not meant to remove the Bible from its general usefulness for future generations but to make it all the more down-to-earth in its general appeal. Unfortunately, some who have missed this point have turned this argument on its head and have felt as if the Bible's particularity removed the text from them. Instead, what

2. Ibid., p. 28.

would have really removed the Bible from us would have been its having been written in some type of metalanguage and located in some otherworldly planet with which we had no contact, feeling, or appreciation. So not every aspect of the Bible's cultural dimensions should be regarded merely as more work for us. It also should give us a certain sense of affinity and identification, just because we too are mortal and share just as detailed and specific needs as these that puzzle us.[3]

THE BIBLE AND CULTURAL RELATIVITY

The Word of God comes to us in the specific cultural and historical language of the pre-Christian and first Christian century. If we are to appreciate the meaning as it was originally intended by its original writers, who after all were the only ones who stood in the council of God and received this message in the first place, we must come to understand what they meant by all the cultural allusions. This is not to say that that ends the process, for there is still the need to link those understandings up with the target culture into which we wish to announce these words, not to mention our need to be aware of our own cultural baggage as interpreters. But let us concentrate here on the problem of the cultural allusions in the text.

First, we must be able to recognize the cultural aspects of the Bible. These usually are the passages that tend to give us problems when we go to apply them directly to our day. The values, associations, and meanings that they may have had in another era will not transfer easily into those of our own day. They also tend to be illustrations of ways in which the truth taught in the text was being applied in another day. Just as we read in Philippians 4:2, "I plead with Euodia and I plead with Syntyche to agree with each other in the Lord," and usually do not stumble over its particularity, so we should act with regard to other cultural elements. Most people, who have never met Euodia and Syntyche, will teach that this passage is an illustration of some principle such as that in Ephesians 4:32: "Be kind and compassionate to one another, forgiving each other, just as in Christ God forgave you." No one assumes that somehow he or she is responsible to do exactly what Paul addressed to both of these women. Why, then, are we so slow to catch on when it comes to handling other matters that in many ways are just as cultural?

Perhaps a list of some possible candidates for the label *cultural* in the Bible might help us to focus on the problem somewhat more accurately. Consider these direct or implied biblical injunctions:

3. See also the Willowbank Report *Gospel and Culture*, Lausanne Occasional Papers no. 2 (Wheaton, 1978), pp. 1–33.

—You also should wash one another's feet. (John 13:14)

—Greet one another with a holy kiss. (2 Cor. 13:12)

—[Should] a woman pray to God with her head uncovered? (1 Cor. 11:13)

—Women should remain silent in the churches. (1 Cor. 4:34)

—Everyone must submit . . . to the governing authorities. (Rom. 13:1)

—If a man has long hair, it is a disgrace to him. (1 Cor. 11:14)

—Put your sword back in its place. (Matt. 26:52)

—Lend [your] money without usury. (Ps. 15:5)

—I wish all men were [single] as I am. (1 Cor. 7:7)

—[Do not] lie with a woman during her period. (Ezek. 18:6)

Most of these examples are well known and may serve as illustrations of the type of issues we confront in interpreting the cultural elements in the Bible. At the center of this search is the problem of distinguishing that which is universal and of enduring authority from that which is cultural and therefore more related to illustrations of the principle being set forth for those times. We need a set of guidelines that will help us not only in determining when we are dealing with a cultural matter but also in understanding their use in our day and in other cultures besides our own. These we will develop later on in this chapter.

THE BIBLE AND CONTEXTUALIZATION

Intimately connected with the topic of cultural exegesis is a new term that has come into increasing prominence in recent theological discussions: *contextualization.* The term appears to have been used first in a document prepared in 1972 by the directors of the Theological Education Fund with reference to offering theological education in the third world. Bruce Nicholls later defined it as "the translation of the unchanging content of the gospel of the kingdom into verbal form meaningful to the peoples in their separate cultures and within their particular existential situations."[4] James Oliver Buswell III offered another way to organize our approach to the issues involved in defining contextualization, suggesting that we break down the term into three categories: "contextualization of the witness, contextualization of the church and its leadership, and contextualization of the Word."[5] In this chapter, we focus mainly on the third in Buswell's list of categories.

4. Bruce Nicholls, "Theological Education and Evangelization," in *Let the Earth Hear His Voice,* ed. J. D. Douglas (Minneapolis: World Wide Publications, 1975), p. 647.

5. James O. Buswell III, "Contextualization: Theory, Tradition, and Method," in *Theology and Mission: Papers Given at Trinity Consultation No. 1,* ed. David J. Hesselgrave (Grand Rapids: Baker, 1978), pp. 89–90.

The theme of contextualization has had many applications in recent years, some that have been good and others that have left the Scriptures lacking in authority to help contemporary cultures. On the more negative side, some have used the idea to support a particular social or political agenda that reflects their own desires (e.g., in some cases the liberation theology of Latin America, some feminist theologies, some Black theologies, and some Asian theologies). When the concerns of the contemporary interpreter supersede those of the text in such a way that the text is used merely as a springboard for issuing what moderns wish to say, the term *contextualization* has been diverted from something useful to being merely the servant of its handlers. The text still must remain prior to and master of whatever context it is being applied to.

Nevertheless, much can be learned from contextualization, even by those of us who are of a conservative bent. Stanley Gundry pondered aloud in his 1978 presidential address at the annual national meeting of the Evangelical Theological society:

> I wonder if we really recognize that all theology represents a contextualization, even our own theology? We speak of Latin American theology, black theology, or feminist theology; but without the slightest second thought we will assume that our own theology is simply theology, undoubtedly in its purest form. Do we recognize that the versions of evangelical theology held by most people in this room are in fact North American, white, and male and that they reflect and/or address those values and concerns?[6]

Our practice of contextualization will affect more than the way we deliver our sermons to different cultures or the way we counsel in those situations; it will have a mighty impact on the way we do theology and the way we present Scripture for ourselves and our hearers. Our perspective cannot be avoided, but it must honestly be acknowledged if we are to be fair to the text, to ourselves, and to others. In all cases, the text as it was intended by the author must sit in judgment on our perspectives and our conclusions that we have drawn from the text.

6. Stanley N. Gundry, "Evangelical Theology: Where Should We Be Going?" *JETS* 22 (1979): 11.

Ethnohermeneutics and Related Concepts

In 1973 Charles H. Kraft advocated developing a new cross-discipline he labeled Christian ethnotheology.[7] In it he wanted to take both Christian theology and anthropology seriously. In 1987 Larry W. Caldwell proposed another field he entitled ethnohermeneutics, which would take seriously the cross-disciplines of hermeneutics and anthropology.[8]

ETHNOHERMENEUTICS

In Caldwell's view, the typical model for interpreting a text could be labeled the two-step method: first one drew from the text what the text meant according to the best grammatico-historical techniques available (Caldwell preferred to call this method the historical-critical method). The second step was then to apply it and say what that text means today. But Caldwell found this two-step model to be thoroughly Western in that it failed to deal with the cross-cultural perspective. In many ways, he was more than justified in making this criticism. No longer would it be possible to discuss the process of interpretation without taking up the cross-cultural implications of what was being read.

Another Western theologian had offered a way to bring that ancient text over into the modern world. Hans-Georg Gadamer emphasized the need for a "fusion of the horizons" between the world of the original text and that of the modern interpreter.[9] This same concept was picked up by several evangelical writers, albeit in a modified form. For example, Anthony Thiselton put this concept into the title of his book *The Two Horizons,* but he too failed to see the need for a cross-cultural perspective in the work of interpretation.[10]

What was really needed was not a model with two horizons but one with three that would include the cross-cultural perspective. It would look like this:

7. Charles H. Kraft, "Toward a Christian Ethnotheology," in *God, Man, and Church Growth: Festschrift in Honor of Donald Anderson McGavran,* ed. A. R. Tippett (Grand Rapids: Eerdmans, 1973), pp. 109–26.

8. See three works by Larry W. Caldwell: "Third Horizon Ethnohermeneutics: Re-evaluating New Testament Hermeneutical Models for Intercultural Bible Interpreters Today," *AJT* 1 (1987): 314–33; "Doing Theology Across Cultures: A New Methodology for an Old Task," *IJFM* 4 (1987): 3–7; "Third Horizon Ethnohermeneutics: Re-evaluating the Apostle Paul's Hermeneutical Methodology for Cross-Cultural Bible Interpreters Today" (Unpublished paper given at the Evangelical Theological Society Meeting on November 19, 1988).

9. Hans-Georg Gadamer, *Truth and Method* (London: Sheed and Ward, 1975) 273.

10. Anthony C. Thiselton, *The Two Horizons: New Testament Hermeneutics and Philosophical Description* (Grand Rapids: Eerdmans, 1980).

First horizon: The culture of the Bible
Second horizon: The culture of the interpreter
Third horizon: The culture of the receptor[11]

In each one of these horizons, a circle of cultural baggage and understandings had to be accounted for, lest any one of the cultures be made normative for the others. Thus far we can agree on the need for such a new program and readily endorse it.

However, a new element arose when some in the new ethnohermeneutical school asserted that the apostle Paul's understanding of the Old Testament was completely revolutionized after his conversion, so that his interpretations of what had been said in the Old Testament were no longer determined by what the text had meant to its original writer, but only by what the present context demanded.[12] According to Caldwell, Paul now determined the meaning of the Old Testament by his own worldview, anthropologically speaking. He now used the rabbinic midrash technique, which simply said, "*That* [Old Testament text] *is this* [new reality in our culture]." What was proposed, then, was that we can do the same type of revising of the text ourselves today in bridging from biblical to modern cultures with the message of the Bible.

All of this seems a bit too cavalier. It tends to elevate one horizon over the others, especially our modern culture, and to make it more normative than the revelation that came from God. That this use of a rabbinic methodology of determining meaning of a text, as a means of legitimating contemporary loosening of the ancient values and meanings of the text, is not an unusual aberration from the current thinking of our times can be shown by citing a 1978 argument by Charles R. Taber. According to Taber:

> The New Testament writers used a hermeneutic in relation to
> many Old Testament citations which was derived from rabbinic
> interpretation but was at the opposite pole from what we would
> consider legitimate today. In our terms, some Old Testament
> passages cited are clearly taken out of context, so that "X" is the
> fulfillment of "Y" may seem to us to mean scarcely more than
> "X" reminds us of "Y." In other words, we today radically
> reject rabbinical hermeneutics of the first century; on what
> grounds? I am aware of various attempts to get around this

11. On these matters, see Eugene A. Nida, *Message and Mission* (New York: Harper & Row, 1960), pp. 33–58; Harvey Conn, *Eternal Word and Changing Worlds: Theology, Anthropology, and Mission in Trialogue* (Grand Rapids: Zondervan, 1984), pp. 188–90; and Donald A. Carson, "Hermeneutics: A Brief Assessment of Some Recent Trends," *Themelios* 5 (1980): 17–20.

12. Caldwell, "Third Horizon Ethnohermeneutics," pp. 8, 11.

uncomfortable fact: that those writers were inspired, so that they could get away with association of ideas that we would not permit in our students today; that there are two or more applications of these passages; and so on. But the fact of the matter is that what they considered proper hermeneutics was part and parcel of their cultural heritage, while what we consider proper hermeneutics and exegesis is part of our western cultural heritage.[13]

We cannot escape Taber's question: Can we reject the rabbinic hermeneutics of the first century as inappropriate for ourselves and yet accept it as being an adequate description of what Paul or the other writers of the New Testament were doing?

Paul doubtless was trained in such rabbinic techniques, for he had the best education available in his day from Gamaliel. But to argue from that agreed-upon fact to the conclusion reached by Charles Taber in the above quote is another matter. How could that type of argumentation have stood Paul in good stead as he entered into apologetical demonstrations that the Jesus he had met on the road was the Messiah of the Old Testament? Can we imagine Paul saying, "The Old Testament does not say what I am drawing from these Old Testament texts, but please allow me to show how on my midrashic principles I can prove that what these texts taught is precisely what happened in Jesus the Messiah"? Would that be an adequate basis for winning people from the Jewish community over to Jesus? Such a claim would call for stretching one's imagination too far.

Put another way, few persons in the church today will object to some rather innocent allegorizing and other types of subjective handling of the biblical text for devotional purposes. Should the same methods be used to foster new or what we would regard as heretical doctrines on us (as the Jews surely regarded Paul's teaching), the demand for a return to what is written in the text would come faster than anyone could say "sensus literalis."

It is one thing, then, to use midrash and pesher methods of exegesis for devotional teachings on which everyone is already agreed, but it hardly fits the facts to imagine that the apostles used such techniques in trying their best to argue that what had happened in Christ was neither new nor unanticipated! It simply does not fit the evidence of either the Old Testament context or the New Testament fulfillments to say that the former texts merely reminded the apostles that the later New Testament connections might be true. Would that be enough to stake one's life on and for the apostles to die for?

13. Charles R. Taber, "Is There More Than One Way to Do Theology?" *GiC*, 1, no. 1 (1978): 8.

I am afraid that scholarship has tended to apply the rather remarkable discoveries from the hermeneutical methodologies uncovered in the Dead Sea Scrolls of Qumran to more areas than are warranted by the facts of the case. There has been a tendency to think that all interpretation in the first century matched that of this one chance find (a form of reductionism!) Moreover, everyone admits that the group that produced these scrolls and used this pesher and midrashic type of interpretation (perhaps, the Essenes) were themselves a cult out on the fringes of even Jewish society and hardly represented any standard of authorial intentionality! Such a solution should not be made the answer for most of the problems we have in interpretation in that era, nor as a wedge for dividing between what the writer meant and what the culture derived from the text.

CONDESCENSION, ACCOMMODATION, AND ACCULTURATION

Rabbinic exegesis is not the only wedge that has been used to try to open up a way to summon the three horizons and introduce ethnohermeneutics. Earlier approaches spoke of "condescension," "accommodation" or "acculturation." For example, the early church father Chrysostom used the notion of God's "condescension" (Greek, *synkatabasis*) to speak of the fact that the writers of Scripture used one inexactitude or another in order to speak in such a way as to be understood by their hearers. In Chrysostom's view, condescension was not a roundabout way of declaring that a bit of innocent error had crept into the scriptural text, nor was it a way of excusing the human writers of Scripture, who must have been accused of what is said to be true of mortals, namely, "To err is human"

But such a conclusion is incorrect on both accounts. It is one thing to approximate a matter while still pointing just as really and accurately to it; it is another to use that which would be misleading and deceptive, or just plain wrong, in representing the same matter. The prophets and apostles took the former course and not the latter. And if it be protested that the writers of Scripture were surely just as human as all of us are, we agree. But the objection about the humanity of the writers has missed the claim of the Bible. As B. B. Warfield pointed out long ago, the pure light of God's revelation will not be distorted coming through such admittedly human channels, just as God's pure sunlight is not bent and distorted by its being filtered through a stained-glass window, for the originator of the sunlight is also the architect who designed the stained-glass windows.

The preparation that went into the lives, experiences, vocabularies, and outlook of the writers of Scripture was enormously significant. Thus, by the time they came to write Scripture, so authentic were the expressions that they used that any of us who might have known them prior to their writing of the text of Scripture would have instantaneously recognized that that is precisely how each writer spoke. The idioms, vocabularies, styles, and the like were uniquely their own, yet the product was precisely what God wanted as he stayed with each writer in such a way that there was a living assimilation of the truth—not a mechanical dictation of the words, such as a whispering in the writer's ear or an involuntary movement of their hands as they automatically wrote.

In 1 Corinthians 2:13 Paul claimed that he was "taught" these truths "in words." That is, what he wrote had become thoroughly a part of him. It was roughly similar to what happens to our students today when it's hard to say where the teacher's ideas end and the student's ideas begin. In this case, however, the total product was exactly what God wanted, for he stayed with the writers all the way up to their verbalizing of the truths that they had assimilated under the tutelage of the Holy Spirit.

Furthermore, there is a type of condescension that does not necessarily involve error—namely, our Lord's condescension. In this regard, then, a parity can be set up between "he who did no sin" as the incarnate Word and the protection that was afforded those who wrote the written Word (1 Cor. 2:6–16, esp. v. 13).

What has been said about condescension is equally true about accommodation and acculturation. The cultural aspects of the message were not meant to make it more difficult for us to interpret, or to deceive us, but to make the truth all the more accessible and part of each person in each succeeding era of history. The particularity of the text, in that it introduced culturally relevant materials, was intended to aid us in applying the text to our own day as we saw vivid illustrations as to how the principles in the text were applied in that day and culture, rather than acting as an obstacle to our contemporary appreciation for what was being said.

What then remains, if we admit that there are numerous cultural allusions in the biblical text? Is nothing abiding? Are there no fixed points of reference? Paul Beauchamp has helpfully called attention to the scope of the biblical message:

> Now according to the Bible, these communal signs [as signaled in Jer. 20:10 and Ezek. 26] of spiritual and physical welfare are the place where God speaks to man, to all men regardless of their culture. On this basis, we could attempt a definition of the common element in culture: what in flesh is related to spirit, what in precarious conditions is related to eternity, what in time is related to what is beyond time. Because of this, cultures contain something of the Logos, of his propensity, so to speak,

to become flesh. The concept of Wisdom, as used in the Bible, conveniently fits this tentative definition. Wisdom is both immanent and transcendent, present in time and eternal. But one fact gives abundant matter for wonder to the Old Testament reader. Israel is acutely conscious of Wisdom as a universal gift of God to man, not to Israel alone. Wisdom herself . . . claims that from the beginning she has been "rejoicing in the inhabited world and delighting in the sons of men" (Prov. 8:31), not in the sons of Israel alone. . . . As a matter of fact, we may observe that, except for a few late cases, Wisdom literature consistently avoids mentioning Israel's history and contains precepts which receive an easy approval everywhere in the world.[14]

This is indeed an excellent reminder. The Bible begins in Genesis 1–11 with a universal outlook. Not until the call of Abraham does the theme of Israel's election come to the fore. But it is to the themes of creation and the universalism of Genesis 1–11 that the books of Wisdom return, thus making a statement that transcends all cultures and times. I am afraid we have neglected the Wisdom books and their materials too long, and therefore we find ourselves somewhat shorthanded when it comes to answering questions about culture and about what abides as permanent. In Wisdom we have a transcultural element that points the way for finding values that all cultures and times can embrace without feeling that their own culture has been compromised or cheated.

Practical Guidelines for Cultural Interpretation

It is clear from Hebrews 1:1 that God has spoken in his Word to our fathers by the prophets "at many times and in various ways." While acknowledging the diversity of method, however, we affirm the profitability (2 Tim. 3:16–17) of *all* Scripture—cultural parts included! Therefore, when it comes to handling the cultural and historical aspects of Scripture, the guidelines below should be helpful.

Before starting this list, however, notice how we are presented with three options in every one of these situations that involve a cultural or historical side to the revelation being considered.

14. Paul Beauchamp, "The Role of the Old Testament in the Process of Building Up Local Churches," in *Bible and Inculturation,* vol. 3, in *Inculturation: Working Papers on Living Faith and Cultures,* ed. Ary A. Roest Crollius (Rome: Pontifical Gregorian University, 1983), pp. 6–7.

1. *We may retain both the theology taught* (i.e., the principle affirmed in the text or contextually implied) *along with the cultural-historical expression of that principle.* Thus, the principle of some type of divinely authorized lines of responsibility in the husband-wife, parent-child, sovereign-citizen relationships seems to be affirmed in Scripture. If this understanding is correct, even to a limited degree, then here would be some examples of cases where the theological principle was also combined with the particular custom expressing that principle. How far the principle would continue to be included in a given culture would be subject to some variation within various systems of interpretation. But the concept that both the principle and some, or all, aspects of its historical-cultural manifestations are often retained is definitely taught.

2. *We may retain the theology of a passage* (i.e., the principle) *but replace the behavioral expression with some more recent, but equally meaningful, expression.* That there are biblical precedents for such replacements can be seen from the way that the so-called civil and ceremonial law of Moses functions as illustrations of the abiding moral law of God. For example, in 1 Corinthians 5 the principle of the sanctity of marriage and human sexuality remained, even though the sanction of stoning to death had been changed for the mother and son guilty of incest to excommunication from the body of believers. Behind the moral law of God (as found, for example, in the Ten Commandments and the law of holiness in Leviticus 18–20) stood God's holy character. That is what made the theological principle unyielding; the sanctions, or penalties, however, were subject to modification.[15] Thus behind both the Old Testament and the New Testament rule against incest stood the holy character of God and the sanctity of marriage; the principle stood even though the cultural application varied.

3. *Some may even replace both the principle* (e.g., the so-called principle of economic subordination) *and the practice.* For example, the practice of wearing veils and using certain hairstyles may be replaced with what is believed to be a more egalitarian concept. It replaces what some regard as older hierarchical or even patriarchal concepts of family relations. This is not to say that the mere decision to do so is thereby legitimized, for modernity and eddies of contemporary thought are never in themselves adequate justification for the truthfulness or authority of the positions adopted. There may be some cases where what some have regarded as a crucial point of theology is nothing more than additional expressions of the culture and the times in which it was written, but all of this must be demonstrated from the text and not just

---

15. For further elucidation on this critical point, see Walter C. Kaiser, Jr., "God's Promise Plan and His Gracious Law," *JETS* 33 (1990): 289–302.

declared to be so on the basis of one's own word. The text will normally supply its own clues as to which of these three options are to be used.

To give further help in handling cultural issues, we turn now to the following five guidelines.

OBSERVE THE REASON WHY A COMMAND, CUSTOM, OR HISTORICAL EXAMPLE IS GIVEN IN THE TEXT

If the reason for a questioned practice or command has its basis in the unchanging nature of God, then that practice or command will have permanent relevance for all in all times. For example, Genesis 9:6 commands that all who shed a person's blood, by deliberately lying in wait for them with premeditation, must suffer capital punishment. The reason given is fixed in the nature and character of God: "because God made man in his own image." Consequently, as long as men and women are still in the image of God, they continue to have worth, value, and esteem in the eyes of God.

But what about the sanction of capital punishment? Is that punishment necessarily mandated even for our day just because we agree on the abiding nature of the reason given for the prohibition against taking another person's life? The force of this moral and theological reason cannot be appreciated until we notice how closely the penalty is linked with the abiding theology of the text of Gen 9:6. "Whoever sheds the blood of man, by man [presumably, as later specified, by the hands of the state] shall his blood be shed, for in the image of God has God made man." So valuable is that murdered person's life that mortals (in this case, the state, to protect society against vigilantes) owes back to God the life of the murderer.[16] This is how the reason for a command or custom helps us to know if both the cultural form and the content are still in vogue.

IN SOME CASES, MODIFY THE CULTURAL FORMS BUT RETAIN THE CONTENT

For example, the principle of humility remains as a permanent injunction for all times, even though the specific application of washing one another's feet has changed (presumably because of our location in history, shoe styles, and our type of roads). John 13:12–16 is clear about what Jesus did and about his command, but his main point is just as well preserved in Mark 10:42–45—"[The] rulers of the Gentiles lord it over them, and their

16. For further substantiation of this exegesis, see Walter C. Kaiser, Jr., *Toward Old Testament Ethics* (Grand Rapids: Zondervan, 1983), pp. 165–68. See also idem, *Hard Sayings of the Old Testament* (Downers Grove, Ill.: InterVarsity, 1988), pp. 40–45.

high officials exercise authority over them. Not so with you. Instead, whoever wants to become great among you must be your servant, and whoever wants to be first must be slave of all. For even the Son of Man did not come to be served, but to serve, and to give his life as a ransom for many."

Similarly, James urged believers to observe the principle of nonpartiality (James 2:1–4), yet the form that it took may not always persist in all cultures. In James's case, it consisted of having the poor sit on chairs in the church services while the rich stood or sat on the floor. While the principle remains, the form of its application will take a multiplicity of forms.

REFUSE PRACTICES THAT WERE INTEGRAL PARTS OF THE SURROUNDING PAGAN CULTURE

Some practices are just basically and inherently wrong because they spring from the pagan religions and culture and, in many instances, carry with them that which the Bible opposes on moral, ethical, and theological grounds. In some cases, the retention or adoption of some of these practices could be a bridge that could lead the practitioner back into the paganism from which he or she came or, in other cases, introduce them into that form of paganism.

The Bible's strong condemnation of bestiality, homosexual behavior, transvestism, and deliberate flaunting of one's nudity are often connected with what these practices meant in paganism. Each one of these Canaanite practices offended one aspect or another of God's moral nature and his attributes. In these cases there could be no doubting the fact that the form was so inextricably bound up with the content and meaning of the pagan religion and its practices that the believer could have no part of any of it.

RETAIN PRACTICES THAT ARE GROUNDED IN THE NATURE OF GOD

Some forms that might at first glance appear to be mere cultural expressions are nonnegotiable commands based on the nature of God. Accordingly, the issues of divorce and remarriage, obedience to parents, and the legitimate respect owed to government are some examples of injunctions grounded either in the nature of God or in the ordinances of creation that have universal and enduring appeal. So it is that "what God has joined together, let no man separate" (Matt. 19:6). That is how it has been and remains since God gave his original directive at creation.

Interestingly enough, the moral responsibility for deciding whether to pay one's taxes to a government that one believes is in opposition to accepted moral law (or some other equally principled objection) is lifted from the shoulders of believers. The reason one is relieved of this moral responsibility is because Romans 13:7 places taxes in the same category as paying for services rendered by people who work for us in the service professions. We do not aid and abet the possible unsavory way of life of some plumbers, electricians, and carpenters who may work in our home from time to time when we pay them the full amount that they request on their bill without deducting that percentage that we might suspect they use for gambling, buying booze, or chasing after women other than their wives. Likewise, when we pay our taxes, we render to Caesar what is due; we have no basis for deducting that percentage that goes to a war that we cannot support or to abortion clinics that we cannot morally justify. Over against this illustration of taxes, however, stand those commands that are grounded in the moral nature of God or his creation ordinances.

NOTICE WHEN THE CIRCUMSTANCES ALTER THE APPLICATION OF A LAW
OR PRINCIPLE

There is indeed biblical precedent for saying that circumstances may alter the application of the laws of God that do not rest on his nature (i.e., on the moral law of God), but that are true because he spoke them in a particular context. Law based not on the nature of God but on his particular sayings on a special occasion is called positive law.

An example of such a change in the *application* of a command can be seen in the command given to Aaron and his sons. Originally they alone were to eat the bread of presence set out before the Lord in the tabernacle (Lev. 24:8–9). But when an emergency arose in the case of David and his men who were without any food, Ahimelech offered this sacred and forbidden food to David and his army (1 Sam. 21:1–6).

But there is more to this illustration of how positive law can have its application changed when the circumstances demanded it. Jesus himself used the very same illustration to justify his performing deeds of mercy on the Sabbath, which some people saw instead as violating its sacredness (Matt. 12:1–5; Mark 2:23–25; Luke 6:1–4). What appeared, at first blush, to allow no exceptions (such as doing what some considered to be working on the Sabbath day), actually had a condition of "all other things being equal" attached to it.[17] This is not to say that we have now confused the moral law (which we said was to be found in part in the Ten Commandments) with positive law, for the commandment about the Sabbath is the only one in the Ten Commandments that is mixed with both moral and positive aspects. It is

17. See J. Oliver Buswell, *A Systematic Theology of the Christian Religion,* 2 vols. (Grand Rapids: Zondervan, 1962), 1:368–73.

moral in that it says that God is owner of all time and therefore has a right to receive back a portion of our time in worship of himself. But it is positive, or ceremonial, in that it spells out the seventh day as that time.

There is absolute loyalty in Scripture to the principles founded on the nature of God, but there is a good deal of flexibility in applying positive commands, such as sanitary laws and dietary laws (see Mark 7:19 and Acts 10:15, where all foods are declared clean). Likewise, the same flexibility holds true in cases of ceremonial regulations, such as the instance of 1 Kings 8:64, where Solomon used the middle of the temple court to sacrifice the numerous animals during the dedication ceremony, instead of the prescribed brazen altar, which was too small for the occasion (cf. 2 Chron. 4:1; 1 Kings 9:26). Nevertheless, the principle of worship remained even though the means varied.

One must watch carefully for positive commands, noting their attachment to particular historical occasions but also observing the principles they inculcate. It will do little good to observe in a formal way such alleged normative commands as "Get into the boat," "Loose the colt," or "Launch out into the deep." The context will help us to see that they had specific reference to specific people, even if the principles observed remain for all who followed in their train.

Conclusion

This area of the cultural and historical application of the biblical message is not easily resolved in every case. When deadlocks remain, then we must remember the need for humility. We likewise can profit from keeping in mind the three horizons of Bible interpretation.

THE CASE FOR HUMILITY IN CASES OF UNCERTAINTY

Robert C. Sproul has given the following good advice about handling uncertainty in matters of interpretation:

What if after careful consideration of a biblical mandate, we remain uncertain as to the question of its character as principle or custom? If we must decide to treat it one way or the other but have no conclusive means to make the decision, what can we do? Here the biblical principle of humility can be helpful. The issue is simple—would it be better to treat a possible custom as a principle and be guilty of being over-scrupulous in our design to obey God; or would it be better to treat a possible principle as a custom and be guilty of being unscrupulous in demoting a transcendent requirement of God to the level of a mere human convention? I hope the answer is obvious.[18]

In other words, it is better to err on the side of being humble and refusing to be (or what could later be exposed as being) cavalier with the text than it is to always assume that the more risky the stand, the more acceptable it is among those who prize creativity as being whatever is new and novel for its own sake.

THE CASE FOR THE THREE HORIZONS

We return, as we conclude this chapter, to the point made in the beginning. There are indeed three definite horizons: that of the Bible, the interpreter, and the receptor. By now it should also be clear that each of these three horizons has a context as well.

The Bible was written within the confines of certain cultures and times. No interpreter has the right to make that text say whatever he or she wants it to say. The text must be allowed to say what it wants to say, but with due respect for the particular setting and culture in which it was based. While some have pointed to the New Testament's use of the Old Testament as legitimizing certain types of intuitive approaches, it can hardly be claimed that the New Testament writers were not interested in the natural sense of the older Scriptures, especially when it came to forming doctrine based on those same texts, or when it came to using them for apologetic purposes to show that Christianity was not some new fantasy just dreamed up by someone.

Interpreters also must be aware of the way that their culture forces certain questions while leaving them blind to other, perhaps equally provocative, questions. Furthermore, when interpreters arrive at a text, they have already formed a kind of hermeneutical spiral that has a forceful way of imposing categories or ways of looking at certain questions and the like. Interpreters must constantly go through periods of self-examination to see just how free they really are and to consider how much each of these points previously adopted has indeed affected the exegesis.

Finally, readers, listeners, and the contemporary audience to whom the ancient Word is being proclaimed must likewise confess that they too each have a circle of culture and personal commitments. No one is an island, and no one arrived on the scene innocent and with a *tabula rasa*. To the degree that prejudices have been built up, to that degree we must expect that our depravity will manifest itself. In fact, the closer each one of us gets to that

18. R. C. Sproul, "Controversy at Culture Gap," *Eternity* (1976): 40.

central religious or philosophical mainspring of our lives, the closer we come into potential conflict with opposing cultural and spiritual viewpoints. One could build a sliding scale of cultural and spiritual interaction that would begin at the far-out reaches of mathematics, where both Beelzebub and a saint could reach agreement on the answers to straightforward math problems, and move all the way through the natural sciences, the social sciences, and then finally to the arts and humanities, where tremendous conflict would increase, the closer we got to that on which our souls were riding. Since theology and the interpretation of Scripture are located on this latter end of the scale, rather than on the other end with mathematics, it behooves us to proceed carefully and to be fully open to rigorous self-examination of the cultural context in which we stand.[19]

19. For this section, see C. René Padilla, "The Interpreted Word: Reflections of Contextual Hermeneutics," *Themelios* 7 (1981): 18–23.

The use of theology in the interpretive process often turns what otherwise would have been a dry and sterile wandering into a vital and powerful experience. Two tools are available for this task: the analogy of faith and the analogy of Scripture.

The analogy of faith, though variously interpreted and often abused, requires us to interpret all Scripture so that it is in agreement with the entire teaching of the Bible. It presupposes (1) the coherence of Scripture, (2) the organic nature of the Bible, and (3) the canonical closure of Holy Writ. Used in this manner, Scripture interprets Scripture, especially in the use of verbally parallel passages and topically parallel passages. Usually, however, use of the analogy of faith is held until one is ready to check one's interpretation of a passage against the rest of Scripture.

The analogy of Scripture refers to the exegetical use of earlier texts that "inform" the later passages by giving backgrounds, depth, and poignancy to the words used. They include technical terms, direct quotations, indirect citations, allusions to previous events, persons, or institutions, or previous covenants.

It is useful to focus on certain key chapters that act as "chair" passages, or "seats of doctrine." These chapters will contain the largest amount of teaching in one place on that respective doctrine.

Some of the key principles underlying the fruitful theological use of the Bible are (1) exegesis is prior to any system of doctrine, (2) doctrines must not go beyond scriptural evidence, (3) only what is directly taught in Scripture is binding on the conscience, and (4) theological interpretation must be responsive to the church.

CHAPTER 11

Putting It All Together
THE THEOLOGICAL USE OF THE BIBLE

WALTER C. KAISER, JR.

The Analogy of Faith

Biblical interpretation is one of the fields of study most critical for the theological task. Any failure in the interpretive mission immediately affects the results obtained in theological construction.[1]

Seen from another angle, hermeneutical practice involves both an exegetical and a theological component if it is to be carried out to its completion. The exegetical part of the interpretive process examines the grammatical, historical, and literary aspects of the text. But once these tasks have been concluded, they need to be related to the overall thought of the individual book being studied and to the whole canon of Scripture. It is at this juncture that the theological component of the interpretive enterprise comes to the forefront, typically introducing the often-abused concept of the analogy of faith.

The analogy of faith (*analogia fidei*) is a concept that has many advocates, but few have paused long enough to define it carefully.[2] This concept comes from a phrase in Romans 12:6—"We have different gifts,

---

1. For a more detailed development of some of the matters in this chapter, see Walter C. Kaiser, Jr., "Hermeneutics and the Theological Task," *TJ*, n.s., 12 (1990): 3–14.
2. A notable exception is Henri Blocher's careful study "The 'Analogy of Faith' in the Study of Scripture," *SBET* 5 (1987): 17–38.

according to the grace given us. If a man's gift is prophesying, let him use it *in proportion to his faith* [*kata tēn analogian tēs pisteōs*]." Two other passages are usually cited: Romans 12:3, where Paul says that one is not to think of one's self more highly than one should; rather each is to think "so as to have sound judgment, as God has allotted to each *a measure of faith* [*metron pisteōs*]"; and 2 Timothy 1:13—"What you have heard from me, keep as *the pattern of sound teaching.*"

In Romans 12:6, Paul makes the point that the gift of prophecy must be "in agreement with" or "in proportion to" the faith. Three main ways of interpreting this phrase have been suggested: It could refer to one's personal faith in Christ. Accordingly, prophets should prophesy in accordance with the standard of their own apprehension and response to God's grace in the gospel.[3] Second, it could refer to what is mathematically proportional; the prophet's gift is to be exercised within the limits of faith as restricted to the prophet's own purpose and sphere.[4] The third view understands Paul as requiring the prophet to speak in accord with previously revealed truth found in the Word of God. This third definition would support the often-used rule that a true prophet was never to contradict existing revelation (Deut. 13:1–5; 18:20–22; Acts 17:11; 1 Cor. 14:37; 1 John 4:1–6).[5]

Each of these three views presents some kind of standard against which the prophecy is to be judged. In that sense, then, Paul's use of the phrase *analogy of faith* is not that far from the way many have used it in the history of interpretation. Our preference, however, is with the third view, for the reasons cited. Henri Blocher nicely summarizes the situation in commenting, "The apostle, when dictating Romans 12:6, barely thought of the technical 'comparing Scripture with Scripture'; yet, he concerned himself with the agreement of Christian discourse with the whole body of teaching given by inspiration of God, in its main emphases and overall balance (*analogia*), all parts included. Substantially, his point was not far removed from our conception of the analogy of faith."[6]

The concept of the analogy of faith comes into play in the interpretive process *after* one has established the meaning of a particular passage from its immediate context. Since the analogy of faith scans the entirety of Scripture without concerning itself with sequence, it is best to use it only by way of summary at the conclusion of investigating each paragraph or basic unit of

3. C. E. B. Cranfield, *A Critical and Exegetical Commentary on the Epistle to the Romans,* ICC, 2 vols. (Edinburgh: T. & T. Clark, 1975–79), 2:621.

4. As represented by John Murray, *The Epistle to the Romans,* 2 vols. (Grand Rapids: Eerdmans, 1959–65), 2:123.

5. As represented by Leon Morris, *The Epistle to the Romans* (Grand Rapids: Eerdmans, 1988), 441.

6. Blocher, "Analogy of Faith," p. 28.

exegetical work. The analogy of faith gathers verses from throughout the canon into a bouquet that is truly biblical in its derivation. The doctrines that are affirmed and the support that is claimed for each doctrine from the assemblage of the verses cited is only as useful and valid as the exegesis that underlies this work of assembling the texts and definitions.

The Analogy of Scripture

Before we take a further look at how the analogy of faith is to be used in the interpretive process, we must consider the parallel term *analogy of Scripture*.[7] It was John Bright who noted that most biblical passages have within them some facet of theology expressed in such a way that marks them part and parcel of the fabric of the whole Bible.[8] The roots for this theology have often been laid down in scriptural texts that appeared earlier than the text under examination.

The clues to such an antecedent theology within the text were

1. The use of certain *terms* that have already acquired a special meaning in Scripture (e.g., seed, servant, rest, inheritance);
2. The use of *direct quotations* from writers that precede the text being examined (e.g., the frequently mentioned tripartite formula: "I will be your God, you shall be my people, and I will dwell in the midst of you");
3. The use of *indirect citations or allusions* to previous events, persons, or institutions (e.g., the Exodus, the epiphany on Mount Sinai, or the giving of the law); and
4. A reference to the *covenants and their contents* (e.g., the Abrahamic, Davidic, or New covenants).

In each case, the interpreter would be well advised to pay close attention to the earlier context. In such cases the author of Scripture was building on the backdrop of the Bible that was already available to him. In the words of John Bright, these earlier passages "informed" the later text and gave it more poignancy and depth.

Modern-day examples are not hard to come by. For example, mention

---

7. For further discussion, see Walter C. Kaiser, Jr., *Toward an Exegetical Theology: Biblical Exegesis for Preaching and Teaching* (Grand Rapids: Baker, 1981), 134–40.

8. John Bright, *The Authority of the Old Testament* (Nashville: Abingdon, 1967), pp. 143, 170.

"Watergate" or the names of any of those who were involved in this scandal during the American presidency of Richard Nixon, and a flood of memories, associations, and even a special phrase or two immediately comes to mind. This one event colors all the characters, events, and writings of American history in 1973 and following.

In a similar manner, when the prophet Hosea mentions in Hosea 2:15 that God "will give [Israel] back her vineyards, and will make the Valley of Achor a door of hope," he is referring directly to the sin of Achan in Joshua 7. In that incident one man brought enormous grief to all Israel, so they stoned him in the Valley of Achor (Josh. 7:24), for he had brought "trouble" or "disaster" (= *achor*) on the people. But in God's grand announcement through Hosea, God promises to turn what previously had been a place of trouble or disaster into "a door of hope"! By noting this "informing theology," we see the true depth and poignancy of Hosea's allusion.

An interpreter can best grasp the analogy of Scripture by consulting editions of the Scriptures that have antecedent references in the margins, such as the *Thompson Chain Reference Bible,* the *Dickson Reference Bible,* and many modern editions that have such references to the earlier allusions and citations. One must be careful, however, to eliminate all the marginal references that cite passages written after the text under investigation.[9]

The Use of the Analogy of Faith

Sometimes, amid all the emphasis on the details, parts, and minutiae of Scripture, modern interpreters have jettisoned three vitally important elements that may seem out of date: (1) the coherence of Scripture, (2) the organic nature of Scripture, and (3) the canonical closure of Scripture. Against such "modernization" Blocher argues, "If Scripture were a collection of independent sayings, all of them right, but simply juxtaposed, on topics unconnected with one another, how could the analogy [of faith] come into play? . . . But Scripture [is] like ordinary speech and even more so."[10]

Here is where the analogy of faith enters the process again. Since the Mind governing Scripture is one, is it not appropriate and fair to God the

9. Such "topical Bibles" have their use in another arena (specifically, the analogy of faith), but not in the formative stages of the interpretive enterprise. One especially replete source for all antecedent references is *The Treasury of Scriptural Knowledge* by R. A. Torrey, which contains more than five thousand such references. Torrey's work continues to be reprinted and used long after his death in 1928.

10. Blocher, "Analogy of Faith," pp. 32–33.

Holy Spirit to gather his total thinking on a particular subject, much as we might do with the writings of a human author? And if communication is assumed, do we not grant that the writer exhibits coherence and unity in his or her thought until proven otherwise? Why should biblical scholars assume less, unless they reject the idea of a unified divine mind behind the entirety of Scripture? The presumption against the unity of the Bible, more than any other factor, has spoiled evangelicals and turned them away from searching for any inner unifying principles in biblical theology or biblical ethics and from appreciating the legitimacy of systematic theology. Success in the analytical methods of scholarship has taken evangelicalism away from focusing attention on synthetic and synoptic types of study to the degree they are needed for interpreting the Bible theologically.

The unity of the Bible, however, can be argued from at least three points of view.

COHERENCE

The argument for coherence can be found in part in the way that one biblical writer after another directly and indirectly refers to those portions of the biblical text that have preceded him. Thus, Daniel "understood from the Scriptures" that what Jeremiah had said less than a century before was "according to the word of the Lord" (Dan. 9:2, quoting Jer. 25:11–12 and 29:10 to the effect that the captivity of Judah in Babylon would last for seventy years). It is on this model of seventy years, then, that Daniel is given his revelation of "seventy 'sevens'" (Dan. 9:24). The biblical writers' clear dependence on, and concordance with, each other is evident throughout the text.

ORGANIC NATURE

There is an organic nature to revelation in that often the earlier forms contain the seminal or germ forms of the ideas that are to come to full expression later on in the progress of revelation. Accordingly, as O. Palmer Robertson has pointed out:

> The permeation of [Hab. 2:4—"The just shall live by faith"] with Gen. 15:6 ["Abram believed the LORD, and he credited it to him as righteousness"] . . . [is a] deliberate echo of Genesis 15:6 in Habakkuk 2:4b . . . and provides the basis for a proper understanding of the text. The same terms for the root concepts of faith and legal right-standing [*he 'ĕmîn, 'ĕmună; ṣĕdāqă, ṣaddîq*] occur in both passages. In the context of Habakkuk, a test of

faith similar to that experienced by Abraham due to non-fulfilment of divine promises is evident.[11]

Thus, the texts separated by centuries were organically related one to the other, and the seed of what was to come to full fruition later on was already present in the earlier text.

CANONICAL CLOSURE

The third part of the argument for the unity of the Bible involves consideration of canonical closure. In recent years new attention has been given to the status of the canon. This has opened up the way for a partial rediscovery of the concept of a beginning and an end to the revelation of God. This concept of wholeness provides an overarching context that completes the picture of what the organizing mind of Scripture envisioned.

The very idea of a canon implies a standard or authoritative measuring device by which a collection of books is recognized as norms for the community. Implicit within that recognition is not only the idea of a beginning and ending point but the suggestion that there are linking notices and devices within that corpus as well. Thus, while the individual parts of the canon are individually valuable, only as the entire corpus is viewed as a whole can the whole mind of God be finally declared on any topic that several of the books may address.

The Theological Task of the Interpreter

The phrase *analogy of faith* is not common in patristic and medieval writings. But the concept did appear under a variety of names, being referred to as the faith, the rule of truth, the measure of faith, the catholic faith, or the apostolic institution of the church. In all of these terms, the concept of unity of Scripture is prominent. Such a unity was based on four pillars: (1) the fact that Scripture has one single, divine Author; (2) the fact that Christ is present in the Old Testament, not only virtually or implicitly, but directly, since the prophets speak of him; (3) the fact that Christ is the center of the Scriptures; and (4) the fact that the doctrines within the Scripture are linked together throughout the text and tend to build one upon another.[12]

The Enlightenment and the advent of the higher-critical method have

11. O. Palmer Robertson, " 'The Justified (by Faith) Shall Live by His Steadfast Trust'— Habakkuk 2:4," *Presbyterion* 9 (1983): 65.

12. I am indebted for this list to Robert D. Preus, "The Unity of Scripture," *CTQ* 54 (1990): 1–23.

led many within the church to reject the unity of Scripture as a viable doctrine or a usable hermeneutical feature. This has left many contemporary readers of the Bible bewildered and without any organizing principle or method by which to put the whole story of the Bible together. These principles must be revived once again, and that is our intention in what follows:

THE PERSPICUITY OF SCRIPTURE

The principle of the perspicuity of Scripture (see also chap. 9, pp. 163–70) states that the message of the Bible is clear enough so that even the most unlearned person can understand the basic message of salvation that the Bible presents. The classic statement of the perspicuous ("plain to the understanding"), or clear, nature of the Bible does not mean to say that all the parts of the Bible are equally clear and free of all difficulty. Perspicuity was never intended to be a shortcut or a skeleton key to unlock all the teaching or interpreting of the Bible. How this principle has been misunderstood and misused is well stated by Bishop Herbert Marsh:

> Another expression used by our Reformers, namely, "the *perspicuity* of the Sacred Writings," has been no less abused than [other] similar expression[s] [such as "the Bible is its own interpreter"]. When [the Reformers] argued for the *perspicuity* of the Bible, they intended not to argue against the application of Learning, but against the application of Tradition to the exposition of Scripture. . . . No! said our Reformers; we need not the aid of your Tradition; to use the Bible is sufficiently perspicuous without it. . . . They never meant to declare, that the Bible was alike perspicuous, to the learned and the unlearned. If they had, they would never have supplied the unlearned with *explanations* of it.[13]

SCRIPTURE INTERPRETS SCRIPTURE

Often what is obscure in one part of the Bible is made clear in another part. The hermeneutical tool to be used here is that of parallel passages. When the immediate context does not assist interpreters in discovering the meaning of a passage, they may utilize two kinds of parallel passages found elsewhere in Scripture.

VERBAL PARALLEL PASSAGES. Often the same word, phrase, clause, or expression appears in two or more passages in a similar connection and with

---

13. Bishop Herbert Marsh, *A Course of Letters . . . in Theological Learning* (Boston: Cummings and Hilliard, 1815), 18, italics his.

reference to the same or a closely related subject. It is most important for the interpreter to demonstrate such relation, for the mere presence of the same words and expressions is not by itself sufficient evidence for linking the two passages.

One illustration of a verbal parallel passage is 1 Kings 19:9, 11, which deals with Elijah on Mount Horeb—"There he went to the cave and spent the night. . . . The LORD said, 'Go out and stand on the mountain in the presence of the LORD, for the LORD is about to *pass by.*'" Now the area to which Elijah had just come in his flight from Queen Jezebel was the same as Mount Sinai, where Moses had received the two tables of the law. The use of the article with "cave" in 1 Kings 19:9 is no doubt an allusion to the "cleft in the rock" mentioned in Exodus 33:22. More important, in this earlier passage, the Lord told Moses, "I will cause all my goodness to *pass by* in front of you, and I will proclaim my name, the LORD, in your presence" (Exod. 33:19).

Besides the relation of Elijah's cave to Moses' cleft in the rock, then, the mention in both passages of the Lord's *passing by* connects the two and enhances our understanding of the Lord's relation to Elijah in this incident. The despondent prophet clearly needed exactly what Moses received from the Lord, namely, a whole new view of the living God as God caused his presence and his attributes to pass in review as a reminder of who and what he is. In this manner, examination of verbal parallels can add depth to one's teaching and preaching of biblical texts.

TOPICAL PARALLEL PASSAGES. A topic parallel passage is one that deals with the same facts, subjects, sentiments, or doctrines as the passage being compared, without using the same words, clauses, or expressions. Prime examples of this type of phenomenon can be found in the synoptic materials of the Gospels and of Samuel, Kings, and Chronicles. In addition to these synoptic accounts, there are also pairs of duplicate passages, including Psalms 14 and 53, Psalm 18 and 2 Samuel 22, Psalm 96 and 1 Chronicles 16, and Jude and 2 Peter.

The eight so-called fugitive psalms of David represent another kind of topically parallel passages:

Ps. 18, when David was delivered from the hand of Saul (2 Sam. 22)
Ps. 34, when David feigned insanity (1 Sam. 21)
Ps. 52, when Doeg told Saul about David (1 Sam. 22)
Ps. 54, when the Ziphites went to Saul (1 Sam. 23)
Ps. 56, when the Philistines seized David (1 Sam. 21:10–15)
Ps. 57, when David fled into the cave (1 Sam. 22)
Ps. 59, when Saul's men watched for David (1 Sam. 19:11–17)
Ps. 142, when David was in the cave (1 Sam. 24)

As the interpreter studies these psalms as a unit, along with the relevant passages from Samuel, elements of the experience and theology of David can come to light that would otherwise remain hidden.[14]

Finally, consider Jesus' word in Luke 14:26 that those following him must "hate" their father and mother. We receive help in interpreting this "hate" by referring to the topically parallel passage in Matthew 10:37, where Jesus requires that his disciples not love their parents "more than me."

THE "CHAIR" PASSAGES OF SCRIPTURE

We have argued already that studies based on the analogy of faith must not be used as a substitute for the hard task of exegeting particular passages of Scripture on their own terms. Rather, such studies are most useful toward the end of the interpretive process, when similar themes, passages, and doctrines can be brought to bear as a test for the general sense of the rightness of the interpretation proposed. Use of the analogy of faith serves, then, both as a check on the conclusion reached in the exegesis and as an indication on what direction the same teaching took in the course of later revelation.

Along with studying related passages in terms of the analogy of faith, it is useful also to focus on certain key chapters of Scripture that contain major treatments of various issues, such as the following:

> Genesis 1–2: The creation
> Isaiah 40: The incomparability of God
> Isaiah 53: The nature of the Atonement
> 1 Corinthians 15: The Resurrection
> 2 Corinthians 5:1–10: The nature of the intermediate state
> Philippians 2:1–11: The nature of the Incarnation

A chapter such as one of the above has been referred to in church history as *sedes doctrinae,* or "a seat of doctrine." These passages, which we may call chair passages, can well function as boundary setters for interpreters as they seek guidance about the correct interpretation of texts that are textually or topically parallel. These chair passages contain the largest amount of material in one place on the respective doctrines. In a sense they represent a self-policing function of Scripture, one particularly important for Protestants, who

---

14. This study obviously depends on the antiquity and authenticity of the Psalm titles. These titles are older than the third century B.C., as attested by the fact that the Septuagint writers were unable to translate many of the terms in the titles, resorting instead to transliteration. Such evidence can be a presumption in favor of their antiquity.

have typically rejected external limitations (e.g., by the church or by tradition) on their interpretations of the Bible.

A Summary of the Principles

If God indeed is the author of a genuine revelation from himself to mortals, it is natural for us to think that the Scriptures are capable of being used for doctrinal and theological teaching. In fact, 2 Timothy 3:16–17 lists "doctrine" as the first of a list of profits that will come from Scripture. The apostle Paul speaks to this same point in mentioning the Romans' obeying doctrine from their heart (Rom. 6:17). The same apostle warned young Timothy twelve times in his two letters to him to be careful to maintain sound doctrine. All of this emphasis on doctrine and teaching was not a late invention of some evangelical movement, or some overreactionary propositional theologians, for the same emphasis on teaching marked our Lord's own ministry. The people were astonished at his teaching (Matt. 7:28). In fact, he flatly declared that his doctrine came from the Father (John 7:16). Therefore, the doctrinal use of the Bible cannot be set aside lightly or played down. It is, instead, that which gives substance and form to the whole of the Christian faith. Doctrine is possible only because God has spoken in the Scriptures.

In this final section we summarize key principles that underlie a fruitful theological use of the Bible.

1. THE MAIN BURDEN OF DOCTRINAL TEACHING MUST REST ON THE CHAIR PASSAGES

This principle is to be preferred over any reductionistic one such as that which says we must take the New over the Old Testament, or the Prophets over the Law, or the Epistles over the Gospels. Every one of these alternatives has been played out in history, many with disastrous effects. Such a deference to what comes latest as being superior over what preceded it would impugn the character of the revealing God and create a canon within a canon. Throughout both canons the revelation of God time and again comes to its fullest measure on one doctrine after another. Consequently, it is important that we go to each of these chair passages and there, as it were, cut our teeth on the fullest expression of what God had in mind for each of these great didactic truths.

2. EXEGESIS IS PRIOR TO ANY SYSTEM OF THEOLOGY

The Scriptures themselves are not a textbook of theology, any more than the natural world around us comes complete with a textbook in geology, physics, or chemistry. Even though all creation is from the hand of God, just as all Scripture is from his hand, we were given the created order already operating, rather than the book of operations. The human propensity to organize, classify, and arrange this data, both natural revelation and supernatural revelation, probably reflects the fact that we are made in the image of God.

But when that propensity to form a theology turns instead to extrabiblical sources, there is no end of trouble. Such sources can become grids dropped over the text that act as a bit and bridle do in the mouth of a horse.

These grids may represent philosophies such as pantheism or existentialism, or they may represent loyalties to organizing principles that form a separate analogy of faith from that offered from a reading of the Bible itself. In this latter category are our systems of dispensationalism or covenantal theology, Calvinism or Arminianism, charismatic or cessationist theologies. This is not to say one system is right and the others are wrong or that all of these are wrong; rather, it is to caution that the system comes second and the exegesis of the Bible comes first. In other words, we often tend to make our systems fit the Bible, not the Bible our systems—in which case we shall all be arguing and reasoning in a circle.

3. DOCTRINES MUST NOT GO BEYOND SCRIPTURAL EVIDENCE

The temptation to say more than Scripture says is always a hazard, for we mortals are a most curious lot. But in addition to our curiosity, we also have a deep-seated desire to pretend that we know more than others do on matters pertaining both to this world and the next. It is at these points that we begin to extrapolate from the evidence that we have in hand in order to make what we believe are consistently logical deductions on some of the doctrines where moderns ask questions for which the text has no direct answers. Unfortunately for the cause of the gospel, we often begin to major in these theological extrapolations, forcing others to agree with our distinctives or to give up their association with "our group."

4. THE ANALOGY OF SCRIPTURE MUST TAKE PRIORITY OVER THE ANALOGY OF FAITH

As we have already presented the case in some detail on both analogies, we will be succinct here. My concern in stating this principle is to give priority to exegesis and to what was known already from the previous revelations of God before we add, by way of summary, everything that the Lord later revealed on a particular topic. In other words, we need to read the Bible forward in time, lest we fall into the error of eisegesis, that is, "reading [back] into" the text what we hoped or wished was there.

The use of "informing theology" from the analogy of Scripture can make a powerful difference in an exegesis that would otherwise be anemic and listless without this input. Thus, when Elijah took up "twelve stones" (not ten) in order to build an altar representative of the twelve tribes and declared, "Your name shall be Israel," he clearly was calling to the minds of the people the first time where such words occurred. In Genesis 32:28 and 35:10, Jacob twice—but some thirty years apart—was told by God that he would no longer be called Jacob, but "Your name will be Israel." In both cases (once as he wrestled with the angel of the Lord at Peniel and once when he worried whether the Canaanites were going to kill off his family after the Dinah–Shechemite affair), Jacob was warned to turn away from his dependence on himself and his idols.

Now, almost a millennium later, Elijah had to teach the same lesson to Jacob's descendants all over again. "Get rid of the foreign gods you have with you," decreed the Lord in Genesis 35:2. Elijah issued a similar cry in 1 Kings 18:21. Thus the informing theology strengthens and enriches our exegesis of biblical texts. Now it is possible—and most desirable—to introduce similar teaching on the same topic raised in our exegesis of a passage from later Scripture as they form a total analogy of faith. The order of employing the analogy of (antecedent) Scripture first and then using the analogy of faith in the summary of each of the main points of a sermon is of primary importance.

5. ONLY WHAT IS DIRECTLY TAUGHT IN SCRIPTURE IS BINDING ON THE CONSCIENCE

As with theology, so it is in the area of morality and ethics. Once again there is a tendency to place as much confidence in human extrapolations and personal deductions from Scripture in the shaping of an ethic and morality as there is in the text of Scripture itself. This is not fair to the primacy of Scripture or to the body of believers.

To bind the consciences of believers to that which is not *directly* taught in Scriptures is to come perilously close to raising up a new form of tradition that vies for equal recognition with Scripture itself. We rightly object when cults and sects add to the Scriptures merely human ideas. We should likewise protest when the human interpretations of the Bible are raised to the level of Scripture. Moreover, such interference is an infringement of our Christian liberty in Christ.

One must be careful in applying this principle, for some have avoided the ditch on one side of the path only to fall into the ditch on the other side. Thus, what is directly condemned in Scripture, we must condemn. And what is condemned by immediate application of a principle we must also condemn. But where neither of these two conditions appear, Christian conscience cannot be bound by others. In these cases where the matters become more debatable (e.g., in scriptural teachings where it is suspected that cultural backgrounds are involved, such as the command to wash one another's feet in John 13:14), our interpretation must remain more tentative, at least as far as binding the consciences of others is concerned.

6. NO DOCTRINE SHOULD BE BASED ON A SINGLE PASSAGE OF SCRIPTURE,
A PARABLE, AN ALLEGORY, A TYPE, A SENSUS PLENIOR, OR AN UNCERTAIN TEXTUAL
READING

Doctrinal teaching is too valuable to entrust it to those areas of interpretation where the subjective biases of the reader might shine through more brightly.

The Mormons, for example, have enshrined 1 Corinthians 15:29 as a key doctrine and formed one of their distinctives from this text—"Now if there is no resurrection, what will those do who are baptized for the dead?" Probably Paul was only arguing ad hominem at this point. One would be hard pressed to assert that this one verse was adequate evidence to build a doctrine for the baptism of the dead. No matter how Paul was arguing at this point, it is extremely dangerous to take one verse and formulate a doctrine from it.

I well remember the day that a man opened his Testament to the book of Acts and declared that he belonged to the "Jesus Only" church, because that is how they were baptized in Acts 8:16—"Only they were baptized in the name of the Lord Jesus" (AV). Never mind what the rest of Scripture said about the Trinitarian formula; his mind and denomination had already been made up.

Likewise, it is just as risky to settle on a doctrine that rests solely on a point allegedly made in a parable, an allegory, a type, a so-called *sensus plenior,* or an uncertain textual reading. For example, some have based the doctrine of the Trinity on 1 John 5:7–8. The evidence, however, comes from late manuscripts of the Latin Vulgate that added about twenty-five words, including those translated "the Father, the Word, and the Holy Spirit." This reading cannot be sustained as being a part of the original text; therefore it should not be used for theology and doctrine. Such procedures are cases of "proof-texting," a method that uses texts simply because they have a certain word or idea in them but gives no consideration to the context or the way in which the original author was using the text.

7. THEOLOGICAL INTERPRETATION MUST RECOGNIZE ITS RESPONSIBILITY
TO THE CHURCH

The Holy Spirit did not begin to work just as *we* reached this stage of history and began to interpret the Bible. For centuries, reaching back into the Old Testament, there has been the faithful accumulation of the gains, insights, and understandings of the believing body of the people of God.

Once again there is a ditch on either side of the road. One can be so beholden to what the church and former believers have learned from Scripture that it is raised to the status of tradition and becomes another scripture. But the opposite problem is just as real. Some will cut themselves off from all previous insights and work, as if they had been sealed in a vacuum and all doctrinal knowledge began with them.

The doctrinal teaching of Scripture is to be shared. The work of theologizing must be done in the spirit of inviting other believers to inspect our work and to measure it by the standard of Scripture itself. This need to work together is not due to the inadequate nature of Scripture, but it has more to do with the inadequate nature of the readers and interpreters of the Bible.

The Reformers set forth a dual system of checks and balances when they announced the priesthood of all believers along with their appeal to the original languages of the Bible. If the former took precedence, then anarchy might result, as each did what was right in his or her own eyes. If the second was elevated over the first, then we might have been left at the mercy of the scholars, who would constitute the final court of appeal as to what a text was or was not saying. Mercifully, the Reformers insisted on both the priesthood of all believers and the appeal to the original languages of Scripture. This made for a balance and a need for both the scholar and the layperson to depend on each other.

PART 4

The Search for Meaning:
Further Challenges

A knowledge of the history of interpretation can be one of the best protections against interpretive error. That history begins with the Jewish *Targums,* which employed both the plain and hidden sense of the Mosaic law. Three important groups helped to formulate different aspects of Jewish interpretation. Rabbi Hillel epitomized the first group with his seven rules, which for the most part were logical extensions of the plain sense. Later Rabbi Eliezar extended Hillel's seven rules into thirty-two rules by including a number of mystical techniques to obtain deeper meanings of the Scriptures. The Essenes of the Dead Sea Scrolls developed the *pesher* method, which transformed persons and events into contemporary values and meaning merely by alleging them to be so. The third group was composed of the Jewish diaspora, best remembered by Philo, who emphasized the *hyponoia,* i.e., the deeper sense of Scripture, which could be uncovered by allegory.

The New Testament writers used almost three hundred citations from the Old Testament along with hundreds (some say thousands) more allusions to it. It is doubtful, however, that Jesus and the apostles used the allegorical interpretation or even a *pesher* or midrashic values for the Old Testament text in order to establish their claim that the Old Testament doctrine and Messiah had been fulfilled in Christ and the church.

Three schools dominated the early Christian centuries: the Alexandrian, the Antiochian, and the Western. The Alexandrian specialized in the allegorical system of interpretation built on a doctrine of correspondence between earthly and heavenly realities, while the Antiochian built its case on a doctrine of *theoria* that claimed that Scripture had one meaning that embraced both the literal and the spiritual, the historical and the typological. The Western school was more eclectic, embodying principles from both schools, as represented by men such as Jerome and Augustine.

The Middle Ages produced the Victorines of Paris, Stephen Langdon, Thomas Aquinas, and a converted Jew, Nicholas of Lyra. Nicholas influenced Luther and the Reformation with his insistence on the plain meaning of the text. Reuchlin and Erasmus laid the groundwork for the Reformation, but Luther and Calvin led the charge against the allegorical interpretation. In the post-Reformation age, the pietist emphasized the application of the Scriptures to one's own personal faith and practice, while Rationalism began a trend that eventually led to forms of historical-critical study of the Bible.

CHAPTER 12

A Short History
of Interpretation

WALTER C. KAISER, JR.

An understanding of the history of the interpretation of the Bible can be an enormous assistance to the student of the Scriptures. For example, it can serve as a warning against repeating some of the errors of the past. It can also trace what influences led to some of the misunderstandings of God's Word. Moreover, it can acquaint the interpreter with some of the outstanding exegetes of the past and demonstrate some of the methods they used in approaching the Scriptures. In any case, no matter what one's motivation is for peering over the shoulders of those interpreters who have gone before us, surely a careful study of their work will save the student from losing valuable time and running down unfruitful rabbit trails that have already been tried and found wanting.

Almost from the very beginning it can be said that many listeners and readers of the message of the Bible were slow to apprehend the spiritual truth it contained. The prophets repeatedly complained that Israel was a foolish, senseless, and rebellious audience, "who had eyes to see, but [did] not see, who had ears to hear, but [did] not hear" (Jer. 5:21; cf. Isa. 6:10; Ezek. 12:2). Nor was the situation that different in the New Testament times. Paul has to write to the Thessalonians, asking them "not to become easily unsettled or alarmed by some prophecy, report or letter supposedly to have come from us" (2 Thess. 2:2). And, yes, Paul's letters indeed "contain some things that are hard to understand, which ignorant and unstable people distort, as they do the other Scriptures, to their own destruction" (2 Peter 3:16). People will

211

distort not only Paul's letters but the "other Scriptures" as well. Hence the need for a short history of interpretation of the Bible.[1]

Jewish Hermeneutics

The great advantage that the Jewish people possessed was conceded by Paul in Romans 3:1–2; namely, they "have been entrusted with the very words of God." But this treasure had not always governed the thoughts and actions of the people, for the law was ignored and the prophets were persecuted.

It was necessary, therefore, when the people returned from the Babylonian exile, to have the *Targums* (from a word meaning "to explain") so that they could be guided in interpreting the Scriptures. Thus oral teaching became a fixed and growing supplement to the biblical text, possessing an authority equal to that of the Scriptures. The claim was that this tradition was handed down faithfully from the scribe Ezra and the members of the Great Synagogue, who in turn were alleged to have received it by divine revelation.

As the Christian era dawned, it was customary for the Jewish rabbis to distinguish between the two senses of the text: the *peshat,* the "clear," "plain," or "simple" (hence the literal or historical) meaning of a Bible passage; and the *remaz,* the hidden sense of the Mosaic law and of the Halakah. There also was the *derûsh* ("searched") meaning of Scripture, that is, the allegorical sense expressed in the form of Haggadoth or legends. From this latter word was obtained the noun *midrash,* "exegesis." The fourth method used in Jewish interpretation was the *sôd*—the mystical or Cabalistic sense of a passage.

The exegesis dealing with historical and dogmatic subjects was called *haggadic midrash.* This type of interpretation was more illustrative, practical, and mixed with a wealth of allegory, legend, and colorful biblical history. It was mainly a homiletic approach to the study of the Bible.

In contrast, the exegesis dealing with legal matters was called *halakic midrash.* This form of interpretation attempted to apply the law by analogy and by a combination of texts to those exceptional cases for which there was no special enactment in Moses' law.

Jewish interpretation was determined, to a large degree, by its own theological framework and the goals of the community in which the

1. For another summary of this history, with a few differences in perspective, see Moisés Silva, *Has the Church Misread the Bible? The History of Interpretation in the Light of Current Issues* (Grand Rapids: Zondervan, 1987), esp. chaps. 2–3.

Scriptures played a role. Three important groups helped to formulate different aspects of Jewish interpretation: the rabbis, the Qumran sect of the Dead Sea Scrolls, and the Jewish Diaspora.

THE RABBIS

After the days of Ezra and the teachers, or *Tannā'îm* (as they were called after A.D. 30), who came after the Maccabean revolt, a tradition began that eventually resulted in the great written collections that in the Christian era were called the *Mishnah, Gemara,* and the *Talmud.*[2] In the beginning, this tradition of oral law developed as a parallel to the Torah. But as time went on, the validity of this tradition had to be proved by referring to the biblical texts themselves. Thus there developed a kind of coordination of the biblical text, tradition, and contemporary application.

The principles for coordinating all three of these concerns were set forth in several sets of rabbinic rules known as *middôt.* The source of these rules is not known for certain, but most say that the oldest set of seven *middôt* came from the famous Rabbi Hillel, an older contemporary of Jesus (ca. 30 B.C. to A.D. 15). These seven rules of Hillel are[3]

1. *Inference from the lighter meaning* (= minor premise) *to the heavier* (= major premise), *or an a fortiori argument.* It simply says that what is true of the lesser is true also of the greater. Thus, since the Sabbath was more important than the other festival days, a restriction placed on an annual festival day was even more applicable to the Sabbath day.

2. *Analogy of expressions.* Ambiguous passages were explained by drawing an inference from the analogy of expressions, that is from similar words and phrases used elsewhere. Accordingly, since Leviticus 16:29 requires Jews to "afflict [their] souls" on the Day of Atonement, without explaining what the nature of that affliction is, it was interpreted to mean that Jews should abstain from food on Yom Kippur, since the same expression is used in Deuteronomy 8:3 with explicit mention of hunger.

3. *Application by analogy with one provision, or the extension from the specific to the general.* In this rule, texts were applied to cases if they were

---

2. Some parts of the Talmud can be traced back to the second century B.C., when various teachings began to be handed down orally and constantly augmented in each generation. Then in the second century A.D. Judah Ha-Nasi collected these teachings in written form. This work, which consists of sixty-three tractates, became known as the Mishnah. In the course of time, the Mishnah itself was the subject of a written interpretation, the Gemara. The combination of the Mishnah and the Gemara is generally referred to as the Talmud.

3. For further explanations of these rules, see *Mikra: Text, Translation, Reading, and Interpretation of the Hebrew Bible in Ancient Judaism and Early Christianity,* ed. Martin Jan Mulder (Philadelphia: Fortress, 1988), pp. 699–702. Also see Karlfried Froehlich, *Biblical Interpretation in the Early Church* (Philadelphia: Fortress, 1984), pp. 30–36.

similar in nature, even though they were not directly covered in the Scripture cited. In other words, a general principle was constructed on the basis of a teaching contained in one verse. So, for example, the case of the accidental killing of a fellow woodsman in Deuteronomy 19 could be applied to any accidental death resulting from two men working together in a public place.

4. *Application by analogy with two provisions.* This rule is similar to the previous rule, only here it is strengthened by giving two provisions, or two verses, for the general principle. For example, Exodus 21:26–27 provided that a slave that had his "eye" or "tooth" destroyed could go free. By analogy, this rule could be extended to all other parts of the body.

5. *Inference from a general principle to a specific case or example.* This rule may be used either way—from the general to the specific or vice versa. Thus, Exodus 22:9 states that if a man lends another his ox, ass, sheep, garment, "or any other thing," he must pay double restitution if it is lost. But since the generalizing term "any other thing" is used, it shows that the ox, the ass, the sheep, and the garment were only examples, and thus the law applies to any borrowed thing that is lost, living or dead; it must be refunded for twice its value.

6. *Explanation from another passage.* Similar to the second rule, this rule explained one passage by appealing to another Scripture. The question arose for Rabbi Hillel whether the Passover lamb was to be slain on a Sabbath if the fourteenth of Nisan fell on the Sabbath day. He replied that since Numbers 28:10 decreed that the "daily" sacrifices had to be offered also on the Sabbath, then by analogy the Passover lamb had to be slain on the fourteenth of Nisan, regardless of what day it fell on.

7. *Application of self-evident inferences from the context.* A passage must not be taken as an isolated statement, but only in the light of its context. Therefore, the apparently absolute prohibition against anyone going out of his or her house on the seventh day in Exodus 16:29 must be interpreted in its context to apply only to the situation of gathering of manna in the wilderness, which was to have been provided for by gathering double on the day before.

Later, in the second century A.D., Rabbi Ishmael ben Elisha increased Hillel's rules to thirteen.[4] Rabbi Eliezar ben Josē elaborated them into thirty-two rules. At this point additional techniques were included such as *gematria*, the computation of the numerical values of letters in order to obtain deeper

4. David Daube, "Rabbinic Methods of Interpretation and Hellenistic Rhetoric," *HUCA* 22 (1949): 239–64, argues quite convincingly that these rules by and large reflect the logic and methods of Hellenistic grammar and rhetoric. Also see Bernard Rosensweig, "The Hermeneutic Principles and Their Application," *Tradition* 13 (1972): 49–76; and J. Weingreen, "The Rabbinic Approach to the Study of the Old Testament," *BJRL* 34 (1951–52): 166–90.

meanings by comparing them with other words yielding the same combination of numbers; *nōtrikon,* the breaking up of one word into two or more, or the reconstructing a word by using the initials of many words, or even suggesting a new sentence by using all the letters of a single word for the initial letters of the other words of the new sentence; *temura,* the permutation of letters by using three Cabalistic alphabets; and *sôd,* the search for the mystical or allegorical sense. These latter departures from Hillel's seven rules, which previously had generally reflected the *peshat,* or direct sense of the text, eventually culminated in the *Cabalistic* system of the thirteenth century.

THE QUMRAN SECT

The Qumran community is best known from the library of Dead Sea Scrolls that were found in 1947 and following years. Most identify the sect that copied these texts with the Essenes mentioned in Josephus, Philo, Strabo, and other ancient writers.

These Essenes were avid readers of the Bible. Several of their commentaries have been found along with the copies of the Scriptures that they made, especially their commentary on Habakkuk. Usually their commentaries quoted a brief passage of one to three verses. This was followed by the phrase "Its *pesher* is . . ." (from the Aramaic word *pǐr,* "to interpret"). The unique aspect of the interpretation that they supplied, especially in the prophetic books, was that everything from the past was transformed and given a contemporary value and meaning. For example, the "righteous" in Habakkuk 1:4 was the "Teacher of Righteousness," or the founder of the Essene sect. And the "wicked that surround the righteous" of 1:4 was the "wicked priest," or "the man of lies," who persecuted the Teacher of Righteousness. The "Chaldeans," or "Babylonians," of 1:6 were the Romans, whom the cult referred to under their biblical name, "Kittim." So went the Pesher exegesis of this cult.

THE JEWISH DIASPORA

The third form of Jewish hermeneutics was that which arose among the Jews of the Diaspora, especially those in Alexandria, Egypt. The most representative person was probably Philo (ca. 20 B.C. to A.D. 50). In this Hellenistic capital, the Jewish canon of Scripture was the Septuagint, the Greek translation of the Bible. Much of the inspiration for the Hellenistic scholarship was derived from the concept that the Scriptures bore a deeper truth, or a spiritual sense, called the *hyponoia.* This deeper truth lay under the human words and had to be uncovered by means of allegorical interpretation.

This allowed the text to say something other than what the words meant. Even Homer and Hesiod, two well-known and beloved Greek authors, were scrutinized for the deeper ethical and cosmic truths contained under the veil of the narratives about the gods and goddesses.

The model that Philo used for his hermeneutical principle was a Platonic division of the world and persons into two spheres—one visible and the other emblematical. The literal meaning of the text was the visible, or that which corresponded to the body; the deeper meaning, or the *hyponoia,* was the symbolical, or that which corresponded to the soul. Whenever Philo was confronted with what he perceived were impossibilities, impieties, or absurdities in the biblical text, he carefully searched for clues such as mysterious numbers, etymologies, peculiar expressions, or the like that could unravel the real teaching of the *hyponoia* behind the surface meaning of the text.[5] Only by taking such steps as these, it was thought in the rarified Hellenistic culture in which the scattered Jewish people were living at that time, could the Jews survive and also make the law of Moses attractive to the Greek mentality.

The New Testament Use of the Old Testament

There are 224 direct citations of the Old Testament in the New Testament, each introduced by a definite quotation formula.[6] Seven other cases are introduced by "and"; nineteen cases of paraphrase or summaries of Old Testament texts appear to depend on quotations; and forty-five instances of striking similarity also indicate that they too depend on the Old Testament. There is little agreement as to the exact number of all the allusions to the Old Testament in the New: C. H. Toy counted 613, Wilhelm Dittmar argued that there were 1640, while Eugene Huehn thought he found 4,105! The point is that the New Testament writers were thoroughly conversant with the Old Testament and felt that they were in direct continuity with it.

How, then, did the New Testament interpret the Old? Did they reflect all three types of Jewish hermeneutics we have just identified, as it is so frequently charged?

5. Philo called this type of interpretation the "Laws of Allegory" (*On Abraham,* 68). Philo's twenty-three rules were arranged under four headings by Charles A. Briggs: Grammatical Allegory, Rhetorical Allegory, Allegory by Means of New Combinations, and Symbolism. See Charles Augustus Briggs, *General Introduction to the Study of Holy Scripture,* rev. ed. (1900; reprint, Grand Rapids: Baker, 1970), pp. 434–36.

6. See Roger Nicole, "The New Testament Use of the Old Testament," in *Revelation and Inspiration of the Bible,* ed. Carl F. H. Henry (Grand Rapids: Baker, 1958), pp. 137–51.

Many of the seven rules of Hillel show up in the teachings of Jesus, for the rules are usually fair to the intentions of the author that wrote in the older testament. Excellent examples of our Lord's practice, in this regard, can be found in Mark 2:25–28 and John 7:23; 10:34–36. But Jesus gives us no examples of midrashic or pesher exegesis. Some have attempted to view the formula in the Sermon on the Mount "You have heard that it was said . . . but I say unto you" as pesher exegesis, much like Qumran used. However, instead of finding a change in the meaning of what the older revelation taught, in each case one finds agreement and further substantiation of the same points made by Moses and the prophets. It is likewise doubtful whether one can find an allegorical approach in Jesus' use of parables. Since the parable is based on the simile, comparisons are direct analogies rather than the more indirect allegories.

What about Paul and the apostles? Did not Paul confess that he had allegorized Sarah and Hagar in Galatians 4:24–31? There is a fine line of distinction between Paul's using allegory and his allegorizing the Old Testament. The critical point is found in Galatians 4:24. There Paul used a most unusual Greek expression which may be translated, "all of which things may be put into an allegory." At that point, Paul had decided that he wanted to get his message over so badly that he decided to adopt, for the moment, the method that so many Jews in his audience were familiar with; however, he never pretended in that act to be interpreting what Genesis had said about these two women or that that is what Genesis taught in a deeper sense of a *hyponoia*. Therefore, on closer examination, this alleged example disappears.[7]

A much more frequent view is that the apostolic writers of the New Testament frequently used the pesher or midrashic method of interpreting the Old Testament. For example, it is said that Paul's use of 1 Corinthians 10:1–6 was based on the rabbinic legend of a rock-shaped, movable well, about the size of an oven or a beehive, that rolled along after the wanderers in the wilderness as they went over hill and dale. Its waters, according to this legend, quenched thirst, healed others, and sent forth rivers with grass at its edges which served as an effective deodorant!

But to confuse the "rock" of 1 Corinthians 10:1–6 with this sort of rolling caisson is to make associations where there are no grounds for doing so. True, the rock is said to be "spiritual," but that denotes its origin, not its nature. It was supernatural in its origins, as the events of Exodus 17:6 demonstrate, when the Lord himself stands by the rock, from which water

7. The other example commonly cited—Paul's comment in 1 Corinthians 9:9 about not muzzling an ox—also fails to show a commitment to allegorizing. See the detailed rebuttal of this example in Walter C. Kaiser, Jr., *The Uses of the Old Testament in the New* (Chicago: Moody, 1985), pp. 203–20.

flowed under his direction. In this sense, then, Christ accompanied Israel with his real presence just as Isaiah saw Christ in the heavenly temple (Isa. 6; cf. John 6:41).

Likewise the argument in Galatians 3:16, wherein Paul insists that the Old Testament did not use the plural word *seeds*, but *seed*, is not a halakic midrash. Paul is making the same point that the Old Testament insisted on when he shows that the word is a singular collective that points first to the representative of the whole group, Christ, and then to all who are incorporated in that collective singular, all who believe (Gal. 3:29). This argument is so endemic to the Old Testament that it is a marvel to hear how many New Testament scholars miss it entirely!

Many other examples could be raised at this point. It is critical to heed the wisdom of Frederic Gardiner as he speaks from more than a century ago:

> In all quotations which are used argumentatively, or to establish any fact or doctrine, it is obviously necessary that the passage in question should be fairly cited according to its real intent and meaning, in order that the argument drawn from it may be valid. There has been much rash criticism of some of these passages, and the assertion has been unthinkingly made that the Apostles, and especially St. Paul, brought up in rabbinical schools of thought, quoted Scriptures after a rabbinical and inconsequential fashion. A patient and careful examination of the passages themselves will remove such misapprehension.[8]

The Interpretive Methods of the Early Church Fathers

The interpretation of the patristic period of the early Christian centuries tended to fall into three main schools: the Alexandrian, the Antiochian, and the Western.

ALEXANDRIAN

The first great teacher of the Alexandrian school was Titus Flavius Clement. Clement adopted the allegorical method of Philo and propounded the principle that all Scripture must be understood allegorically. "For many reasons," he argued, "the Scriptures hide the sense. . . . Wherefore the holy mysteries of the prophecies are veiled in parables" (*Miscellanies* 6.15).

8. Frederic Gardiner, *The Old and New Testament in Their Mutual Relations* (New York: James Pott, 1885), pp. 317–18.

Elsewhere he taught, "Almost the whole of Scripture is expressed in enigmas" (*Stromata* 6124.5–6). The motto of the Alexandrian School was, "Unless you believe, you will not understand" (a mistranslation and misapplication of Isa. 7:9 in the Septuagint).

Clement's disciple Origen (ca. A.D. 185–253/54), was probably the greatest theologian of his day. He is more to be honored for his prodigious work in the area of textual criticism than for his work in biblical interpretation. Origen also followed Philo's allegorical method, but he gave it a biblical basis and declared that Scripture had a threefold sense: the corporeal or fleshly, the psychical, and the spiritual. He outlines these senses in *On First Principles*, the first technical treatise on Christian hermeneutical theory:

> Indeed, it seems to us that the correct method of approaching the Scriptures and grasping their sense is the following, taking it from the texts themselves. In the Proverbs of Solomon we find this kind of directive concerning divine doctrines in Scripture: "And you, write down those things threefold in your counsel and wisdom that you may reply with words of truth to those who ask you [so the Septuagint and Latin of Prov. 22:20–21]. This means, one should inscribe on one's soul the intentions of the holy literature in a threefold manner; the simpler person might be edified by the flesh of Scripture, as it were (flesh is our designation for the obvious understanding), the somewhat more advanced by its soul, as it were; but the person who is perfect and approaches the apostle's description: "Among the perfect we impart wisdom although it is not a wisdom of this age. . . ." [1 Cor. 2:6–7], by the spiritual law which contains "a shadow of the good things to come" [Heb. 10:1]. For just as the human being consists of body, soul, and spirit, so does Scripture which God has arranged to be given for the salvation of humankind. (4.2.4)[9]

All biblical texts, according to Origen, have a spiritual sense, but not all have a literal sense as well. The fact that there were so many stumbling blocks with a strictly literal rendering of the Old Testament forced Origen into reading the text for a deeper understanding. The method Origen used for his biblical hermeneutics was that of *anagōgē*, ("ascent"), the ascent of the soul upward from the level of the flesh to the realm of the spirit.

Origen's successors built on the foundations he had laid. When Origen was driven from Alexandria by persecution, he made his home in Caesarea, in

9. As newly translated by Karlfried Froehlich, *Biblical Interpretation in the Early Church* (Philadelphia: Fortress, 1984), pp. 57–58.

Israel. The most distinguished in this new school at Caesara was Gregory Thaumaturgus, followed by Pamphilus and Eusebius. So devoted was Eusebius of Caesarea to Pamphilus that he is also known as Eusebius Pamphilus.

Eusebius of Caesarea went so far as to claim that Moses and the prophets did not speak to their day at all. Gregory of Nyssa (ca. 335–94) wrote *Life of Moses,* which illustrates the anagogical or mystical understanding of biblical texts in probably its purest form.

It seems quite possible that lists of allegorical equivalents existed for many teachers and preachers who belonged to the Alexandrian school. Such allegorical keys existed in Philo's works, and now the Greek Papyrus Inventory 3718 of the University of Michigan, dated by paleographers to the seventh century A.D., has been uncovered and seems to confirm further the existence of such lists.[10] From this document we learn, for example, that John 2:1 ("On the third day a wedding took place at Cana in Galilee") has the following allegorical values: "the day" is Christ; "the third" is faith; "a wedding" is the calling of the Gentiles; and "Cana" is the church. Proverbs 10:1 ("A wise son brings joy to his father, but a foolish son grief to his mother") is allegorized as follows: "a wise son" is Paul; the "father" is the Savior; the "foolish son" is Judas; and the "mother" is the church.[11] Surely this document, though later than most evidences for the Alexandrian school, no doubt belongs to the same tradition.

The allegorical system of interpretation is built on a doctrine of correspondences. Simply stated, it claimed that for every natural or earthly object or event, there was a corresponding spiritual or heavenly analogue that went with it. The idea was derived in the main from Plato, who divided the world into two: one world was visible and the other emblematic; one actual and the other invisible. In its broadest application, it asserts that all of life and all of secular history is allegorical and descriptive of spiritual or heavenly things; others restrict its application only to Scripture. However, it must be noted that the Bible nowhere teaches such a doctrine of shadows and images or a doctrine of correspondences. Those doctrines are drawn directly from the secular philosophy of the day; therefore, Scripture must not be blamed for advocating such a view.

---

10. Ibid., pp. 79–81.
11. There are sixteen other such verses that this document, fragmentary though it is, also comments on in a similar fashion.

ANTIOCHIAN

Over against the Alexandrian school was the Antiochian. The actual founder of the Antiochian school was probably Lucian of Samosata, around the end of the third century A.D. Others regard the distinguished presbyter Diodorus as the founder around 290. Whichever it may be, there is no doubt about the two greatest disciples of this school: Theodore of Mopsuestia and John Chrysostom.

The watchword of the Antiochian school was *theōria,* coming from a Greek word meaning "to see." They contended that the spiritual sense was in no way separable from the literal sense, as it was in the Alexandrian school. The exegetes of the Antiochian school were united in their single-minded concern to preserve the integrity of history and the natural sense of a passage. But they were just as concerned about being overly literalistic as they were worried over the excesses of allegory and what they called "Judaism." Both extremes were equally dangerous; only *theōria* could offer the middle road out of the dangers on both sides.

Whereas the Alexandrians saw at least two distinct meanings juxta-posed in every event, the Antiochians claimed that an event in Scripture had only one meaning—a meaning that, to the trained eye of the "theoretic" exegete, was at once both literal and spiritual, historical and typological.[12] The Antiochians placed great emphasis upon the idea that *theōria* referred primarily to the fact that there was a vision or perception of spiritual truth at the heart of a historical event that the writers of Scripture were recording, and that this linking of the historical event with the spiritual truth was not a double sense or meaning but a single sense as originally intended by the writers of Scripture.

The fathers of Antioch would not have shared the basic assumptions of modern historical criticism that the science or art of exegesis is essentially a historical discipline rather than a theological one. Instead, *theōria* contended that the historical event itself was the necessary vehicle for that spiritual and theological truth. But unlike allegory, it insisted that the historical event was indispensable as the means God had chosen to bring his eternal truth to expression. Therefore the aim of exegesis was just as involved with spiritual and doctrinal enlightenment as it was with historical and philological facts.

12. The finest discussion of these matters is perhaps John Breck, *The Power of the Word in the Worshiping Church* (Crestwood, N.Y.: St. Vladimir's Seminary Press, 1986), pp. 25–113. Also, Bradley Nassif, "The 'Spiritual Exegesis' of Scripture: The School of Antioch Revisited," *ATR* 75 (1993): 437–70.

WESTERN

The third school in the patristic period was called the Western school. It appeared to be more eclectic in its methods of interpretation, for it harbored some elements of the allegorical school of Alexandria but also embodied some principles from the Antioch. Its most distinctive feature, however, was that it advanced an element that heretofore had not been a major issue: the authority of tradition in interpreting the Bible.

The key representatives of this school are Hilary, Ambrose, and especially Jerome and Augustine. Jerome is famous because of his translation of the Vulgate Bible. Jerome knew Greek and Hebrew, whereas Augustine's knowledge of the original languages was deficient. Accordingly, Augustine specialized more in systematizing the truths of the Bible than he did in their exegesis.

Augustine worked out his hermeneutical principles in his *De Doctrina Christiana*. He stressed there the need for the literal sense as the necessary basis for the allegorical meaning. But Augustine was not hesitant to indulge in a rather free use of the allegorical method. The deciding factor for Augustine, whenever the sense of Scripture was doubtful, was the *regula fidei* ("rule of faith"), by which he meant the collection of doctrines of the church. It is at this point that the authority of tradition began to play a major part in Augustine's interpretive skills, for the proper use of the *regula fidei* presupposes that the meaning of the text has already been established sufficiently in order to recognize that the passage being considered does belong to the doctrine being used as a "rule of faith" to measure it; otherwise, the danger of eisegesis is enormous.

Unfortunately, Augustine argued for a fourfold sense of Scripture: historical, aetiological (an inquiry into the origins or causes of things), analogical, and allegorical.[13] The set of four terms that eventually won out in the Western school of hermeneutics was literal, allegorical, tropological (moral), and anagogical (mystical or eschatological). The standard illustration of this fourfold sense first appeared around A.D. 420 in John Cassian's *Conferences* (14.8): Jerusalem *literally* means the city of the Jews; *allegorically*, Jerusalem is the church (Ps. 46:4–5); *tropologically*, Jerusalem is the soul (Ps. 147:1–2, 12); and *anagogically*, Jerusalem is our heavenly home (Gal. 4:26). Cassian made it clear that the fourfold sense would not fit every passage of Scripture; attention must always be given first to the literal sense as emphasized by the Antiochian school. But the anagogical and allegorical

---

13. Augustine, *On the Usefulness of Belief*, 3.5–9. Augustine worked on this list for the Old Testament based on the Greek technical terms of a rhetorical analysis of language.

senses kept alive the central concerns of the Alexandrians for the mystical and spiritual aspects of the text, while the tropological allowed Jewish and Christian moralists to uncover moral and ethical teachings from the text.

Interpretation of the Bible in the Middle Ages

The Middle Ages were not the most brilliant of times for the church or biblical hermeneutics. In fact, many of the clergy, not to mention the laity, remained in ignorance of what the Bible even said. But to the degree that there was an awareness of the Scriptures, to that degree the fourfold sense of interpretation continued as it had been set forth by the Western church fathers.

What did increase in importance, however, was the principle that the interpretation of the Bible had to adapt itself to the traditions and doctrines of the church. For example, Hugo of St. Victor (1096?–1141), one of the most learned interpreters of Scripture in this period, declared, "Learn first what you should believe, and then go to the Bible to find it there!" However, even though Hugo lived more than a hundred years before Aquinas, he seems to have grasped one of Thomas Aquinas's principles that the clue to the meaning of prophecy and metaphor was the writer's intention, for the literal sense included everything the writer of the sacred text meant to say.

The key figures during the long years between 600 and 1500 were the Victorines from the Abbey of St. Victor in Paris. Hugo, as already mentioned, was probably the greatest of that school, but his disciple Andrew of St. Victor was also rather remarkable in that he furthered this emphasis on the literal meaning by utilizing the Vulgate text for his Christian meaning of the Bible and the Hebrew text for his Jewish explanation.[14]

Another leading light in this period was Stephen Langdon (1150–1228), archbishop of Canterbury. It was he who divided the Bible into its present chapters. But he also interpreted the Bible to conform to the doctrines of the church. For him the spiritual meaning was preferred over the literal meaning, since he thought it more helpful for preaching purposes and for the growth of the church.

The major figure of this whole era, however, was Thomas Aquinas (1225–74). He defended the literal sense as the basis for all the other senses of Scripture. But, he argued, the interpreter must realize that the Bible has

---

14. The best discussion of the exegesis of the Middle Ages is Beryl Smalley, *The Study of the Bible in the Middle Ages* (Notre Dame, Ind.: University of Notre Dame Press, 1964).

symbolic meanings as well, since heavenly things cannot be put in earthly terms without using some form of symbolism. Furthermore, the history of Israel was leading up to the New Covenant. Thus the old doctrine of correspondences, which had been so much at the heart of the allegorical sense of Scripture, was still a major factor in exegesis during the Middle Ages.

One other person stands out in this time frame: Nicholas of Lyra (1270–1340). As a Jewish convert to Christianity, Nicholas had a thorough knowledge of Hebrew. What made his work distinctive was that he, more than any others since the days of the Antiochian school, gave preference to the literal sense of Scripture. Constantly Nicholas urged that the original languages be consulted; and he complained that the mystical sense was being "allowed to choke the literal." Only the literal, he insisted, should be used to prove any doctrine. It was his work that influenced Luther and affected the Reformation so profoundly. As the aphorism says, "Si Lyra non lyrasset, Lutherus non saltasset" (If Lyra had not piped, Luther would not have danced).

Interpretation of the Bible in the Reformation

The groundwork for the Reformation was prepared further by two men from the Renaissance period at the beginning of the sixteenth century: Johannes Reuchlin and Desiderius Erasmus. Reuchlin, an uncle of Philipp Melanchthon, deserves his title as the father of Hebrew learning in the Christian church, for he published a Hebrew grammar, a Hebrew lexicon, a work on Hebrew accents and orthography, and a grammatical interpretation of the seven penitential psalms. No wonder people said of Reuchlin, "Jerome is born again."

Erasmus (1467–1536) published the first critical edition to the Greek New Testament in 1516. He also published his *Annotations,* and his *Paraphrases* of the Gospels, after being stimulated by John Colet (1467–1519) to apply to the Scriptures the new humanistic emphasis of historical and philological learning. Erasmus's Greek New Testament became the basic tool of Luther during his formative and polemical years of the Reformation.

Martin Luther rendered a great service to the German people when he translated the Bible into the German vernacular from the original languages. Luther's hermeneutical rules were better than his practice, for he insisted on the literal meaning as the only proper basis for exegesis. In characteristic phrases Luther defamed the allegorical meaning of Scripture by saying that "Origen's allegories are not worth so much dirt," for "allegories are empty speculations ... the scum of Holy Scripture." "Allegories are awkward, absurd, invented, obsolete, loose rags." To use such a method for interpreting the Bible, he warned, would be to "degenerate ... into a mere monkey game." "Allegory is a sort of beautiful harlot, who proves herself specially seductive to idle men."[15] "The Holy Ghost," declared Luther, "is the all-simplest writer that is in heaven or earth; therefore his words can have no more than one simplest sense, which we call the scriptural or literal meaning."[16]

No less strident in his view on this matter was John Calvin. In his commentary on Galatians 4:21–26 he complained that it is "a contrivance of Satan" to introduce numerous meanings into Scripture. And in his introduction to his commentary on Romans, he warned: "It is an audacity akin to sacrilege to use the Scripture at our pleasure and to play with them as with a tennis ball, which many before have done.... It is the first business of an interpreter to let his author say what he does say, instead of attributing to him what we think he ought to say."

Although the doctrines of *sola fide* and *sola gratia* ("by faith alone" and "by grace alone") constituted the *material* principle of the Protestant Reformation, the *formal* principle was *sola Scriptura*. The norm for all doctrine was not to be found in tradition or the church but in "Scripture alone." That was a reversal of the strategy for interpretation that had begun in the Western school of the church fathers.

Much could be said of Melanchthon, Zwingli, Bucer, Beza, and others, but the principles of interpretation in the Reformation are perhaps best summarized by William Tyndale, translator of the first New Testament printed in English (1525).

> Thou shalt understand, therefore, that the Scripture hath but one sense, which is the literal sense. And that literal sense is the root and ground of all, and the anchor that never faileth, whereunto if thou cleave, thou canst never err or go out of the way. And if thou leave the literal sense, thou canst not but go out of the way. Neverthelater, the Scripture useth proverbs, similitudes, riddles, or allegories, as all other speeches do; but that which the proverb, similitude, riddle, or allegory signifieth, is ever the literal sense, which thou must seek out diligently.[17]

15. Martin Luther, *Lectures on Genesis,* in *Luther's Works,* vols. 1–3, ed. Jaroslav Pelikan (St. Louis: Concordia, 1958– 61), comments on Gen. 3:15–20.

16. As quoted in Frederic W. Farrar, *History of Interpretation,* Bampton Lectures, 1885 (Grand Rapids: Baker, 1961), p. 329.

17. William Tyndale, *The Obedience of a Christian Man* (Parker ed., *Doctrinal Treatises,* 1928), pp. 307–9.

Bible Interpretation in the Post-Reformation Age

The two most significant movements for the history of interpretation in the seventeenth century were pietism and rationalism. Pietism was a protest against the doctrinal dogmatism and institutionalism that exhibited an absence of personal faith and pious Christian practice in one's life-style. In addition to such leaders in the movement as Philipp Jacob Spener and August Hermann Francke, the most valuable contributions to interpretation were made by John Albert Bengel (1687–1752). He was the first to classify the Greek New Testament manuscripts into families, based on their similarities. He also published his famous *Gnomon of the New Testament* (1742), a model for future commentaries, in that it stuck close to the natural meaning of the text while placing some one hundred figures of speech, with definitions, in the appendix of the fifth volume of this commentary.

Philosophical rationalism found its beginnings in René Descartes (1596–1650), Thomas Hobbes (1588–1679), Baruch Spinoza (1632–77), and John Locke (1632–1704). Theological rationalism, however, was directly linked to three chief sources: Christian von Wolff (1679–1754), Hermann Samuel Reimarus (1694–1768), and Gotthold Ephraim Lessing (1729–81). Wolff attempted to tie biblical revelation into natural revelation, while Reimarus made natural revelation the source of Christianity. Lessing added to this new set of problems by arguing that the contingent truths of history could never be a proof for the necessary truths of reason. Thus, to these men can be traced much of what later developed in liberal Christianity, including the destructive form of biblical criticism of the nineteenth and twentieth centuries.

The eighteenth century saw a continuation of both pietism and rationalism. However, pietism at first received more visibility through the ministry and preaching of John Wesley (1703–91). In particular, the Wesleyan revivals called men and women to individual and group study of the Bible.

Nevertheless, in spite of all these gains in Bible study and interpreting the Bible according to its single, natural, or literal sense, an underlying current of protest broke out again in the writings of Immanuel Kant (1724–1804) and Friedrich Schleiermacher (1768–1834). Kant wanted to break into the upstairs "noumenal realm" (the realm of universals, God, and immortality) from the downstairs "phenomenal realm" (the realm of our everyday lives). Ultimately, after writing three books, he decided that this was impossible, except for a "categorical imperative," a "thou shalt," that remained inside all mortals.

Schleiermacher, in contrast, emphasized *Gefühl* (human feelings), as the seat of a person's consciousness of God. Religion no longer was to originate from a book, reason, or anything external; its primary source was to be found in our feelings of ultimate dependence on someone outside ourselves. Sin, in this recasting of definitions and removal of the authoritative source of the Bible, was a disruption of this sense of feeling dependent on God, not a rebellion against a God who had revealed himself in the Scriptures or in Jesus Christ.

Joining Schleiermacher's rejection of a person-religion, as revealed in an event in history or in a book like the Scriptures, was Albrecht Ritschl (1822–89). Ritschl argued instead that Christianity was based on a value judgment. The chief emphasis of religion ought thus to be the moral and ethical value of Christianity.

The climax of much of this line of thought came in Adolf von Harnack (1851–1930). He called for a return to the religion of Jesus, but not a religion *about* Jesus. Therefore, he purged the Gospels of everything he thought represented Hellenistic accretions that had been subsequently attached to them.

There was little time in all these debates for the question as to how we were to interpret the Bible, for as liberalism and modernism grew, interpretation became a nonquestion for most observers and practitioners. The energies of the scholarly world would be taken up with rationalistic, historical, and critical questions about the Bible and the faith until the middle of the twentieth century.

From this point on, the issue suddenly becomes exceedingly complex as a number of agendas arise for scholars and Bible readers to contend with simultaneously. We thus come to the subject of contemporary theories of interpretation, the topic of the following chapter.

The field of biblical interpretation has undergone dramatic changes during the twentieth century, largely because of the work of such scholars as Karl Barth and Rudolf Bultmann, but also because of developments in other fields, including literary criticism, philosophy, and even science. To a large extent, these changes signaled a reaction to the historical-critical method that flourished in the nineteenth century. This method focused on the historical meaning of the Bible so intensely that it often seemed to exclude its present relevance.

The rise of the so-called New Criticism (in American literary studies) shifted attention to the view that literary texts have significance in themselves, that is, independently of the author's original intention. Especially when applied to the Bible, this approach minimizes the historicity of the narratives. In addition, a growing emphasis on the role of the reader has injected a strong element of subjectivity into the work of interpretation. Although it may be true that we should not identify the meaning of a text totally and exclusively with what the author consciously intended to communicate, it is a serious error to dispense with the concept of authorial intention or even to relegate it to secondary importance.

CHAPTER 13

Contemporary Approaches to Biblical Interpretation

Moisés Silva

Key Developments in the Twentieth Century

It is no exaggeration to say that the contemporary interest in hermeneutics signals a new epoch in the scientific study of the Bible.[1] Observers commonly see the beginning of that epoch in the work of Karl Barth (1886–1968), one of the most influential theologians of modern times. Barth had been trained by highly respected scholars in the classical liberal tradition. Nevertheless, as he left the academic world and took up a pastorate, he found that his training was of little value for the life of the church.

Then in 1914 came the tragedy of World War I, which affected theological developments quite directly in Europe. Liberalism, believing that the proclamation of a "social gospel" would bring God's kingdom of peace to the earth, had relied heavily on an optimistic view of human nature. Those hopes were crushed by the war. Barth was of course personally affected by these events. But there was an additional element. He saw his revered teachers adopt political positions that, he felt, contradicted the very principles they had taught. The only course left open to him was to break with his theological past, and this he did in a rather unusual way.

---

1. This chapter is a revised and abbreviated version of Moisés Silva's article "Contemporary Theories of Biblical Interpretation," in *The New Interpreter's Bible*, vol. 1 (Nashville: Abingdon, forthcoming). Used by permission.

Soon after the war, Barth published a commentary on Paul's epistle to the Romans that sent shock waves through academia. As someone said, it was as though a bomb had been dropped in the garden where the theologians were playing. Even today his book seems somewhat strange. It bears little resemblance to a typical exegetical commentary. Instead of focusing on the historical meaning of the text, Barth seemed to ignore that meaning because of his preoccupation with the *relevance* of the text for today's reader. Predictably, the commentary made no advance on Romans scholarship. His bold approach, however, set in motion a dramatic change in the way theologians view biblical interpretation.

Enter Rudolf Bultmann (1884–1976), whose relationship with Barth was rather friendly at the beginning. Primarily a New Testament scholar with special interest in the history-of-religions school, Bultmann shared with Barth a deep concern about the relevance of Christianity. For a variety of reasons, however, they soon parted company. One important factor was Bultmann's adoption of existentialism, particularly as set forth by the philosopher Martin Heidegger.

Among Bultmann's articles, few are more interesting than one entitled, "Is Exegesis without Presuppositions Possible?"[2] The answer to his own question was no. To be sure, Bultmann was not suggesting that readers of the Bible may decide ahead of time the specific meaning of a text: he always believed that objectivity (properly understood) is the aim of the exegete. His point, however, was that all of us bring a worldview to the text and that suppressing that worldview is out of the question. Boldly, Bultmann went on to argue as follows:

> The historical method includes the presupposition that history is a unity in the sense of a closed continuum of effects in which individual events are connected by the succession of cause and effect. . . . This closedness means that the continuum of historical happenings cannot be rent by the interference of supernatural, transcendent powers and that therefore there is no "miracle" in this sense of the word.

Bultmann was quite right to argue that it is impossible to interpret the Bible (or any other text, for that matter) without presuppositions.[3] The kind

---

2. Rudolf Bultmann, "Is Exegesis without Presuppositions Possible?" in *Existence and Faith: Shorter Writings of Rudolf Bultmann*, ed. Schubert M. Ogden (New York: World Publishing, 1960), pp. 289–96. The quotations that follow are from pp. 291–92.

3. This emphasis was hardly unique to Bultmann. Many challenges to the supposed objectivity and impartiality of the scientific enterprise have been raised by scholars in a variety of fields. In theology, note in particular the work of Cornelius Van Til; building on the philosophy of Abraham Kuyper, he developed a system of apologetics in which the role of presuppositions

of neutral objectivity that earlier scholars had aimed for does not exist. It is another issue, however, whether Bultmann's own presuppositions were in line with the presuppositions of the biblical writers. A genuine Christian commitment, one could argue, must be compatible with the faith of those through whom the Christian revelation came. The inevitable question is thus raised, Just what sense does it make to hold on to our Christian identity if our most basic assumptions (the question of God's so-called interference in this world) conflict with those of the Christian Scriptures?

Note, however, that Bultmann's theological aims, like Barth's, were greatly affected by a concern for relevance. If we moderns cannot believe in miracles, he argued, then we must reclothe the primitive Christian message in terms that are understandable to us. This principle led Bultmann to develop a hermeneutical method known as *demythologization* (but perhaps more accurately described as *remythologization*). He believed that the early Christians used mythical categories to give expression to their Easter faith. One must not think of myths as fabrications intended to deceive. Indeed, Bultmann's approach did not precisely involve rejecting the myths but translating them into modern myths. By this Bultmann meant primarily the categories of existentialist philosophy.

Some of Bultmann's disciples, though dissatisfied by various elements in their teacher's ideas, sought to build on those ideas during the 1950s and 1960s. For example, a movement that came to be known as "the new quest for the historical Jesus" attempted to bring the Jesus of history and later Christian faith closer together than Bultmann had allowed. More significant for our purposes was the development of the "New Hermeneutic." This movement had very little to do with the traditional concerns of hermeneutics,[4] except in the rather general sense that it focused on the concept of understanding. Indeed, the scholars representative of the New Hermeneutic seldom discussed the methods by which we determine the historical meaning of the biblical text. They were rather interested in developing a theology that built on certain Continental views about language and thought, mainly the teachings of the existentialist philosopher Martin Heidegger (1889–1976). Because these ideas have broad implications, however, the movement has

was fundamental. Cf. especially his book *The Defense of the Faith*, 3d ed. (Phillipsburg, N.J.: Presbyterian and Reformed, 1967; repr. 1985).

4. The very use of the singular form, *hermeneutic*, reflects the changed perspective. The term "can become coterminous with Christian theology as the statement of the meaning of Scripture for our day" (James R. Robinson, "Hermeneutic since Barth," in *The New Hermeneutic*, vol. 2 of *New Frontiers in Theology*, ed. J. M. Robinson and John B. Cobb, Jr. [New York: Harper and Row, 1964], pp. 1–77, esp. p. 6). The term *hermeneutics* had been used in a much narrower sense to refer to a discipline that deals with the principles and methods of interpretation.

made a significant impact on subsequent discussions about biblical interpretation.

Even as these developments were taking place in biblical and theological scholarship, a parallel set of ideas was coming to expression in the field of literary criticism. As early as the 1930s, an important group of literary scholars were arguing that the traditional approach to criticism was unsatisfactory—in particular, that the usual concern with the author was misguided. What a poet may have intended in writing a poem, for example, may be of some historical interest, but that has little relevance to our understanding of that poem. Known as the New Criticism, this approach treated the text as an artifact independent of its author and thus reopened the fundamental question of textual meaning.[5]

The interrelationship among the disciplines of literary criticism, philosophy, and theology has deeply affected the debate during the past several decades. Perhaps the most prominent figure has been the German philosopher Hans-Georg Gadamer, whose name is usually (though not always fairly) associated with a relativistic approach to interpretation. Indeed, Gadamer went so far as to give the impression that truth in interpretation is a matter of personal taste.[6]

It is important to keep in mind, however, the context of his argument. What Gadamer was most concerned to refute was the claim that the scientific method alone is able to arrive at the truth. At the root of this method is doubt—specifically, doubt about anything that has not been repeated and verified. Accordingly, tradition is "prejudice" and must be eliminated. But the humanities, and history in particular, are not subject to this kind of repetition and verification, so the inference might be drawn that the humanities cannot arrive at the truth.

Over against that viewpoint—which was almost a commonplace a few decades ago and even today continues to be assumed in some quarters— Gadamer argued that "prejudice" cannot be eliminated. Indeed, prejudice is essential for consciousness and understanding. His intent was to rehabilitate tradition (particularly the classics), which provides the presuppositions that can be tested as they are applied to the texts. In the development of his conception, however, Gadamer also placed much emphasis on the view that

5. See the somewhat different discussion of the New Criticism, authorial intent, and the work of Hans-Georg Gadamer, Paul Ricoeur, and E. D. Hirsch in chapter 2, "The Meaning of Meaning."

6. According to Joel C. Weinsheimer, *Gadamer's Hermeneutics: A Reading of Truth and Method* (New Haven: Yale University Press, 1985): "Whether an interpretation is true is a matter of taste. If this seems to denigrate truth, that is only because we have denigrated taste as a cognitive capacity able to arrive at the truth. It is only because we have thought truth is exclusively something that has been or can be proven" (p. 111).

the past is not fixed, that prior events and texts change inasmuch as they are continually being understood. If so, it is not possible to identify the meaning of the text simply with the author's intention.

Ironically, soon after the publication of Gadamer's work, modern science itself underwent some radical changes, largely as a result of the work of Thomas Kuhn.[7] Though many scientists perhaps continue to do their work as though nothing had happened, it is now generally recognized that the sciences are not so fundamentally different from the humanities. The former no less than the latter are deeply involved in hermeneutics, so that no field of study can escape some measure of relativity. In any case, Gadamer's thought had a deep impact not only on philosophical discussion but also on the study of literature and therefore on theological and biblical scholarship.

Particularly well known in this connection is the work of Paul Ricoeur. Among his numerous suggestive ideas, we should take note of his emphasis on the distinction between the relations of speaking-hearing and writing-reading. In spoken discourse, the meaning of the discourse overlaps the intention of the speaker. "With written discourse, however, the author's intention and the meaning of the text cease to coincide. . . . The text's career escapes the finite horizon lived by its author. What the text means now matters more than what the author meant when he wrote it."[8] While Ricoeur himself is not a biblical scholar, he is deeply interested in religious thought, and thus many theologians and biblical students have been affected by his work.

J. S. Croatto is an especially interesting example, since his writings, which arose in the context of Latin American liberation theology, have become popular in the English-speaking world.[9] According to Croatto, the Bible must not be viewed as a fixed deposit that has already said everything— it is not so much that the Bible "said" but that it "says." In committing their message to writing, the biblical authors themselves disappeared, but their absence means semantic richness. The "closure" of authorial meaning results

7. Thomas S. Kuhn, *The Structure of Scientific Revolutions*, 2d ed., International Encyclopedia of Unified Science 2/2 (Chicago: University of Chicago Press, 1967). For the relevance of Kuhn's work to hermeneutics, see Vern S. Poythress, *Science and Hermeneutics: Implications of Scientific Method for Biblical Interpretation*, Foundations of Contemporary Interpretation 6 (Grand Rapids: Zondervan, 1988), chaps. 3–4.

8. Paul Ricoeur, *Interpretation Theory: Discourse and the Surplus of Meaning* (Fort Worth: Texas Christian University, 1976), pp. 29–30; see also *Essays on Biblical Interpretation*, intro. by Lewis S. Mudge (Philadelphia: Fortress Press, 1980). Among various important assessments of Ricoeur, see especially Kevin J. Vanhoozer, *Biblical Narrative in the Philosophy of Paul Ricoeur: A Study in Hermeneutics and Theology* (Cambridge: Cambridge University Press, 1990).

9. J. Severino Croatto, *Hermenéutica bíblica. Para una teoría de la lectura como producción de sentido* (Buenos Aires: La Aurora, 1984), esp. pp. 7, 23–24, 73. English translation by R. R. Barr, *Biblical Hermeneutics: Toward a Theory of Reading as the Production of Meaning* (Maryknoll, N.Y.: Orbis, 1987), pp. ix, 17, 66.

in the "opening" of new meaning. Croatto even tells us that the reader's responsibility is not *exegesis*—bringing out a pure meaning the way one might take an object out of a treasure chest—but properly *eisegesis*, that is, we must "enter" the text with new questions so as to produce new meaning.

One can hardly overemphasize the radical character of these developments. To a practitioner of the historical method it is simply shocking to hear that eisegesis may be a permissible—let alone the preferable!—way to approach the text. For nineteen centuries the study of the Bible had been moving away from just such an approach (especially in the form of allegorical interpretation), so that with the maturing of the historical method a great victory for responsible exegesis had been won. But now we are told that historical interpretation is passé. Although no one is arguing that we should return to the uncontrolled allegorizing of some ancient and medieval interpreters, the search for a meaning other than that intended by the original author does seem, at first blush, as though one is giving up centuries of hermeneutical progress.

The situation is even more complicated. During the past several decades we have witnessed the arrival of a variety of more specialized, even esoteric, approaches, such as structuralism, poststructuralism, deconstruction, and so on (see below, the section "The Role of the Reader"). At their most extreme, some schools question the very foundations of Western thought and thus suggest the impossibility of interpreting texts.

To be sure, there have been some eminent defenders of "authorial intention" in the contemporary scene, best known among them being E. D. Hirsch. Arguing for a distinction between *meaning* (the invariable sense intended by the writer) and *significance* (the changeable application of a writing to different contexts), Hirsch believed he could preserve the crucial role of the original author against the attacks of thinkers like Gadamer.[10] Moreover, the vast majority of books and articles dealing with the biblical text continue to place priority on its historical meaning. Especially puzzling is the fact that, from time to time, one may hear a scholar at a professional meeting who seems to adopt the newer approach at least theoretically but whose actual interpretive work does not appear substantially different from

10. E. D. Hirsch, Jr., *Validity in Interpretation* (New Haven: Yale University Press, 1967). This work has been embraced by many evangelical writers, including W. C. Kaiser, Jr., *The Uses of the Old Testament in the New* (Chicago: Moody, 1985), and some other biblical scholars concerned with the objectivity of historical meaning, but Hirsch has not been well received by the mainstream of philosophical and literary thinkers. For a brief criticism cf. Anthony C. Thiselton, *New Horizons in Hermeneutics: The Theory and Practice of Transforming Biblical Reading* (Grand Rapids: Zondervan, 1992), p. 13. Ben Meyer, *Critical Realism and the New Testament*, Princeton Theological Monograph Series 17 (Allison Park, Pa.: Pickwick, 1989), chap. 2, defends the intended sense of texts while recognizing weaknesses in Hirsch's argument.

standard historical exegesis. In other words, the abandonment of authorial and historical interpretation would be difficult to document from the usual articles published in the recognized journals of biblical scholarship.

Nevertheless, it would be a mistake to infer that the contemporary debates in hermeneutics are mere games. The challenges to traditional approaches are serious and need to be weighed carefully. In particular, these challenges have a direct bearing on the relevance of the Bible for the communities of faith. After all, whatever the scholars may be doing in their specialized publications, one must still ask what the responsibility of preachers is as they address their congregations and also how individual believers should approach their reading and study of Scripture.

The Historical-Critical Method

Before looking in greater detail at the various aspects of the current debate, we must be clear as to what contemporary thinkers are reacting *against*. Unfortunately, the terminology is not always as precise as one might hope. Up to this point I have used phrases such as historical interpretation and biblical criticism to represent the work done by the mainstream of biblical scholarship. Understood in a general way, this approach fairly characterizes the vast majority of scholars, even though their theological views about the character of the Bible may differ from each other in fundamental ways.

At this general level, perhaps the best descriptor is *grammatico-historical exegesis* (cf. the discussion in chap. 1). This old phrase focuses attention on the detailed analysis of the text in conformity with the original language and the original historical situation. The approach was developed in self-conscious opposition both to allegorical interpretation and to the natural tendency we all have to interpret the text on the basis of English (or some other modern language) and in the light of our own customs and experiences. An important corollary of this approach was that before using, say, Romans 8 for our needs, we first had to set aside our prejudices and ask what the original author meant. According to this viewpoint, in other words, only after we have figured out what Paul wished to communicate to the Roman Christians could we claim the right to *apply* that passage to our situation.

Is this viewpoint, however, to be equated with the "historical-critical method"? Many students of the Bible, including important scholars, have rejected this method on the grounds that it is incompatible with the divine character of Scripture. Here is where the confusion begins, since the label *historical-critical* is not used in precisely the same sense by everyone. Scholars who reject the method—usually referred to as conservative or evangelical—certainly do not object to reading the Bible historically. Quite the contrary, they have been among the most vocal supporters of historical, authorial meaning in opposition to current trends. Moreover, there are many aspects of "critical" study in which they have participated without misgivings.[11]

Unfortunately, there is a deep ambiguity in the term *criticism*. Even apart from the negative associations the word has in popular use, several meanings have to be distinguished. In the fields of art and literature, it refers to the skill of evaluating the artistic quality of specific works (the application of this skill to the Bible has been spotty in the past but is gaining momentum). When used with reference to biblical scholarship, the primary idea is that of investigating in scientific fashion the historical origins, text, composition, and transmission of literary documents. For anyone who acknowledges that the Bible has human as well as divine characteristics, there can be no objection to such a study.

The problem arises, however, because of the close ties between the critical method and the principles of the Enlightenment. The priority given to human reason during that period had a direct impact on the issue of religious authority. This priority dictated that the Bible must be treated "like any other book," a phrase that need not be offensive to evangelicals as long as it is also recognized that the Bible is uniquely divine in origin, and so, with respect to this factor, it must be treated *unlike* any other book. As far as the Age of Reason was concerned, however, such a qualification was unacceptable; obviously, it would have been destructive of the principle of human autonomy. Accordingly, "biblical criticism" came to mean not simply the scientific investigation of biblical documents but a method that assumed from the start the critic's right to pass judgment on the truth claims of the Bible. Thus, for example, to interpret the Bible historically meant almost by definition to acknowledge that it contains contradictions; indeed, one of the standard textbooks on the subject simply assumes that any approach is unhistorical that does not accept those contradictions.[12] In short, assent to the view that the Bible was not totally reliable became one of the operating principles of the "historical-critical method."

Anyone who was theologically committed to the traditional view of inspiration obviously could not do "criticism" in this sense. Subsequent

---

11. Among the most prominent conservative scholars of the last two centuries are such New Testament specialists as J. B. Lightfoot, Theodore Zahn, Bernhard Weiss, J. Gresham Machen, Herman Ridderbos, and F. F. Bruce. In the field of Old Testament, note such names as E. Hengstenberg, Franz Delitzsch, Robert Dick Wilson, Edward J. Young, and the Jewish scholar Umberto Cassuto.

12. W. G. Kümmel, *The New Testament: The History of the Investigation of Its Problems* (Nashville: Abingdon, 1972), pp. 29–31 and throughout.

developments, however, created further complications. The formulations of so-called higher criticism[13] regarding the historical origins of biblical documents tended more and more to denigrate the religious value of the Bible. By the beginning of the twentieth century, "conservative" and "liberal" approaches had become almost totally polarized, though the former continued to make extensive use of critical studies insofar as these could be integrated into the framework of theological orthodoxy.

The significance of these developments for the present chapter is fairly obvious, but two points need emphasis. In the first place, the fundamental antitheses between the conservative and critical schools must not obscure their common goal of discovering the historical meaning of the text. Committed to the priority of authorial intent, both sides assumed the need for an objective, unbiased, scientific approach, which was to be distinguished from the task of application.

In the second place, ironically, this history also reminds us that theological commitments can hardly be separated from decisions about hermeneutical principles. Given the claims of the Bible and the religious expectations it places on its readers, theological neutrality is a mirage. This is not to deny that people with widely differing theological assumptions can come to the same conclusions on numerous points of detail and even on significant issues. But we fool ourselves if we think we can approach the text of Scripture with unprejudiced minds. Current emphasis on the role of the reader's "preunderstanding" is therefore a salutary development that must not be ignored.

The Autonomy of the Text

Only a little reflection helps us appreciate that determining the meaning of a text is not a simple task. For interpretation to take place, there must be an author, a text, and an interpreter (reader or hearer), and it is precisely this three-pronged relationship that can create confusion. Even when we come across a statement whose meaning seems to be obvious, the truth is that an enormous amount of previous knowledge and experience has prepared our minds to handle the new information. There is no guarantee, however, that our minds are in fact ready to process the message.

For example, in the process of determining the meaning of a specific

---

13. This label served to distinguish the more controversial approaches from investigations focusing on language and textual transmission, which were referred to as lower criticism.

word or sentence in the letters of Paul, interpreters often ask themselves, Would the original readers of the letter have grasped such-and-such a meaning? Not infrequently, a particular interpretation will be rejected precisely on the grounds that those readers could not have been expected to come up with it. Probably all scholars, however, acknowledge that some of the apostle's richer or subtler nuances would have been beyond the reach of his original audience.

In the introduction to his famous dictionary of New Testament Greek, Walter Bauer raised

> the possibility that what . . . Paul said, conditioned as he was by his Jewish past, was not always understood in the same terms by his gentile Christian hearers, who were also unable to dissociate themselves entirely from their previous ways of thought. . . .
>
> With this in mind we might conclude that sometimes there are two meanings for the same passage, one from the standpoint of the writer and another which becomes evident when one puts one's self in the place of the recipient, intellectually and spiritually; the lexicographer naturally feels an obligation to draw the proper conclusions. The way a passage is understood by its first readers has an immediate effect upon its later interpretation.[14]

While this quotation raises several interesting questions, we need only note at this point the recognition that an appeal to the original readers does not always work—that in itself such an appeal is not a satisfactory solution to problems of interpretation. In other words, we have to cope with the possibility of a "disturbance" between two points of the interpretive triangle: the author and the reader.

The moment we acknowledge this problem, however, we have also conceded that writing a text (and, in somewhat different ways, speaking an utterance) involves a risk. That text, as it were, has a life of its own. It is subject to being understood in ways different from those intended by the author. This complication increases the further that text moves (geographically, temporally, culturally) away from its author, particularly as one loses the possibility of asking the author for an explanation.

Biblical scholars interested in the original author's historical meaning have not been unaware of this problem, though one may wonder whether they have fully realized its implications. For them, however, the problem was simply a challenge to be overcome. At times the definitive solution may be

14. BAGD, p. xxiv.

beyond the interpreter's reach, but one makes every effort to discover what the author meant.

With the rise of the New Criticism, however, American students of literature began to see this phenomenon not as a problem to be solved, but as an opportunity for interpretive creativity.

> Instead of asking "Does the text mean this or that?" with a "Tea or coffee?" intonation, implying that only one answer can be chosen, critics began to ask "Can the text mean this or that?" with a "Cigarettes or liquor?" intonation, seeing a text as a bag of mysteries not advertised on the surface. (There is some debate whether the author knows what he has packed.) To take an example, in Marvell's lines:
>
>> Meanwhile the mind, from pleasure less,
>> *Withdraws into its happiness*
>
> should we understand that the mind is less because of pleasure or that because of pleasure the mind withdraws? The answer now was to be "Both—and what else can you find?"[15]

Freed from the constraints of authorial intent, critics could now proclaim the autonomy of the text. This perspective became dominant in American literary criticism through the 1940s and 1950s, though its impact on biblical scholarship was slow in coming. When finally it did come, other currents of thought, such as French "structuralism," were entering the picture as well.

One of the more controversial elements in this modern emphasis on the autonomy of the text has been the tendency to downplay the extraliterary, particularly the historical, reference of literary works. In other words, an emphasis on the text's autonomy means that the text is cut off not only from the author but also from the extralinguistic reality to which the text apparently refers.

Earlier biblical scholarship (both "liberal" and "conservative") is often criticized for paying too much attention to the question of historicity. If conservative scholars wonder what may have motivated a biblical character to act in a particular way, they are chastised for focusing on the historical event rather than on the literary skills of the biblical author. If liberal scholars take to task a conservative reading of some historical portion, they too are criticized for missing the point. In short, the very asking of historical

---

15. G. W. Turner, *Stylistics* (Baltimore: Penguin, 1973), pp. 100–101. It is important to note that this approach focuses primarily on poetry, a medium that frequently uses deliberate ambiguity and thus invites imaginative response.

questions is seen as basically irrelevant. One proponent of this point of view suggests that "the new literary criticism may be described as inherently ahistorical." He further comments: "Consideration of the Bible as literature is itself the beginning and end of scholarly endeavor. The Bible is taken first and finally as a literary object."[16]

As is usually the case when a provocative new idea makes its appearance and is embraced by enthusiastic thinkers, so the notion of the autonomy of the text has proven to be a mixed blessing. Both positive and negative results are clearly discernible. Predictably, formulations that appear extreme tend to prejudice our acceptance of the positive elements. Even the most objectionable views, however, are likely to reflect some important truth, and the effort must be made to do justice to it.

Undoubtedly, historical exegesis—in spite of some notable exceptions—has tended to ignore the intrinsic literary quality of the biblical documents. The New Criticism and later developments related to it have taught us to pay attention to the "texture" of biblical literature. One must not view this quality as the beginning and end of our interest. To do so would be to undermine what traditionally has been recognized as a foundational element of biblical religion, namely, its essentially historical character.

Nevertheless, biblical narrative, as well as other biblical genres that include historical reference, should not be treated as neutral in character, free of interpretive and theological "bias." (Belief in biblical inspiration and infallibility does not preclude—in fact, it intensifies—the importance of this interpretive element.) Now the theological perspective of the biblical authors is seldom expressed in explicit terms; rather, it is reflected in their composition of the text. Accordingly, close attention to the literary quality of narrative, even if considered in relative independence from its historical reference, can be of immense value in understanding the significance of the history which that narrative presents.

The Role of the Reader

Throughout the centuries people have assumed without a second thought that our perception of data corresponds exactly with objective reality. If we see a black horse, it *must* be black—and it certainly must be a horse! After all, how could the work of science proceed without such assurance? What is true of the scientific observer is presumably true as well of someone interpreting literature, though it might be recognized that in this case there is

16. D. Robertson, "Literature, the Bible as," in *IDP Sup,* pp. 547–51, esp. p. 548.

more room for ambiguity and misunderstanding. Biblical interpreters prior to this century were indeed conscious of the role played by personal bias, but they simply took for granted that such a bias could be overcome.

No more. If there is anything distinctive about contemporary hermeneutics is precisely its emphasis on the *subjectivity* and *relativity* of interpretation. The roots of this perspective may be found in the philosophy of the eighteenth-century thinker Immanuel Kant, whose work was undoubtedly a major turning point between modern thought and everything that preceded it. The effect of Kant's contribution was so broad and so fundamental in character that no intellectual discipline could escape its impact—not even biblical interpretation, though it took a while for exegetes to figure out what was happening.

To put it in very simple terms, Kant was deeply preoccupied with the unbearable tension that the Enlightenment had created between science and religion (i.e., the old philosophical problem of reason vs. faith in new dress). His own solution to the problem was to divorce the two by circumscribing their roles. Religion, for example, must recognize its limitations: the basic tenets of faith cannot be proved by theoretical reason. But science is also restricted: observers never see things as they are in themselves, since the mind is no mere receptacle molded by physical sensations, but rather an active organ that brings order to the chaotic stream of data it confronts. One might as well admit that the world *as we know it* is a world created by our own ordering of sensations.

To be sure, most scientists went about their work in blissful ignorance, but the seed had been sown for fundamental changes in scientific outlook. Indeed, some of the most significant questions debated in twentieth-century philosophy of science have to do with the relativity of scientific thought. As already mentioned, the controversial writings of Thomas Kuhn have served to sensitize the scientific community to this issue. Kuhn's primary interest was to understand the human process by which major changes in our interpretation of the natural world have taken place. If we look carefully, for example, at the "scientific revolution" associated with the work of Galileo and Copernicus, we do not find a simple change of opinion based on the impartial investigation of objective data. In the face of newly discovered evidence, respectable scientists continued to hold on to traditional views of physics and astronomy. They managed to integrate some of the new evidence into their general interpretation; when they could not, they treated the discoveries as anomalies—that is, data for which they did not yet have an explanation.

As part of his argument, Kuhn called attention to a fascinating psychological experiment. In it, the experimenters used a deck of playing cards that contained a few anomalies, such as a *red* six of spades or a *black* four of hearts. The cards were quickly displayed one by one, and the subjects were asked to identify them. As a rule, the subjects did not even seem aware of the anomalies, as *they readily integrated the new facts into a system that was incompatible with those facts.* With somewhat lengthier exposures, most of the subjects became aware of a problem but were unable to figure out the anomaly. With increased exposure they were able to identify the cards correctly. A few subjects, however, even after exposures many times longer than the others required, continued to experience difficulties and became very anxious. For them, it was as though an interpretive inflexibility prevented them from accepting the new evidence.[17]

The old retort, "I've made up my mind—don't bother me with the facts" is usually spoken tongue-in-cheek, but there is more truth to it than we realize or are willing to admit. This is not necessarily a matter of willful obstinacy or dishonesty. When some one misinterprets what we say, we may find solace in the fact that "people hear what they want to hear." Perhaps more accurately, we could say that people hear only what their minds are already prepared to hear. It is impossible for us to understand and assimilate new information except by relating it to what we already know, that is, by filtering it in a way that fits our "preunderstanding." True, some of us are more adept at this process than others. A few wise individuals, moreover, seem able to identify an anomaly quickly, to recognize that they are unable to assimilate it, and to adjust their interpretive framework in a way that takes account of the new fact.

In any case, the point is that contemporary thinkers have learned to accept the role played by the subjectivity of the observer in scientific research.[18] But now, if these things are true in the "hard sciences," where objective measurement lies at the core of research, what shall we say with regard to the humanities, and particularly the interpretation of literature, where the subjective factor seems so much more prominent? For one thing, these developments tell us that we probably have overestimated the differences between the sciences and the humanities. In both of these broad disciplines, the researcher is faced with a set of data that can be interpreted *only in the light of previous commitments;* in both cases, therefore, an interpreter comes—consciously or unconsciously—with a theory that seeks to account for as many facts as possible. Given the finite nature of every human interpreter, no explanation accounts for the data exhaustively. In many, many

17. Kuhn, *Scientific Revolutions,* pp. 62–64.
18. I must leave out of account here many other relevant developments, such as the implications of the uncertainty principle in the field of quantum physics.

cases, it is a set of prior commitments, rather than the weight of the evidence, that determines the final conclusion.

That much is widely agreed upon in our day. Some thinkers, however, will argue that, at least in the case of literary interpretation, we need to go further. It is even suggested that the role of the reader is and should be virtually the only thing that matters. For practitioners of both the historical method (which emphasized the original author's meaning) and the New Criticism (which disregarded any such authorial intention), the one thing that could be relied on was the objectivity of the text. For proponents of "reader-response theory," however—at least in its more extreme forms—there is no such thing as an objective text. Insofar as every reader brings an interpretive framework to the text, to that extent every reader generates a new meaning and thus creates a new text.

Unquestionably, current emphases on the role of the reader cover a wide variety of approaches. Included under the general category are profound insights into the process of interpretation as well as faddish ideas.[19] The danger is that, troubled by what appear to be extreme formulations, we may close our eyes to the invaluable contributions made by this movement. Such an overreaction would be particularly unfortunate in view of the character of Scripture as a book that speaks to all generations. If there is anything demonstrable in the history of biblical study, it is the vigor and consistency with which believers have "actualized" its teachings in their lives.

This relevance is not the result of the Bible's timelessness, if we mean by that a transcendent meaning totally unconditioned by historical factors. On the contrary, the very fact that the biblical message has proven relevant to remarkably diverse people living in different ages and different lands is itself evidence of its essentially historical character. It was given to people in the context of their life situation and it has been readily *contextualized* by subsequent readers. (This is hardly an accident. After all, the same Holy Spirit who authored the Scriptures is the one who brings understanding to the reader.)

Some thinkers view the concept of contextualization as a relativizing of the Bible that deprives it of its authority. Although the concept perhaps has

---

19. Especially influential has been the work of Stanley Fish, *Is There a Text in This Class? The Authority of Interpretative Communities* (Cambridge, Mass.: Harvard University Press, 1980), pp. 301–21. Arguing that his viewpoint does not imply an "infinite plurality of meanings," Fish notes that "sentences emerge only in situations, and within those situations, the normative meaning of an utterance will always be obvious or at least accessible, although within another situation that same utterance, no longer the same, will have another normative meaning that will be no less obvious and accessible" (pp. 307–8). Again, "It is impossible even to think of a sentence independently of a context, and when we are asked to consider a sentence for which no context has been specified, we will automatically hear it in the context in which it has been most often encountered" (p. 310).

been abused in specific instances, biblical authority can just as easily be undermined by minimizing the reality of historical variation. The divine authority of Scripture comes to human beings in their concrete situations, which are susceptible to change. The absoluteness of God's commands thus would not be preserved but rather compromised if those commands were so general and vague that they could be applied to all situations in the same way.

These comments are merely to acknowledge the intense involvement of the reader in the process of interpreting Scripture. We therefore should not be misled by the apparent novelty, or even avant-garde quality, of reader-response theory. While the current preoccupation with the reader is very much a modern phenomenon, the newness in question has to do mainly with the self-conscious and explicit character of the descriptions. But there is unquestionably a reality to which those descriptions point, and that reality has always been there.

Whether we like it or not, readers can—and routinely do—create meanings out of the texts they read. That being so, several options are available to us (other than ignoring the reality!). At one extreme, we could legitimize all reader responses, or at least the ones that have the authority of some community behind them; it is doubtful, however, whether the integrity of Christianity can be preserved within such a framework. At the other extreme, we could attempt to suppress the reader's prejudice. In effect, this is what historical exegesis has had as its goal: total objectivity on the part of the interpreter so as to prevent injecting into the text any meaning other than the strictly historical one. But such objectivity does not exist. And if it did exist it would be of little use, because then we would simply be involved in a bare repetition of the text that takes no account of its abiding value. Paradoxically, the success of modern biblical criticism was obtained at the great cost of losing biblical relevance.

The historical method was not necessarily wrong in *distinguishing* what the Bible originally meant from what it means today. In practice, however, it also *separated* the two. The new approach teaches us, or rather reminds us, that if we do not know what the Bible means today, it is doubtful that we know what it meant then. At all stages of interpretation

> some human need is being met. None of those activities presents us with a "purely objective" truth that is removed from all human questions and concerns. Every request for "meaning" is a request for an application because whenever we ask for the "meaning" of a passage we are expressing a lack in ourselves, an ignorance, an inability to use the passage. Asking for "meaning" is asking for an application of Scripture to a need; we are asking Scripture to remedy that lack, that ignorance, that inability.

Similarly, every request for an "application" is a request for meaning; the one who asks doesn't understand the passage well enough to use it himself.[20]

In short, it is not necessary to suppress our present context to understand the text. On the contrary, at times we need to approach Scripture with our problems and questions if we would truly appreciate what it says. We thus recognize that in order to value the text, the reader must have a commitment to it. Commitment, however, entails preunderstanding, and such a "prejudice" is not only permissible—it is required (cf. Ps. 119:33–34).

Authorial Intent

There is undoubtedly a certain legitimacy to the claim that the meaning of a text should not be identified with the author's intention *in an exclusive and absolute fashion.* Every teacher, for example, has probably experienced the delight of having a student ask a question that rephrases, interprets, and expands points mentioned in a lecture. Although it would not be quite right to say that all of what the student says was part of the teacher's conscious intention, the instructor is happy to take credit for the "new" meaning insofar as it is a legitimate inference from the lecture.

May we say that the student's interpretation was part of the meaning of the lecture? In some sense, yes, and we can confirm that by the very fact that the instructor accepts the interpretation. Now, if the same interpretation had arisen in a conversation among the students, with the instructor being absent and thus unable to confirm it, it would still have been part of the meaning. This potential for semantic expansion increases in the case of a written document, for now the text becomes widely available to a large and diverse number of people who are more and more removed from the original setting of the author. The apostle Paul, let us say, could not have possibly anticipated certain specific problems in twentieth-century Christian churches. Whether we admit it or not, the "application" of a Pauline statement to those problems entails a decision about the meaning of the text that certainly was not part of the original author's conscious intent.

The matter becomes even more pressing for believers who regard God as the ultimate author of Scripture. This conviction of a dual authorship— both human and divine—has been the motivating factor behind many

20. John M. Frame, *The Doctrine of the Knowledge of God* (Phillipsburg, N.J.: Presbyterian and Reformed, 1987), p. 83.

controversial uses of the Bible throughout the centuries. Whether we think of the strand of Jewish exegesis associated with Rabbi Akiba that saw a significant meaning in every detail, or the allegorical program of Origen of Alexandria, or the so-called typological approach of the Antiochenes, or the appeal to *sensus plenior* ("fuller meaning"), or simply the common devotional reading of thousands of believers—all of these assume that there is "more" to the biblical message than is apparent on the surface. Indeed, anyone who believes that the primary origin of the Bible lies in an omniscient and foreseeing God can hardly doubt that there is considerable meaning in the biblical text that the human authors were not fully aware of.[21]

In short, my own position, on both literary and theological grounds, is that the meaning of a biblical passage need not be identified *completely* with the author's intention. It is quite a different matter, however, to suggest that authorial meaning is dispensable or even secondary. While in certain cases the task of identifying what the biblical author meant is not the *only* legitimate way of proceeding, such a task is *always* legitimate and indeed must continue to function as an essential goal.

One could argue that this is the only honest way of proceeding before further considerations are brought to bear on the text. Our social interaction with one another is anchored on this principle. We all recognize that it is utterly unjust to take a conversation we have just heard and interpret the words of one of the speakers in a sense different from—let alone contradictory to—the sense meant by that speaker. Indeed, we routinely denounce that sort of thing as morally unacceptable behavior. The notion that such a principle can simply be suspended in the case of written documents cannot be justified.

Consider, for example, liberation theologian Croatto's claims (summarized early in this chapter) that interpreters should read into the text their own meaning. One suspects that Croatto would be deeply offended (and rightly so) if we were to interpret his book to mean that the best kind of hermeneutics is the fundamentalist approach, or that his book sets forth a capitalist ethics on the basis of which the United States is justified in exerting imperialist pressures on Latin America. Such an interpretation of Croatto's work would be deplorable and a personal insult.

In response, some may suggest that he was only referring to works that have become classics, whether religious or otherwise. There is no doubt a

---

21. Professor Kaiser, to be sure, has argued that the divine meaning must be the same as the human meaning, because otherwise the real meaning of Scripture would be inaccessible to us; after all, grammatico-historical exegesis is our only way to determine what the actual text says (*The Uses of the Old Testament in the New* [Chicago: Moody, 1985], pp. 63–66). For a different viewpoint, see Vern S. Poythress, "Divine Meaning of Scripture," *WTJ* 48 (1986): 241–79.

measure of truth in this argument. A classic work becomes part of a given community whose members, by their very use of the work, put their own impress upon it. But to admit that much is a far cry from what some moderns are suggesting. Can it reasonably be argued that the more important a work is, the greater liberties we may take with it? That the more we respect a text, the more justified we are to disregard its author? Whatever other functions a classic may have, it continues to be a historical document, requiring historical interpretation.

Part of the difficulty arises from the role played by poetry in most societies. When someone composes a poem or produces a painting—that is, a purely artistic product—the creator is indeed inviting us to interpret that work in a variety of ways. But the biblical texts are not art in this sense. Even the Hebrew poetry of the Old Testament cannot be reduced to pure art. Whatever literary and artistic features we may find in Scripture, its primary purpose is to communicate an intelligible message that requires a response.

Conclusion

Exposure to contemporary theories of meaning and interpretation not only can prove dizzying; they can also create personal angst about the uncertainty of human experience. We need to keep in mind, however, that the same scholars who challenge the determinacy and objectivity of meaning go on in their daily lives assuming that interpretation is both possible and essential. They engage in conversations with the clerk at the bank and believe that the money they were told had been deposited is really there. They read the newspaper account of a fire in another city and do not experience an emotional crisis wondering whether the fire actually took place in the very house where they are reading the newspaper. They even write books about the death of the author and expect the reader to believe that they themselves are alive and kicking.

The view that it is the reader who creates meaning calls to mind the old question whether a tree falling in the forest would produce a noise even if no one were there to hear it. Suppose that I receive a letter but, afraid of what it might tell me, decide to burn it without reading it. It could be argued that, since the very reader for whom the letter was intended never read it, there was no meaning at all. Yet the objective reality of the communication is not undone by my reaction—and it certainly would be folly to think that I am personally unaffected as a result of the decision not to read the letter (which happened to say, "You must come in for an operation this Friday or you will die").

For those who believe what the Scriptures claim to be—God's very message to us—an additional consideration must be brought to bear. The Bible presents God as the Creator of all things, including human speech. In fact, the ability of men and women to speak appears to be closely related to their being created in the image of God, who made the world by speaking the word of command, "Let there be. . . ." The reality and effectiveness of human communication is a reflection of God's own speaking. To be sure, human speech is finite and, more important, it is deeply affected by the presence of sin. Not surprisingly, therefore, legitimate questions arise concerning the interpreter's subjectivity, the relative features of culture, and ambiguity in meaning. These are problems that must not be ignored or set aside by an appeal to theological considerations.

Nevertheless, the purposes of the Creator, who is also the Savior, cannot be thwarted by human weakness. Indeed, just as the snow and the rain do not return to the sky without producing fruit on the earth, "so is my word that goes out from my mouth: It will not return to me empty, but will accomplish what I desire and achieve the purpose for which I sent it" (Isa. 55:10–11). For the Christian, the meaning of that revelation is inextricably bound to Christ, who came to "explain" or "interpret" (*exēgeomai*) the Father and whose words, we are assured, will never pass away (John 1:18; Mark 13:31).

The exegetical work of John Calvin, as well as the theological system associated with his name, can be of great help as we seek to develop principles and methods of interpretation. Calvin's commentaries are a model of clarity and excellence. In addition, his work—in line with the doctrine of common grace—reflects a critical appreciation for the contribution that unbelievers can make to our understanding of truth, and this feature has some interesting implications for modern evangelical scholarship.

A more controversial question has to do with the relationship between theology and exegesis: While biblical scholars tend to ignore or even reject the value of systematic theology for their work of interpretation, it can be argued that theological commitments inevitably affect the process of exegesis and that such an influence is both essential and desirable.

Finally, among the doctrinal distinctives of Calvinism, none is more fundamental than an emphasis on the sovereignty of God. An appreciation for this teaching will greatly enhance our understanding of biblical narrative. It will give us, through the concept of covenant, a sharpened focus on the meaning of Scripture as a whole; it will even help us to see how the very process of interpretation itself is guided by the wisdom of a loving and all-powerful God.

CHAPTER 14

The Case for Calvinistic Hermeneutics

Moisés Silva

The word *Calvinistic* in the title of this chapter (aside from any negative connotations it may have for some of my readers) contains an ambiguity. Am I interested here in the methods of interpretation used by John Calvin, the sixteenth-century Protestant reformer, in his biblical commentaries? Or does the title refer to the system of theology that, originating in Calvin's *Institutes of the Christian Religion,* was brought to full expression a century later by the Westminster Confession of Faith?[1]

The ambiguity is deliberate, since one of my aims here is to stress the close connection between biblical interpretation and systematic theology. True, it would be an exaggeration to claim that Calvin's exegetical method in the commentaries is absolutely identical to his use of the Bible in the *Institutes,* but one must recognize that during the course of over two decades, Calvin's theological thought guided his exegesis, while his exegesis kept contributing to his theology. (The first edition of the *Institutes* appeared in

---

1. In North America, the Calvinism of the Westminster Confession was further developed by the Puritans, especially Jonathan Edwards, and then by the great Princeton theologians of the nineteenth and early twentieth century, Charles Hodge and B. B. Warfield. (The latter wrote the article "Calvinism" for *The New Schaff-Herzog Encyclopedia of Religious Knowledge* [reprint, Grand Rapids: Baker, 1977], 2:359–64, which may serve as a brief but useful introduction.) After 1929, this theological tradition became associated primarily with Westminster Theological Seminary, particularly because of the work of John Murray and Cornelius Van Til. There is more than a verbal coincidence between the title of this chapter and that of Van Til's book *The Case for Calvinism* (Philadelphia: Presbyterian and Reformed, 1964).

1536 and the last one in 1559, and during those two decades most of the commentaries were produced.)

Again, some might object that there are significant differences between Calvin himself on the one hand and later Calvinism on the other.[2] These differences, however, have been greatly overstated. While undoubtedly there are features that distinguish these two expressions of theology (e.g., organization, formulation, and emphases), such distinctions are far outweighed by the fundamental commitments that bind them together.

In all fairness, the reader should be warned that I teach in an institution that, having derived its name from the Westminster Confession of Faith, seeks to preserve, propagate, and build on the theological position set forth in that document. In other words, my objectivity in this area is open to challenge. It is also worth mentioning, however, that I was not raised in a Calvinistic environment and that my initial training in theology came from quite a different tradition.

Curiously, the very conservative circles of which I was a part—indeed, American evangelicalism generally—have depended *heavily* on the publications of such Reformed scholars as B. B. Warfield, J. Gresham Machen, and E. J. Young but have at the same time been rather critical of the alleged "cold intellectualism" in the Princeton-Westminster tradition and of the distinctively Calvinistic features in their theology. We should, no doubt, be quick to retain what is valuable and reject what is damaging in any book we read. But is it only a coincidence that this theological tradition, more than any other, has furnished the means to preserve the intellectual integrity of evangelicalism? Does it make sense to cast aspersions at the academic rigor of these scholars while freely using the results of their academic labor? And could it be that what evangelicalism finds objectionable in their theology is precisely what has made possible their contribution to conservative scholarship?[3]

Whatever our answer to these questions, we can certainly profit from considering the distinctives of "Calvinistic hermeneutics." Note, however, that I cannot adequately defend here all of my claims, especially since some of them would require extensive theological discussion. (The occasional biblio-

2. Particularly after the rise of so-called neoorthodox theology in the 1920s, it became common to dismiss the orthodox Calvinist theologians of the seventeenth and eighteenth centuries as scholastics who undermined the spirit of the Reformers. Subsequently, some writers have sought to draw a sharp wedge between Calvin and the Westminster Confession. For a criticism of these attempts, see Paul Helm, *Calvin and the Calvinists* (Carlisle, Pa.: Banner of Truth, 1982).

3. The argument can be made, for example, that Warfield's defense of the infallibility of Scripture, though widely adopted by non-Calvinist evangelicals, is intimately related to his commitment to divine sovereignty. See Cornelius Van Til's introduction to B. B. Warfield, *The Inspiration and Authority of the Bible*, ed. S. G. Craig (reprint, Philadelphia: Presbyterian and Reformed, 1964), esp. p. 66.

graphical comments in the notes may be of value to readers who want to pursue these topics.) Neither do I wish to suggest that the positive qualities described below are the exclusive property of Reformed scholarship. If I set Reformed distinctives over against broad evangelicalism, that is only to clarify the issues. Indeed the Calvinistic tradition, which suffers from its own weaknesses, can learn a great deal from Christians of other persuasions.

Excellence and Clarity of Exposition

In attempting to make the case for a Calvinistic approach to biblical interpretation, one must first appeal to those biblical commentaries for which Calvin became justly famous. Numerous scholars, some of whom would be the least inclined to accept Calvinism, emphasize the extraordinary virtues of Calvin as an expositor of Scripture. A brief summary of opinions on this matter is given by Philip Schaff, the dean of nineteenth-century church historians: "Calvin was an exegetical genius of the first order. His commentaries are unsurpassed for originality, depth, perspicuity, soundness, and permanent value. . . . Reuss, the chief editor of [Calvin's] works and himself an eminent biblical scholar, says that Calvin was 'beyond all question the greatest exegete of the sixteenth century.' . . . Diestel, the best historian of Old Testament exegesis, calls him 'the creator of genuine exegesis.'"[4] It is even more remarkable that professional exegetes in our day continue to refer to Calvin as a matter of course when commenting on the biblical text. Quite likely, no commentator prior to the middle of the nineteenth century is alluded to more frequently than Calvin is, even though he lived long before the development of the modern scientific outlook.

Among the characteristic features of Calvin's work as a commentator, none was so important as his desire for clarity and brevity.[5] These were not two separate aims, but rather twin ideals that he pursued in conscious distinction from much of the work that had preceded him. As he looked back on the history of commentary writing, he found that one theologian stood out as a model for biblical expositors, and that was the fourth-century Antiochene

---

4. *History of the Christian Church* (New York: Scribners, 1885–1910), 8:524–25.
5. In a letter to Simon Grynaeus, he states that the interpreter's principal virtue resides *in perspicua brevitate*. See Richard C. Gamble, "*Brevitas et facilitas:* Toward an Understanding of Calvin's Hermeneutic," *WTJ* 47 (1985): 1–17, esp. pp. 2–3. For what follows, see pp. 8–9 and 13–15. Note also that Calvin's sermons are a rich source for illustrating some of the points made here.

preacher John Chrysostom. When compared against Chrysostom's expositions, most subsequent writers appeared verbose.

But if Calvin objected to long-winded commentaries, the reason was
not merely impatience with a particular kind of style—it was rather the
inevitable obscuring of the message of the text that concerned him. The task
of the expositor is to clarify the author's meaning, whereas the accumulation
of material normally moves the expositor away from this goal. In keeping with
this principle, Calvin consciously refrained from dealing with contrary
opinions (unless the omission was likely to confuse the reader) because, he
said, "I have held nothing to be of more importance than the edification of the
church." Moreover, it appears that he sought to write in a style that was
patterned after the Scriptures themselves. The Bible has its own eloquence,
and it is the eloquence of simplicity.

Not all of Calvin's followers imitated him in this matter. The
seventeenth-century Puritans tended to write massive expositions, such as
William Gurnall's influential work *The Christian in Complete Armour,* a
treatment of Ephesians 6:11–20 filling nearly 1,200 pages. In the last couple
of decades, the growth of learning has led many scholars to write lengthy
works as well. It would be foolhardy to ignore the wonderful contribution
that some of these commentaries have made to our understanding of the
biblical text. Still, Calvin's example should remind us of what our primary
goals ought to be. It is all too easy to become mesmerized either by exegetical
problems or by perceived devotional needs; in both cases, we allow the
central and simple message of the text to recede into the background. If,
however, we keep in mind that no motive is more important than the
edification of the church—the basis for which is God's own teaching and not
our imagination—our efforts will remain focused on the historical meaning
intended by the biblical author.

Common Grace

A second feature that distinguished Calvin's method of interpretation
was his full appreciation of human learning. In this respect, Calvin was a child
of the Renaissance and, inevitably, a follower of the humanism associated with
Erasmus.[6] Prior to devoting his life to the Christian ministry, Calvin had been
trained in the humanities and had produced a detailed commentary on *De*

---

6. Cf. Quirinius Breen, *John Calvin: A Study in French Humanism* (Grand Rapids:
Eerdmans, 1931), esp. chaps. 4–5.

clementia, a philosophical work by Seneca, the first-century Spanish Stoic. Whatever else one may think of that commentary, it clearly reveals that Calvin had honed his skills in the best methods of philological and literary analysis available in his day. It is also clear that subsequently, far from abandoning his devotion to classical scholarship (as Jerome did—or so he claimed), Calvin put it to the service of biblical interpretation and theological reflection. As he expressed it in his *Institutes,* "Men who have either quaffed or even tasted the liberal arts penetrate with their aid far more deeply into the secrets of the divine wisdom." And again: "But if the Lord has willed that we be helped in physics, dialectic, mathematics, and other like disciplines, by the work and ministry of the ungodly, let us use this assistance. For if we neglect God's gift freely offered in these arts, we ought to suffer just punishment for our sloths."[7]

Calvin's use of "secular" learning is of special significance because it reflected a key theological concept, namely, his view of so-called *common grace.* This is a crucial point, because Calvin's approach must be distinguished from that of many evangelical scholars who make free use of critical methods, although these have been developed without consideration of (and sometimes in opposition to) biblical faith. The problem here is not precisely that those methods are used, but rather that they are used without careful reflection on their theological implications. To put it differently, one seldom sees an attempt to integrate the principles of critical scholarship with the distinctives of evangelical thought. The impression one usually gets is that, unless a specific conclusion of scholarship explicitly contradicts a tenet of "conservative" theology, we should freely appropriate the work of "liberal" critics. This attitude, however, can only undermine the integrity of evangelicalism. For one thing, the very coherence of the evangelical faith is likely to be crippled as potentially incompatible elements are adopted without critical evaluation. In addition, the approach does not sit well with nonevangelical scholars, who argue, with some justification, that the credibility of conservative thinking becomes suspect.[8] In short, the desire to gain intellectual respectability backfires.

So how was Calvin's approach different? As is well known, the Swiss reformer actually begins his *Institutes* by discussing epistemology, that is, by reflecting on fundamental questions of knowledge: just how can we know God? His answer was that the knowledge of God and the knowledge of

---

7. John Calvin, *Institutes of the Christian Religion,* ed. J. T. McNeill, trans. F. L. Battles, Library of Christian Classics, vols. 20–21 (Philadelphia: Westminster Press, 1960), 1.5.2 (p. 53), 2.2.16 (p. 275).

8. Though not always accurate or fair, James Barr, in his *Fundamentalism* (London: SCM, 1977), esp. chap. 5, raises questions that demand our attention.

ourselves are intimately related. We cannot look at ourselves, he argued, without thinking about God. "For, quite clearly, the mighty gifts with which we are endowed are hardly from ourselves; indeed, our very being is nothing but subsistence in the one God. Then, by these benefits shed like dew from heaven upon us, we are led as by rivulets to the spring itself." Adam's rebellion has indeed brought ruin, but even that fact "compels us to look upward." Nevertheless, he continues, we cannot expect to acquire a clear knowledge of ourselves—inclined to hypocrisy as we are—unless we look carefully at God and judge everything by his standard.[9]

In subsequent chapters, Calvin has much to say about general revelation and about the other evidences of God's grace toward humanity in general. Of special interest for us is his discussion of human learning as a gift of the Spirit:

> Whenever we come upon these matters [art and science] in secular writers, let that admirable light of truth shining in them teach us that the mind of man, though fallen and perverted from its wholeness, is nevertheless clothed and ornamented with God's excellent gifts. If we regard the Spirit of God as the sole fountain of truth, we shall neither reject the truth itself, nor despise it wherever it shall appear, unless we wish to dishonor the Spirit of God. For by holding the gifts of the Spirit in slight esteem, we contemn and reproach the Spirit himself. . . . No, we cannot read the writings of the ancients on these subjects without great admiration. . . . But shall we count anything praiseworthy or noble without recognizing at the same time that it comes from God? . . .
>
> But lest anyone think a man truly blessed when he is credited with possessing great power to comprehend truth under the elements of this world, we should at once add that all this capacity to understand, with the understanding that follows upon it, is an unstable and transitory thing in God's sight, when a solid foundation of truth does not underlie it.[10]

It is essential to appreciate Calvin's balance here. By recognizing at once the marvel and praiseworthiness of human learning as a divine gift and also its basic instability because of the fallen and perverted mind of the sinner, he could do justice to the coherence of biblical teaching.

Later Reformed theology was not always consistent in working out the implications of Calvin's ideas. In the Dutch tradition, however, the doctrine

9. Calvin, *Institutes*, 1.1.1–3 (pp. 35–39).
10. Ibid. 2.2.15–16 (pp. 273–75).

of common grace has played a prominent and controversial role, and few have given more attention to it than Cornelius Van Til. Without attempting to describe his apologetic system, we can point out certain features that are of particular relevance for biblical hermeneutics. Central to Van Til is the importance of presuppositionalism and thus the denial of neutrality. Over against the traditional Roman Catholic distinction between nature and grace—and thus between reason and faith—Van Til argued that, according to Scripture, all human beings know full well that God exists and that his power has created the world. Moreover, they have all rejected that knowledge and rebelled against him (see esp. Rom. 1:18–23). Human beings, therefore, are not neutral observers who need to be persuaded by rational arguments that there is a God so that subsequently they can be brought to faith. On the contrary, they have willfully chosen to worship the creature rather than the Creator, and their whole thinking is distorted by the presence of sin. Readers will note that this formulation is a specific way of expressing the Reformed doctrine of total depravity.

Van Til also emphasizes, however, that men and women are not as sinful as they can be. Sin has fundamentally distorted, *but it has not destroyed,* their character as God's image. To put it differently, they are inconsistent both in their thinking and in their conduct. It is here that the doctrine of common grace shows up clearly. God continues to send the warmth of the sun to this sinful world; he restrains the progress of evil in human society as a whole. As a result, many people who reject God's goodness manage to live apparently exemplary lives, even though their starting point should lead them to full-blown licentiousness. Similarly, their minds, in spite of having spurned the knowledge of the only wise God, accomplish remarkable feats. To the extent that they make intellectual progress, however, they do so only on "borrowed capital," that is, by taking advantage of the very truths that contradict their most basic commitments. Van Til's approach, then, while radically antithetical, does not at all lead to contempt for human accomplishments but makes possible our appreciation for them.[11]

The history of both "Old Princeton"[12] and Westminster exemplifies

---

11. See Cornelius Van Til, *The Defense of the Faith,* 3d ed. (Phillipsburg, N.J.: Presbyterian and Reformed, 1967), chap. 8, and idem, *Common Grace* (Philadelphia: Presbyterian and Reformed, 1947), esp. p. 91, on the correlative character of common grace and total depravity, and p. 95: "It is only when we thus press the objective validity of the Christian claim at every point, that we can easily afford to be 'generous' with respect to the natural man and his accomplishments. It is when we ourselves are fully self-conscious that we can cooperate with those to whose building we own the title." In other words, only if we are unequivocal about the antithesis between the Christian and the non-Christian viewpoint can we legitimately use the work of the unbeliever.

12. Ironically, much of Van Til's work was developed in reaction to the apologetic system that had been used at Princeton. By correcting certain features in the Warfieldian

how this Calvinistic understanding of sin and common grace can affect theological scholarship. The best-known theologians at Princeton Theological Seminary, Charles Hodge (1797–1878) and Benjamin B. Warfield (1851–1921), were not only fully abreast of contemporary progress in the sciences, the humanities, and critical biblical scholarship;[13] it is also clear that their own thinking was positively affected by those advances. While much of their work had a strong polemical edge against unbelieving scholarship, it is undeniable that their own thought reflected an integration of so-called secular knowledge and biblical teaching. This was not, however, a naive adoption of unbiblical ideas but simply a recognition that Calvin was right when he insisted that the Spirit of God is the source of all truth and so we should not despise it, regardless of where it appears; in other words—to use a profound saying that for some has become an ambiguous cliché—"all truth is God's truth."

Specifically in the area of biblical scholarship, no one illustrates this principle more powerfully than J. Gresham Machen (1881–1937), who taught New Testament at Princeton until 1929 and then, because of the modernist-fundamentalist conflicts at that time, led several of his colleagues to found Westminster Theological Seminary in Philadelphia. Having studied under some prominent liberal theologians in Germany, Machen struggled with the challenges brought against the authority of Scripture and the integrity of his evangelical faith. In the end he became the leading intellectual opponent of modernism while at the same time making full use of the biblical scholarship associated with that movement.

Machen's two major works—*The Origin of Paul's Religion* (1925) and *The Virgin Birth of Christ* (1930)—are brilliant examples of evangelical learning, in both of which he attempts to dismantle, logically and patiently, major tenets of liberal theology. It is important to emphasize, however, that Machen did not master liberal scholarship merely to build his intellectual ammunition against it (as more than a few evangelical scholars are wont to do). The seriousness with which he regarded that scholarship is evident on every page, as is the fact that he was not at all afraid to *learn* from it. Not surprisingly, a well-known German critic who disputed Machen's thesis wrote a twenty-page review article of *The Virgin Birth of Christ* in which he described the book as "so circumspect, so intelligent in its discussions, that it must be recognized unqualifiedly as an important achievement."[14] Still, we

approach, however, Van Til was in effect bringing the apologetics of American Calvinism closer to its theology.

13. Cf. Mark Noll, "The *Princeton Review*," *WTJ* 50 (1988): 283–304, esp. pp. 302–3.
14. F. Kattenbusch, review in *TSK* 102 (1930): 454.

cannot ignore the fact that Machen himself viewed his approach as "a thoroughgoing apologetic."[15]

In our day, the growing presence of evangelicals in scholarly forums, such as the Society of Biblical Literature, is at once encouraging and unnerving. Sometimes, one fears, this participation reflects a tendency to compartmentalize the intellect. Commitments to biblical truth are suspended, not merely for the temporary purposes of discussion, but perhaps as a reflection of the view that the issues have a neutral character. (In principle, it is quite proper to engage nonevangelical scholars on a whole spectrum of issues without having to raise the bugaboo of theological presuppositions. The question is rather whether, in the process of discussion, our own thinking becomes independent of our faith.) Apart from the occasional disagreement expressed against specific ideas, one seldom detects an effort, or even a desire, to assess the fundamental character of critical approaches in the light of evangelical faith. Perhaps a consideration of how Calvin and some of his successors have related their study of Scripture to human learning can assist modern conservative scholars as they seek to do the same in these challenging times.

Theology and Exegesis

As the previous section may have suggested to the reader, it is not feasible to separate biblical interpretation from theology.[16] The relationship between exegesis and systematic theology has been one of the most controverted issues in the history of biblical scholarship. Many scholars doubt, or even deny, that it is really possible to use the Bible for the purposes of developing a systematic theology. In their view, the various biblical authors had different, indeed incompatible, theologies, so that the attempt to treat them as a unity can result only in distorting the text.

Evangelical biblical scholars would reject such an approach, but that

15. J. Gresham Machen, *The Virgin Birth of Christ*, 2d ed. (New York: Harper & Row, 1932), p. x. It is sometimes thought that Machen's approach was incompatible with Van Til's; this misconception is adequately handled by Greg L. Bahnsen, "Machen, Van Til, and the Apologetic Tradition of the OPC," in *Pressing Toward the Mark: Essays Commemorating Fifty Years of the Orthodox Presbyterian Church*, ed. C. G. Dennison and R. C. Gamble (Philadelphia: Committee for the Historian of the Orthodox Presbyterian Church, 1986), pp. 259–94. More to the point, however, I wish to suggest that the character of what Machen and some of his predecessors did (whatever their conscious apologetic principles) provided a model for Van Til regarding the proper use of unbelieving scholarship.

16. Some of the material in this section is taken from "Systematic Theology and the Apostle to the Gentiles," forthcoming in *TJ*.

does not mean they have a particularly high view of systematic theology. Exceedingly few of them show much interest in the subject—if anything, it is viewed with suspicion. Particularly objectionable to them would be the suggestion that systematics should influence our exegesis. Yet that is precisely the claim that I wish to make, and here again Calvin provides a remarkable model.

The first edition of the *Institutes* was published when Calvin was a very young man, and the subsequent revisions and expansions reflect both his growing knowledge of historical theology (references to the Fathers and medieval theologians increase sharply in each subsequent edition) and his greater attention to exegetical work. No one is likely to argue that these two sides of his work were independent of each other—as though he forgot about his theology when he exegeted (and that is why his commentaries are good!) or did not pay attention to the Bible when he did theology (and that is why the *Institutes* are so bad!). My own thesis is that both his expositions and his theology are superb precisely because they are related.[17] But even if one has little use for Calvin's system, I wish to suggest that exegesis stands to gain, rather than to lose, if it is consciously done within the framework of one's theology.

Such an approach, admittedly, seems to be diametrically opposed to the aims of grammatico-historical exegesis. Three centuries ago scholars were already arguing, with great vigor, that systematic theology—especially in its classical form—must be kept quite separate from biblical interpretation. Indeed, it was not difficult to show that theological biases had frequently hampered the work of exegetes, even to the point of distorting the meaning of the text. True "historical" exegesis was understood, more and more, as interpretation that was not prejudiced by theological commitments. Leopold Immanuel Rückert, in the preface to his 1831 commentary on Romans, stated that the biblical interpreter must abandon his own perspective.

> In other words, I require of him freedom from prejudice. The exegete of the New Testament as an exegete . . . has no system, and must not have one, either a dogmatic or an emotional system. In so far as he is an exegete, he is neither orthodox nor heterodox, neither supernaturalist nor rationalist, nor pantheist,

17. Calvin himself saw his two projects as complementary. In his introductory statement to the *Institutes* ("John Calvin to the Reader"), he tells us that his aim in this work was to help "candidates in sacred theology" grasp "the sum of religion in all its parts" and thus guide them in the study of Scripture. Such a compendium would make it possible for him, when writing his commentaries, to avoid long doctrinal discussions. In his view, the proper use of the commentaries presupposed that the student was "armed with a knowledge of the present work, as a necessary tool" (pp. 4–5).

nor any other ist there may be. He is neither pious nor godless, neither moral nor immoral, neither sensitive nor insensible.[18]

One of his contemporaries, the great New Testament exegete Heinrich August Wilhelm Meyer, expressed the same idea as follows:

> The area of dogmatics and philosophy is to remain off limits for a commentary. For to ascertain the meaning the author intended to convey by his words, impartially and historico-grammatically—that is the duty of the exegete. How the meaning so ascertained stands in relation to the teachings of philosophy, to what extent it agrees with the dogmas of the church or with the view of its theologians, in what way the dogmatician is to make use of it in the interest of his science— to the exegete as an exegete, all that is a matter of no concern.[19]

Today most people would view these two formulations as strikingly naive. But we should not be fooled. The underlying commitment is alive and well. Moreover, there are plenty of exegetes around who might vigorously disown these statements, but whose work, unwittingly perhaps, is a perfect expression of the same viewpoint. In contrast, I wish to argue that proper exegesis should be informed by theological reflection. To put it in the most shocking way possible: my theological system should tell me how to exegete. Can such an outrageous position be defended? Three considerations make that position not merely defensible but indeed the only real option.

In the first place, we should recognize that systematic theology is, to a large extent, an exercise in contextualization, that is, the attempt to reformulate the teaching of Scripture in ways that are meaningful and understandable to us in our present context. Sometimes, it is true, theologians have given the impression (or even claimed) that their descriptions are no more and no less than the teachings of Scripture and that therefore, being independent of the theologian's historical context, those descriptions have permanent validity. But the very process of organizing the biblical data—to say nothing of the use of a different language in a different cultural setting— brings to bear the theologian's own context. Even Charles Hodge, who claimed with great pride that no original ideas had ever been proposed at Princeton,[20] was a truly creative thinker, and his *Systematic Theology* reflects

18. W. G. Kümmel, *The New Testament: The History of the Investigation of Its Problems* (Nashville: Abingdon, 1972), p. 110.

19. Ibid., p. 111.

20. The reference was specifically to the journal edited by him (see Noll, "The *Princeton Review*," p. 288). Hodge was clearly not as naive as those words might suggest. His use of hyperbole was intended to focus on doctrinal substance, not on the way the doctrines were formulated. Indeed, some modern writers have emphasized—and severely criticized—the

through and through an innovative integration of some strands of nineteenth-century philosophy with classic Reformed theology.

Intrinsically, there is nothing objectionable in attempting to understand and explain an ancient writing through contemporary categories, yet biblical scholars often assume that such an approach is off-limits. As one writer has put it, biblical exposition should be done "in terms of what the text itself has to say.... Resorting to ... later formulations is not only anachronistic but obscures the impact of the specific words [the writer] chose to use on the occasion. In short, such an approach is methodologically indefensible."[21] In fact, however, the very use of English to explain the biblical text means resorting to subsequent formal expressions. If a modern writer wishes to explain Aristotle's thought, for example, we all acknowledge not only the legitimacy but also the great value and even the necessity of doing so by the use of contemporary philosophical terms that make it possible to express clearly an ancient thinker's writings. Someone who merely restated Aristotle's teachings using Greek words, or even strict English equivalents, would fail to explain those teachings precisely because no attempt was made to contextualize them.

In the second place, our evangelical view of the unity of Scripture demands that we see the whole Bible as the context of any one part. An appeal to the study of Aristotle is of help here too. The modern scholar looks at the whole Aristotelian corpus for help in understanding a detail in one particular work. To the extent that we view the whole of Scripture as having come from one Author, therefore, to that extent a systematic understanding of the Bible contributes to the exegesis of individual passages. Admittedly, there are some real dangers in this approach. On the basis of a questionable reading of Romans 12:6, Christians have often appealed to "the analogy of faith" in a way that does not do justice to the distinctiveness of individual writers of Scripture. Moreover, it is all too easy to fall into the trap of eisegesis, of reading into a particular text some broad theological idea because we (sometimes unconsciously) want to avoid the implications of what the text really says. It is therefore understandable that Professor Kaiser wishes to restrict the principle of the analogy of faith to the end of the interpretive process, and then only as a means of summarizing the teaching of the pas-

---

innovative use of Scottish realism made by Hodge. Without denying that some aspects of that background had a negative effect, attention must be paid to the positive benefits as well. In any case, it is my opinion that the indebtedness of Hodge and later Princetonians to realism has been greatly overstated.

21. Clinton E. Arnold, review of Silva, *Philippians,* in *Critical Review of Books in Religion 1991* (Atlanta: Scholars Press, 1991), p. 232.

sage.[22] To do so, however, is to neglect God's most important hermeneutical gift to us, namely, the unity and wholeness of his own revelation.

Third, and finally, my proposal will sound a lot less shocking once we remember that, as a matter of fact, everyone does it anyway. Whether we mean to or not, and whether we like it or not, all of us read the text as interpreted by our theological presuppositions. Indeed, the most serious argument against the view that exegesis should be done independently of systematic theology is that such a view is hopelessly naive. The very possibility of understanding anything depends on our prior framework of interpretation. If we perceive a fact that makes sense to us, the simple reason is that we have been able to fit that fact into the whole complex of ideas that we have previously assimilated.

Of course, sometimes we *make* the fact fit our preconceptions and thus distort it. The remedy, however, is neither to deny that we have those preconceptions nor to try to suppress them, for we would only be deceiving ourselves. We are much more likely to be conscious of those preconceptions if we deliberately seek to identify them *and then use them* in the exegetical process. That way, when we come across a fact that resists the direction our interpretation is taking, we are better prepared to recognize the anomaly for what it is, namely, an indication that our interpretive scheme is faulty and must be modified. In contrast, exegetes who convince themselves that, through pure philological and historical techniques, they can understand the Bible directly—that is, without the mediation of prior exegetical, theological, and philosophical commitments—are less likely to perceive the real character of exegetical difficulties.[23]

The old advice that biblical students should try as much as possible to approach a text without a prior idea as to what it means (and that therefore commentaries should be read after, not before, the exegesis) does have the advantage of encouraging independent thinking; besides, it reminds us that our primary aim is indeed to discover the historical meaning and that we are always in danger of imposing our meaning on the text. Nevertheless, the advice is fundamentally flawed because it is untrue to the very process of

22. See above, p. 195. Other writers are more negative and tend to undermine the coherence of Scripture. Cf. Calvin R. Schoonhoven, "The 'Analogy of Faith' and the Intent of Hebrews," in *Scripture, Tradition, and Interpretation: Essays Presented to Everett F. Harrison by His Students and Colleagues in Honor of His Seventy-fifth Birthday*, ed. W. W. Gasque and W. S. LaSor (Grand Rapids: Eerdmans, 1978), pp. 92–110, esp. p. 105. Much more helpful is Henri Blocher, "The 'Analogy of Faith' in the Study of Scripture: In Search of Justification and Guidelines," *SBET* 5 (1987): 17–38, though I would wish to go a little further than he does.

23. It is perhaps worth pointing out that long before Rudolf Bultmann's emphasis on "preunderstanding" became a popular topic, and certainly before Thomas Kuhn challenged the neutrality of scientific investigation, Cornelius Van Til had, in an even more radical way, exposed the role of presuppositions for all of life.

learning. I would suggest, rather, that a student who comes to a biblical passage with, say, a dispensationalist background, should attempt to make sense of the text assuming that dispensationalism is correct. I would go so far as to say that, upon encountering a detail that does not seem to fit the dispensationalist scheme, the student should try to "make it fit." The purpose is not to mishandle the text but to become self-conscious about what we all do anyway. The result should be increased sensitivity to those features of the text that disturb our interpretive framework and thus a greater readiness to modify that framework.[24]

God's Sovereignty in Biblical Interpretation

Calvin's theology is best known for its stress on divine sovereignty, particularly as expressed in the concept of election. For some people, it seems, that is all Calvin ever taught. The truth, however, is that few theologians have ever been as balanced as Calvin was in attempting to give expression to the breadth of biblical teaching. The very fact that he wrote commentaries on almost every book of the Bible should tell us something. Even in the midst of a strongly polemical setting, he managed to do justice to every theological *locus.*

His balance, ironically, is especially evident in his treatment of election. This doctrine does not have as prominent a place in the *Institutes* as many imagine. It is not covered in the first chapter or even the whole of book 1. One has to wait until book 3, chapters 21–24, and then the treatment consists of forty-four pages, that is, less than 5 percent of the *Institutes.* In short, an understanding of Calvin's doctrine of divine sovereignty in salvation must take into account its place in the context of his whole teaching.

From another perspective, however, this doctrine was even more important to Calvin than is usually understood. The fact that it is not the explicit subject of discussion in books 1 and 2 hardly means that it is not present there. Quite the contrary. Calvin's sense of awe at the majesty and power of God over all creation pervades the whole of his theology in a fundamental way. In the Calvinistic tradition, this emphasis has played a significant role. Far from annulling human freedom, total divine sovereignty alone makes such freedom meaningful.[25] Because only in God do we have our

24. Or so one hopes—at this point, unfortunately, psychological disposition usually takes over!

25. As the Westminster Confession of Faith 3.1 puts it: "God from all eternity did, by the most wise and holy counsel of his own will, freely and unchangeably ordain whatsoever comes

being, freedom outside of his will is inconceivable. Accordingly, in light of our slavery to sin (Rom. 6:16–23), it would be illusory to think that salvation can in any way depend on our effort or will (John 1:13; Rom. 9:14–16).

What bearing does all this have on biblical hermeneutics? Here we can only illustrate its significance with a few examples. With regard to exegetical practice, the doctrine of divine sovereignty makes us particularly sensitive to God's workings in the history of redemption. Biblical narrative nowhere suggests that the divine plan has been frustrated by historical accidents or human obstinacy. While free agency and responsibility are clearly assumed, these human realities are pictured as coordinate with—indeed, subsumed under—God's will for his people. Particularly striking is the description of events in the days of Rehoboam, whose wicked decision to oppress Israel led to the tragedy of a divided kingdom: "So the king did not listen to the people, for this turn of events was from the LORD, to fulfill the word the LORD had spoken to Jeroboam" (1 Kings 12:15). The prophets understood well the significance of this principle:

> The LORD Almighty has sworn,
>   "Surely, as I have planned, so it will be,
>   and as I have purposed, so it will stand."
>
> For the LORD Almighty has purposed, and who can thwart him?
>   His hand is stretched out, and who can turn it back?
>   (Isa. 14:24, 27)

The relevance of these concepts shows up unexpectedly in various exegetical problems. Redaction criticism, for instance, has pointed out how frequently biblical narrative colors and interprets historical events. For some scholars, this characteristic is evidence that the biblical writers have tampered with the facts. Conservative writers, afraid of the implications, often shy away from such features and prefer to downplay, for instance, the differences among the Gospels. Evangelical scholars who do appreciate the value of redaction-critical work have not always grappled with the serious theological challenges posed by this method. The Reformed view of biblical inspiration, however, goes hand in hand with a Reformed understanding of history. The

to pass; yet so as thereby neither is God the author of sin, nor is violence offered to the will of the creatures, nor is the liberty or contingency of second causes taken away, *but rather established"* (my emphasis). This is hardly the place to provide a philosophical defense of the doctrine. Note, however, that a world in which *anything at all* happens outside of God's will is a world inevitably ruled by contingency, that is, radical uncertainty. If God knows for certain what will take place in the future (the fundamental biblical doctrine of foreknowledge), then everything that takes place must take place. If, however, events are not "determined" in this sense, then God cannot know what will take place, which means that *anything* could take place and God would be quite limited as to what he could do about it.

God who controls the events of history is the God who interprets those events in Scripture, and thus there can be no inherent contradiction between the two. This hardly means that we are free to adopt any approach to the narratives even if it undermines their reliability, nor does it provide an automatic solution to many difficult problems. It does mean that we need not "protect" the credibility of Scripture by making sure it conforms to our expectations of history writing.[26]

The doctrine of divine sovereignty also helps us to appreciate the centrality of the concept of covenant in Scripture. As is well known, Calvinism has been characterized by an approach known as covenant theology. The term means different things to different people; it indeed serves as a conceptual umbrella covering a rich and wide variety of emphases, some more clearly biblical than others. Fundamentally, it refers to God's dispositions in his plan of salvation. It is God who takes the initiative in forming a people for himself, so that the assurance "I am your God and you are my people" provides an all-pervasive principle throughout the history of redemption (from Gen. 17:7–8 to Rev. 21:3).

Faithfulness to this principle should guide the exegete at numerous points, as in passages that bear on the doctrine of salvation by grace, or when assessing the function of the Mosaic law in relation to the Abrahamic covenant. The concept evidently has much to say about questions related to prophecy and the place of the people of Israel. Traditionally, for instance, dispensationalism has drawn a sharp distinction between Israel and the Christian church. More recent writers have recognized the important features common to both,[27] but the organic unity of God's people throughout the ages is a distinctive emphasis of covenant theology. This emphasis in turn has profound implications for our understanding of ecclesiology (including questions of church government, baptism, etc.), of the Christian's use of the Old Testament, and much more.

Finally, an appreciation for the Calvinist or Augustinian (indeed, Pauline!) doctrine of divine sovereignty and election affects one's understanding of biblical interpretation as such.[28] It is not sufficient to recognize God's lordship over biblical history without submitting ourselves to that lordship as interpreters. It is in fact quite silly, on the one hand, to affirm that the events

26. I have dealt with this problem in "Ned B. Stonehouse and Redaction Criticism," *WTJ* 40 (1977–78): 77–88, 281–303.

27. In chap. 8, Professor Kaiser seeks to mediate between dispensationalism and covenant theology on this issue. However, it is not clear to me that he has done justice to the emphasis with which the New Testament writers see the promises of the Old Testament fulfilled in the context of the church.

28. For a discussion of this issue in a more general way, see Vern S. Poythress, "God's Lordship in Interpretation," *WTJ* 50 (1988): 27–64.

related in Scripture, as well as the actual writing of Scripture, are a fulfillment of God's will and, on the other hand, to assume that our interpretation of that material has some sort of neutral character or independent status. Yet some students of the Bible seem to think (or at least act as though they think) that God, after "going to all the trouble" of overseeing the writing of Scripture by many different individuals over the course of many centuries, decided to sit back and watch believers try to figure out what to do with it! On the contrary. The divine purposes are being worked out even now in the lives of believers as they listen to the Scriptures no less than when God was overseeing the events of redemptive history.[29]

The implications of this truth are rather far-reaching. If nothing else, it should fill us with a sense of humility before the majesty of God; truly, without him we can do nothing (John 15:5), and it is only because he anoints us with his Spirit that we are able to learn at all (1 John 2:27). This principle also sheds light on the difficult questions surrounding such issues as the proper application of Scripture, the use of allegorical methods, and the claims of reader-response theorists. While I certainly share Professor Kaiser's concern with cavalier approaches to interpretation (especially in the typical church Bible studies), my attitude toward the common, popular study of Scripture is not nearly as negative. Although I neither approve of nor recommend Origen's hermeneutical methods, it is difficult for me simply to dismiss them without inquiring into the burning question: Why has allegorical interpretation spoken to the hearts of countless believers, and why does it continue to meet their needs even today?[30] Similarly, a reader-response approach to the Bible, especially when set in opposition to historical interpretation, can easily turn into a subtle excuse for finding what we are looking for, but the challenges of this new approach are too serious to be ignored.

If we believe that God's Spirit is truly at work as Christians explore the Scriptures, and if his work of illumination is something more than identifying a bare textual meaning, isn't it true, then, that interpreters in some sense contribute to the meaning of the Bible out of their own context? God does not wait for us to become masters of the grammatico-historical method before he can teach us something. Instead, he uses even our ignorance to lead us to himself, and he resorts to our capacity for associations as a means for us to

29. It is important to point out again that, paradoxical though this principle may sound, the doctrine of divine sovereignty in history does not suspend human agency, nor does it render God in any sense responsible for human sin. Similarly, the truth of God's sovereignty in our Christian lives neither guarantees that we will always do right nor excuses us when we do wrong.

30. See my discussion in *Has the Church Misread the Bible? The History of Interpretation in the Light of Current Issues* (Grand Rapids: Zondervan, 1987), chap. 3.

recognize his truth. Not long ago I heard a learned minister testify to God's goodness through a rather trivial incident. In the midst of some discouragement, he came across a branch lying on a sidewalk. For some reason, this sight reminded him of the biblical image of the staff and the various comforting truths associated with it. Shall we condemn this pastor for his allegorical interpretation of that event and forbid him to use such hermeneutics again? Or shall we recognize that God, in his wisdom and sovereignty, delights to work in us at whatever level of "receptivity" we may find ourselves?

The fact that God can use our ignorance for his glory is hardly enough reason to remain as ignorant as we possibly can—and we dare never appeal to divine sovereignty to excuse our failings. Accordingly, we should do everything in our power to help believers appreciate the historical character of Scripture and thus respect its original meaning. But in their reading of the Bible, especially for devotional purposes, do believers need to suppress associations that come to mind? Previous exposure to other parts of Scripture inevitably lead us to make literary connections that are, from an exegetical point of view, far-fetched. But as long as those connections are *biblical* in their own right—and as long as we do not make improper claims about the original meaning of the text we happen to be reading—need we really condemn this commonplace (and "time-honored"!) approach to finding solace and direction from Scripture? Should not a sense of God's power in our interpretive activity affect our evaluation of this problem?[31]

There is one more conclusion to be drawn from the doctrine of divine sovereignty. If we acknowledge God's lordship in our interpretation, that fact should fill us with confidence. There are, to be sure, many things to discourage us as we study the Scriptures. Acquainting ourselves with the history of biblical interpretation can sometimes be a baffling experience. Looking around us even today, we become aware of theological controversies among believers and find them unspeakably depressing. As though all that were not enough, when we examine ourselves, we detect ignorance,

---

31. For similar reasons, I am open to the possibility that the apostles, in their reading of the Old Testament, may have *on some occasions* used approaches that do not conform to what we usually consider "proper" exegetical method. Without for a moment blurring the distinction between the inspired work of the biblical writers and our use of Scripture, we must do justice to the continuity between them and us. Cf. G. Vos, *Biblical Theology: Old and New Testaments* (Grand Rapids: Eerdmans, 1948), 325–36. Professor Kaiser finds it difficult to believe that Paul could have used a scriptural argument that did not represent the *sensus literalis* of the Old Testament text (see above, chap. 10). Admittedly, if the apostolic understanding of the Old Testament was fundamentally flawed, it would be impossible to defend the intellectual viability of the gospel message. But neither can I accept that an occasional "free" or "associative" type of allusion—even in the midst of serious argumentation—necessarily reflects a misunderstanding of the literary work being alluded to. See my article "The New Testament Use of the Old Testament: Text Form and Authority," in *Scripture and Truth,* ed. D. A. Carson and J. W. Woodbridge (Grand Rapids: Zondervan, 1983), pp. 147–65, esp. pp. 157–58.

selfishness, obduracy, deceit—a host of obstacles that would seem to wipe out all hermeneutical hopes!

Yet, a moment's reflection on God's sovereignty ought to set us straight. If the Lord assures us that his word will not return to him empty but rather will accomplish what he desires (Isa. 55:11), can we really think that his purposes will be thwarted and that his people will fail to "reach unity in the faith and in the knowledge of the Son of God" (Eph. 4:13)? May we learn to do all our biblical interpretation with assurance that "he who began a good work in [us] will carry it on to completion until the day of Christ Jesus" (Phil. 1:6).

The central issue on biblical interpretation has not changed much in the last century and a half: It is to leave us alone in company with the author. However, there has been one enormous change: The hermeneutical task is not finished until we have wrestled with the problem of applying the text. Augustine sensed this very dilemma long ago, but his solution led to the unsatisfactory proposal of three additional senses for Scripture along with the literal sense: the allegorical, the tropological, and the anagogical.

As a test case for determining if the single meaning, but multiple significance/application theory advocated here is workable, we use the four major "interpretations" given over the centuries for the parable of the laborers in the vineyard (Matt. 20:1–16). The conclusion is that these are nothing more than four different applications of one principle.

Assistance is given to the interpreter to move from the single meaning/principle to the application/significance of a text. These may be found (1) in the explicit statements made in the pericope, (2) in editorial summaries given by the author of Scripture, (3) in the motivational clauses attached to biblical commands, and (4) in illustrations of the way that Scripture uses earlier Scriptures for edification.

Care must be exercised to apply the principles behind biblical commands, to separate what is taught from what is merely recorded in the Bible, and not to universalize and generalize biblical promises beyond their intended scope of reference.

CHAPTER 15

Concluding Observations

WALTER C. KAISER, JR.

In 1859 Benjamin Jowett, then the Regius Professor of Greek at the University of Oxford, published an essay on the interpretation of Scripture. In that oft-cited work, Jowett set forth the thesis that "Scripture has one meaning—the meaning which it had in the mind of the Prophet or Evangelist who first uttered or wrote, to the hearers or readers who first received it." Interpretations, later accretions of ideas attached to a biblical text, or even later traditions were to be set aside in favor of the single meaning of the text, according to Jowett. "The true use of interpretation is to get rid of interpretation and to leave us alone in company with the author."[1]

In spite of the years that have come and gone since these words were first published, the central issue in interpreting the Bible has, in some ways, not moved very far away from Jowett's central thesis. Yet, in other ways, we have moved beyond that target by leaps and bounds. In our day, the increased role of culture, imagination, the progress of revelation, the role of the listener and reader, the development of the historical-critical theories of understanding the Bible, and new discoveries, both in the scientific world and in communication theory, have complicated matters beyond what Jowett could have even imagined.

1. Benjamin Jowett, "On the Interpretation of Scripture," *Essays and Reviews,* 7th ed. (London: Longman, Green, Longman and Roberts, 1861), pp. 330–433, quotations on pp. 378, 384.

But the more one studies this problem of the single versus the multiple meanings of the text, the more one is tempted to say this quarrel, at least as it exists among evangelicals that hold to the same concepts of revelation, is a disagreement over the problem of *application,* more than over the goal of *interpretation* per se.

One of the largest gains, and unusual benefits, that we have seen in the second half of the twentieth century is the emphasis on the idea that our hermeneutical task is not finished until we, as the contemporary audience, have applied the meaning that we think the author is communicating. There should never have been a gap left, yawning between what the text meant and what it means, between the then and the now. That gap may be said to exist only as an academic convenience for a momentary separation in the task of examining two inseparable parts of one whole. But what the scholar separates, in order to undertake certain studies under the microscope, must be put back together by the interpreter with the understanding that the process is not completed until the text has been applied and its contemporary significance understood.

This writer sympathizes with those interpreters who struggle with, on the one hand, what often appears to be rationalistic attributions of the single meaning of the text on the one hand and, on the other hand, the need for discerning some spiritual significance and theological relevance of narratives as disturbing as the drunkenness of Noah, the murder of Sisera, the choice of Esther as queen, or a psalm of cursing such as Psalm 137. Everyone must struggle with the dilemma of reconciling the surface meaning of such biblical narratives and texts with the need to show how these same texts edify contemporary readers.

Augustine's Solution to the Meaning Problem

Augustine sensed the very dilemma we have posed here. As we saw in chapter 12, he proposed that, since Scripture was given for the edification of the church, in addition to the literal sense the interpreter could appeal to three additional senses, each one corresponding to a virtue. The *allegorical* sense corresponded to faith, since it taught the church what to believe; the *tropological* sense was the expression of love, since it taught individuals what they should do; and the *anagogical* sense pointed to the future and to the virtue of hope. But very seldom at the hand of the best practitioners of the patristic and medieval church did a text exhibit more than one other meaning beside the literal meaning. It appeared that what was being advocated was that a text must also be applied to real-life situations, as well as understood in its original context. One of those applications could be doctrinal (note Augustine's expression of "faith"), another could be moral and ethical (cf. "love"), or another could be related to eschatology and the future ("hope"). Each of the three senses was usually coordinated one at a time with the literal sense, which suggests that the words *meaning* and *sense* were being used by them in ways that approximate our idea of "significance" and "applications," without replacing the meaning that the text bore in and of itself.

But it hardly seems fair to equate such patristic systems of interpretation with the oft-quoted remark of C. S. Lewis, who commented in his own book *Till We Have Faces,* "An author doesn't necessarily understand the meaning of his own story better than anyone else."[2] A multiple application based on a literal understanding of a text is not the same thing as a plurality of truth or distinct levels of meaning in one and the same passage (or even an unknown principle), being applied in ways that are not governed by anything in the text.

A Test Case for Understanding the Single Meaning

Let's explore the difference between (1) a single principle or truth taught by the human writer of Scripture (which may have multiple applications in the areas of doctrine, morals, and future things) and (2) multiple levels of meaning for a given text. As a test case, consider the parable of the laborers in the vineyard (Matt. 20:1–16).[3]

In this parable, the owner of the vineyard hires day laborers to work all day in his vineyard at the standard wage of a denarius. However, he needs additional workers, so he returns to the marketplace at nine, noon, three, and five o'clock and hires whatever workers he can find. The only promise he gives to those he hires at nine, noon, and three is that he will give them what is fair. As for the workers he hires at five o'clock, he sends them into the vineyard without any promise as to what wages they will receive.

When it comes time to pay each worker, the owner instructs the foreman to pay the workers, beginning with those hired last at five o'clock. Instead of giving them only one-twelfth of a denarius, he pays them a full

2. W. H. Lewis, ed., *Letters of C. S. Lewis* (New York: Harcourt, Brace and World, 1966), p. 273.
3. For the outline of the various views set forth here, I am beholden to David C. Steinmetz, "The Superiority of Pre-critical Exegesis," *Theology Today* 37 (1980): 27–38, especially pp. 33–35.

day's wage. When those who have worked from early in the day until the end receive the same amount—a single denarius—instead of a bonus they are hoping for after they see what those who were hired last received, they begin to complain. The owner, however, replies that he has cheated no one, for he has paid them what he had promised. If he wishes to be generous to those who came last, that's his privilege. Jesus contends that that is how the kingdom of God is.

Two main interpretations of this parable exist: one tracing its lines of thought back to Irenaeus, and the other to Origen. Origen saw this parable as a comment on the various ages at which one is converted to Christ, with "day" equaling the life span of an individual. Some have served Christ and loved him since their childhood; others have come to Christ late in life. Irenaeus, however, saw the parable as a reference to the history of salvation, in which various epochs of history—Adam to Noah, Noah to Abraham, Abraham to David, and David to Christ—were depicted, with the owner of the vineyard as the Trinity as a whole and Christ as the foreman. The workers hired at the eleventh hour were the Gentiles. Payday came with the resurrection from the dead, when the Jewish laborers complained because they bore the heat of the day, but God was equally generous to all alike.

The fourteenth-century anonymous author of the *Pearl* proposed a third interpretation, applying this parable to the death of a young girl. Even though she was only two years old and entered the vineyard, as it were, at the eleventh hour (five o'clock), God did not withhold his mercy from her as well.

John Pupper of Goch, a fifteenth-century Flemish theologian, suggested a fourth interpretation. He thought the parable attacked the doctrine of proportional rewards in heaven for service done for Christ. The only people who contend for proportional rewards for work done are those who were the first workers hired in the vineyard. But our Lord rejected the idea that twelve times the work must receive twelve times the payment.

In 1525 Martin Luther enlarged on his earlier essential agreement with this Flemish theologian's interpretation by insisting that the parable celebrated God's goodness that resisted all religion based on law-keeping and good works. All workers are unworthy, even if they are not all unworthy for the same reasons. Salvation is not grounded in human merit but only in the goodness and grace of God.

The question for us now is whether these four major uses of the parable represent four different levels of meaning, or whether they represent one meaning with four different applications? The evidence favors the latter, namely, four applications of one principle, which in turn derives from the parable's natural, or literal, meaning. All four agree that the parable is a declaration of God's generosity and grace to undeserving workers. Once this goodness of God is grasped from the passage, the relationship of Jew to Gentile, the problem of an early decease or a late conversion, and questions about proportional rewards can be seen as various ways in which the same principle is applied to different cultures, times, settings, needs, and personal problems. Each application is effective and valid as long as it is a further explication of the common, underlying principle within the text.

Therefore, rather than speaking of levels of meaning in a text, perhaps what has been sought throughout the history of interpretation, including the present concern with the reader's response, are levels of application and significance, or what one writer has referred to as "consequent meanings." Common to all four major interpretations of this parable was the fact that the vineyard owner was a gracious, generous, benevolent dispenser of his gifts. If that principle were not foundational to all else that was being said, there would be no way of validating the application that was being made. There would also be no authority behind the application that was being attributed to this parable.

Identifying and Using General Principles

A major part of the art of interpreting passages is the task of moving from the specific matters mentioned in the biblical text to the general principles that stand behind those specifics.

Jack Kuhatschek, relating a family story, reminded me of a similar experience that we had as a family with our youngest son, Jonathan.[4] When he grew old enough to be asked to give thanks for the food at the table on behalf of the whole family, Jonathan was delighted. He took the occasion to itemize practically everything that was on the table in his prayer, much to the chagrin of his older brothers and sister. "Thank you for the salt and the pepper. Thank you, Lord, for our spoons, forks, and knives. Thank you for the milk, the salad, the bread. . . ." On and on he went in a veritable marathon as the food began to get cold. Finally—and mercifully in the views of his now exasperated siblings, Jonathan concluded with "Amen."

Instructions to Jonathan on the merits of praying for the food in general either were not understood or were deliberately avoided. However, as the months passed, one day he suddenly surprised us by saying, "Dear

4. Jack Kuhatschek, *Applying the Bible* (Downers Grove, Ill.: InterVarsity Press, 1990), pp. 51–52.

Lord, thank you for the food on our table. In Jesus' name, Amen." Jonathan had learned how to generalize.

The legitimacy of such generalizing practices is affirmed repeatedly in the biblical text itself. Not only did God summarize his whole law in ten commandments (Exod. 20:1–17; Deut. 5:6–21), but he also gave seven other summaries of the law as well. Psalm 15 preserves God's law in eleven principles; Isaiah 33:15 sets it forth in six commands; Micah 6:8 encapsulates it in three commands; Isaiah 56:1 further reduces it to two commands; and Amos 5:4, Habakkuk 2:4, and Leviticus 19:2 each summarize the whole law in one general statement.

Jesus himself continued this same tradition by summarizing the whole law in two principles: "Love the Lord your God with all your heart and with all your soul and with your mind. . . . And the second is like it: Love your neighbor as yourself" (Matt. 22:37–40; Luke 10:26–28; Deut. 6:5; Lev. 19:2, 18).

In order to identify general principles in a biblical text, interpreters must ask three questions: Does the author explicitly state a principle in the passage at hand? If not, does the broader context reveal such a general principle? And, Does the specific situation of the text contain any reasons, explanations, or clues that could suggest what motivated the writer to be so concrete, rather than abstract, in mentioning the specific illustrations that he chose?

The search for principles in the biblical text is usually not to be found in isolated words or phrases, and it certainly is not to be found in verses used as proof-texts. Such principles, rather, are set forth as the controlling theses in paragraphs, chapters, sections of a book, and even whole books of the Bible.

Examples of a specific principle explicitly stated in a teaching block of text are numerous. For example, in the fifth of Zechariah's eight visions, there is the enigmatic appearance of a solid golden lampstand flanked by two olive trees. When the prophet asked, "What are these?" he was told, "This is the word of the LORD to Zerubbabel: 'Not by might nor by power, but by my Spirit,' says the LORD Almighty" (Zech. 4:6). This is the controlling general principle for the whole passage: what is accomplished will not come by the hands of the political or religious leaders; it will come by means of the Holy Spirit.

In 1 Corinthians 8, Paul addresses the matter of buying food that has been sacrificed to idols. In verse 9 he states explicitly the relevant principle: "Be careful, however, that the exercise of your freedom does not become a stumbling block to the weak." This idea governs whatever freedom or restrictions would be exercised in buying meat at markets that were known to have connections with the temple and its sacrificial routine.

But what if the text never comes out and says directly what the principle is? This often happens in narrative texts, which tend to state things indirectly, rather than putting matters into direct speech, as it does in prose. Here we may rely on the general context to help us.

Genesis 37–50 records the story of Joseph. Only once or twice in the long recounting of that story are we given the clue that explains what this whole episode is all about and why God would have wanted it recorded in his Word. When Joseph disclosed himself to his brothers, he concluded, "And now, do not be distressed and do not be angry with yourselves for selling me here, because it was to save lives that God sent me ahead of you. . . . God sent me ahead of you to preserve for you a remnant on earth and to save your lives by a great deliverance" (Gen. 45:5, 7). Joseph later repeated this theme to his brothers, telling them, "You intended to harm me, but God intended it for good to accomplish what is now being done, the saving of many lives" (Gen. 50:20). The principle of God's overriding providence, then, is the key to interpreting this narrative about Joseph. Only the context will reveal it, even though each individual episode or pericope within the story may not directly draw that principle as its own conclusion.

In other cases, neither a direct statement of a principle nor even an indirect statement within the broader context appears. What are we to do then? Here the search for a general principle must proceed with the thoroughness of detectives sifting through a murder scene for clues.

Other literary devices come into play at this point, such as motivational clauses, which are often attached to biblical commands.[5] Motive clauses may be one of at least four kinds (the motive clause appears in italics):

1. *Explanatory*—an appeal to common sense of the listener or hearer. "If anyone curses his father or his mother, he shall be put to death. *He has cursed his father or his mother, and his blood will be on his own head*" (Lev. 20:9; cf. Deut. 20:19; 20:5–8).
2. *Ethical*—an appeal to the conscience or to moral sentiments. "When you build a new house, make a parapet around your roof, *so that you may not bring the guilt of bloodshed on your house if someone falls from the roof*" (Deut. 5:14–15).
3. *Religious and theological*—an appeal to the nature and will of God. "The priests must not desecrate the sacred offerings the Israelites present to the LORD *by allowing them to eat the sacred offerings and so*

5. The first scholar in modern times to point out the function of the motive clause was Berend Gemser, "The Importance of the Motive Clause in Old Testament Law," in *VT*, supp. vol. 1 (1953): 50–66.

bring upon them guilt requiring payment. I am the LORD, *who makes them holy"* (Lev. 22:15–16; cf. Deut. 18:9–12).

4. *History of redemption*—an appeal to the Lord's interventions in the history of his people. "When you harvest the grapes in your vineyard, do not go over the vines again. Leave what remains for the alien, the fatherless and the widow. *Remember that you were slaves in Egypt. That is why I command you to do this"* (Deut. 24:21–22).

Once we have identified the general principle, we must apply that principle to our lives, basically by applying it either to the *same* situation that the text of Scripture introduces or to one that is *similar* or *comparable*.

The book of James illustrates both ways of applying a general principle. This book might well be an abstract of a series of sermons preached by James and based on a portion of the Holiness Law, in this case taken from Leviticus 19:12–18. Every verse in this passage except verse 14 is either cited or alluded to in the book of James.[6]

In James 2:1, the author repeats a portion of the "royal law of love" from Leviticus 19:15, which reads, "Do not show partiality." The principle is clearly stated. It is also illustrated in James 2:2–7 by talking about how the church should seat a rich man wearing a gold ring and fine clothes and how it should seat a poor man in shabby clothes. Now if the poor man is seated on the floor and the rich man is given a good seat, would that not be an improper type of discrimination that offends the principle of not showing partiality? But such seating arrangements do not exhaust all the contexts in which the same nondiscriminatory policy could be urged with just as much authority and biblical precedence. In fact, James 2:9 repeats the principle once more and shows how it fits in with the much larger principle "Love your neighbor as yourself" (Lev. 19:18b; James 2:8). Every other situation that might lead to injuring my neighbor (defined in Scripture as anyone in need) would be one to which the meaning of this passage could legitimately be extended.

The application may thus involve the identical situation where African-American worshipers or those of other ethnic backgrounds would be segregated in a poorer seating area in the church in order to give preference to the dominant racial group or the class that "carries the bills" of that church. Or the application can reach out beyond that identical or same situation to others that are similar and comparable in that they too fall under the outlines of the general principle that has been observed.

6. See Luke T. Johnson, "The Use of Leviticus 19 in the Letter of James," *JBL* 101 (1982): 391–401. Also see "Applying the Principles of the Ceremonial Law: Leviticus 19 and James," chap. 11 in Walter C. Kaiser, Jr., *The Uses of the Old Testament in the New* (Chicago: Moody, 1985), pp. 221–24.

Special Situations in Applying Biblical Principles

Thus far, we have argued that we must identify the general principle in a passage and seek to apply it to the same or to a similar situation in our modern lives. But oftentimes we run into special sorts of problems when we attempt to apply certain types of literary forms in the Bible, especially biblical commands, biblical examples, and biblical promises. Each of these situations should be examined for the one or two unique features that each introduces.

BIBLICAL COMMANDS

First, let us consider the commands of the Bible. It is often reported that the Old Testament has over 600 commands. Actually the number used in rabbinic circles was 613, but nowhere has the text of the Old Testament authorized that exact number. Some modern believers observe some of these commands but not others. Is there any real basis for such a distinction, or is it left up to the instincts and feelings of each believer?

The Scriptures themselves offer us a way of sorting out which commands have continuing relevance for our lives and which ones have been rendered obsolete by God's having declared their usefulness to have ended. Even though the law is one, we are taught in the Bible to distinguish at least three different aspects in that one law. Jesus authorized such a stance when he used the concept in Matthew 23:23 that some things in the law were "weightier" than others. It is this ranking and prioritizing within the law that establishes the *moral* aspect of the law as higher than its *civil* and *ceremonial* aspects. In this verse justice, mercy, and faithfulness are heavier and weightier than the rules for tithing spices, evidently because the former reflects the nature and character of God.

When God gave the instructions for the tabernacle with all its utensils, services, rituals, and ministers, he implicitly put his own time for expiration on it by informing Moses that he was to make and set up all these things "exactly like the *pattern* shown you on the mountain" (Exod. 25:9, 40). Since Moses constructed these things according to the pattern, or model of what God showed him, he obviously did not have the real. That remained apart from Moses and Israel with God, even as the writer of Hebrews later argued (Heb 8:5). When the real analogue for each of these models or patterns came in Christ's first coming, including his death, resurrection, and ministry, we can assume that everything in the old ceremonial law was jettisoned except the application of those principles to our day. The exact forms, rituals, and facilities had been replaced, just as Hebrews 9–10 also taught.

Some teach that only those commands that are restated in the New

Testament are normative for today. But there are many commands that still give directions for the believer that cannot be found in the New Testament, touching on marrying close relatives, rape, bestiality, abortion, and the like. Jesus himself treated the Old Testament as authoritative; therefore we ought to do the same.

A biblical command may still be in force in the principles it embodies even though obedience to that precise form of the law may not be required today. Thus the command to leave the edges of one's fields unharvested so that the poor might glean them is not operative for those who do not live in agricultural areas or own farms; however, even apart from the agricultural economy reflected in the law in Leviticus 19:9–10, we are still obligated to express, in ways open to us, our practical concern for the poor and the alien in our midst. Numerous other texts in the Bible make the same point (e.g., Exod. 22:21–27; Deut. 14:28–29; 15:12–14).

Even the *lex talionis* ("eye for an eye and tooth for a tooth") is still in effect. That law was given to the "judges" (Exod. 21:6; 22:8–9) as a stereotypical formula meaning, in effect, "make the punishment fit the crime"; do not try to take undue advantage of the situation. In settlements on automobile accidents, for example, the rule is to be bumper for bumper, fender for fender; don't try to get tuition for schooling out of the incident.

Whereas the Old Testament tends to give rather specific laws, for which we must formulate or identify the general principle, New Testament commands tend to be stated in their general form already, and thus our task is to identify specific situations where that principle applies today. For example, when Paul urges, "Rejoice in the Lord always. I will say it again: Rejoice! Let your gentleness be evident to all" (Phil 4:4–5), the general nature of these commands is evident. What is not so evident are all the specific ways in which we must manifest the joy of the Lord and gentleness to all with whom we deal.

BIBLICAL EXAMPLES

The second area where the application of general principles becomes enormously important is that of biblical biography and examples. Since one-third of the Bible is cast in historical narrative, this is no small problem.

Some passages tell us precisely what should be approved and imitated about the person being presented. In the case of the two midwives in Egypt, Shiphrah and Puah, it was their fear of God (Exod. 1:17). True, they also lied to Pharaoh, the morality of which the text does not address. This shows us that we must make a distinction between what the Bible approves and what it reports.

In other instances, what is to be taught from the biblical examples is raised implicitly, but not explicitly. For example, what are we to make of the example of Jonah? Never does the text pause and moralize, or point out something good or bad about his character. But the message is implicit from the Lord's question with which the book concludes, "Should I not be concerned about that great city?" (Jonah 4:11). Jonah's reluctance to minister on God's behalf to a people that had treated his people so badly is a central point in the book without the book's saying so in so many words. Thus, we are left with the question dangling over us, as it did over Jonah. God's grace is much larger and more magnanimous than the graciousness of most of God's creatures, who have experienced that same grace.

BIBLICAL PROMISES

Finally, we must look at the area of the promises of the Bible. Often there is much confusion over this area, since many have had songs drummed into them from childhood with words like, "Every promise in the Book is mine." Taken literally, these words overlook the fact that the scope of some promises is not universal and that some promises also have conditions that accompany them. Some promises were made directly to certain individuals or groups and may be extended beyond those persons only when the general principles inherent in those texts provide for such extensions.

A general principle is not the same thing as a promise. A promise is based on what God said he would or would not do; a principle is based on who God is in his character and nature. Therefore, we must ask the following questions when it comes to establishing principles from God's promises: Can I discern from the context a particular person or group to whom this promise is distinctively offered? Does this promise bear any evidence of being offered for a certain time period or under certain set limits of times or conditions? Is this promise qualified in any way in the progress of revelation?

The promise that God would build a "house," or dynasty, out of King David (2 Sam. 7 and 1 Chron. 17) is certainly limited to the Davidic line and to the coming messianic rule and reign of God in his kingdom. There is clearly no warrant here for applying this promise to any physical house (or dynasty) today.

Likewise, other promises have explicit or implicit conditions attached to them. For example, 1 Peter 1:5 affirms that believers are "shielded by God's power," but it also expresses the condition of this happening "through faith." That is similar to Colossians 1:22–23, where we who were once alienated are now reconciled to God and presented as holy in his sight, without blemish and free of accusation—"*if* you continue in your faith, established and firm, not moved from the hope held out in the gospel." Believers are eternally secure, but there are some twenty warning passages in Scripture that must be placed alongside of these marvelous promises.

Especially difficult in this area of finding general principles in the promises of God are the proverbs of the Old Testament. One must be careful not to assume that just because a proverb sounds like a promise that it is one. Proverbs are, instead, Wisdom sayings that apply to situations generally, without listing the exceptions that must often qualify them. This limitation is particularly evident in the pair of proverbs in 26:4–5, which appear to contradict each other in offering the contrary advice "Do not answer a fool according to his folly" and "Answer a fool according to his folly." Likewise, the proverb on child rearing in Proverbs 22:6 is not an ironclad guarantee that if one abides by the rules established there that in every instance all will turn out well for the child. Many a person has come to grief by universalizing the proverbs into unconditional truths or into promises without qualifications. Accordingly, there are times when some have worked their land well, but their crops failed through no fault of their own, even though Proverbs 28:19 seemed to guarantee the opposite results. Therefore, we must be careful to discern just which statements of the Bible are promises and then we must be careful to establish whether they are directed exclusively to certain persons or conditioned by certain qualifications.

Conclusion

It is usually easier to propose theories than to implement them. In many ways, that is also true of books on Bible interpretation. Nevertheless, it is the practice, not the ability to state more theory, that makes perfect in this instance. There is no substitute for attention to detail and experience in more and more biblical texts.

The most important work needed in our day is for legitimate applications that do not go beyond what God has revealed in the principles in that Word. To press texts into our own personal service and for the answering of some immediate questions that we may have is to use the Bible much like the Greeks used the various oracles in their day. It is to play with the Bible as one would play with a tennis ball, lobbing it back and forth at will in the service of our own games.

The Bible is not just a book that is about peoples in the past, or even a book that is written to us; it is a book where we must become identified in a very personal way with the story in all its parts and in all its commands and promises. In doing so, however, we must be constantly on the lookout for the single truth-intention of the human author, who claimed to have stood in the council of God, and thereby must distinctly hear God's own voice for all generations to come.

Glossary

Allegorical interpretation. A method that looks for meanings in a text in addition to the historical (literal, plain) sense of the passage. The phrase is most often associated with Origen of Alexandria, who used Greek philosophical categories to discover these additional meanings.

Amanuensis. A scribe or secretary employed to copy a manuscript or to take dictation.

Apocalyptic literature. A type of writing (such as the book of Revelation or the last chapters of Daniel) that uses symbolism to predict the future, especially the end of the world.

Authorial intention. A phrase used in reference to the meaning intended by the original author of a text, in distinction from other possible meanings that readers may claim to discover in the text.

Chiasm. A literary technique that inverts the elements in two parallel phrases (see examples in chap. 5).

Contextualization. Often used as a synonym of *application* (in the field of missions, as a synonym of *indigenization*), this term refers to the process of understanding and explaining a text or a doctrine by taking into account the interpreter's own historical context (life situation). Although this process is proper and even inescapable, occasionally it seems to include altering the content of the gospel message to fit the modern context, and so the term has acquired a negative nuance in some conservative circles.

Criticism. The evaluation or scientific investigation of works of literature (and art). For many, this term, when applied to the Bible, implies the interpreter's independence from religious authority, including a denial of biblical infallibility. The phrase *higher criticism* refers to the study of the origins and composition of a text; because this approach has often (but not always) reflected a weak view of the authority and reliability of the Bible, the phrase has acquired a negative connotation in evangelical scholarship. The phrase *lower criticism,* which does not have such a negative connotation, is applied to such areas of study as linguistic investigation and textual criticism. The phrase *historical criticism* is roughly synonymous with the scientific approach to biblical study that flourished in the nineteenth century and continues to be used by mainstream scholarship; it often implies a skeptical attitude to the historical claims of Scripture.

Deism. A philosophical movement in the eighteenth century that emphasized morality and natural religion and that denied God's interference with the created world.

Demythologization. A method of interpretation (associated primarily with the name of Rudolf Bultmann) that views much of the Bible as containing primitive forms of thinking and that attempts to translate them into modern categories.

Didactic. Designed to teach. The term is often used in reference to biblical books (such as Proverbs, Ecclesiastes, and the New Testament Epistles) that have a strong instructional purpose.

Eschatology. The study of the last things. The adjective *eschatological* is often used to describe portions of Scripture that emphasize the theme of fulfillment. The phrase *realized* (or *inaugurated*) *eschatology* refers to the initial and partial fulfillment of events associated with the end of the world.

Etymology. The origin and historical development of words.

Exegesis. The analysis and explanation of a text, usually with reference to detailed, scientific ("critical") interpretation. The term is often distinguished from *hermeneutics* in that the latter refers to principles of interpretation, whereas *exegesis* has to do with the practice of explaining texts.

Existentialism. A modern philosophical movement that focuses on the individual's existence and plight in a world that cannot be understood. Some important theologians have sought to understand the Bible using the categories of existentialism.

Genre. A type of literary composition distinguished by such features as content or a specific form.

Grammatico-historical exegesis. A method of interpretation that emphasizes the need to take into account the original languages and the historical context of Scripture. Because the phrase is used in opposition to allegorical exegesis, it is roughly equivalent to literal interpretation.

Hermeneutics. The study of principles and methods of interpretation. The term is sometimes used to emphasize the present relevance of the text. (The form *hermeneutic* often refers to a specific theological perspective that may guide one's interpretation.) The phrase *general hermeneutics* refers to principles that are applicable to the interpretation of any text; *special hermeneutics* deals with issues that are distinctive to a particular text (or group of related texts).

Inclusion (also **inclusio**). A literary technique used to indicate the boundaries of a literary unit by beginning and ending it with the same or parallel terms.

Leitwort (German for "leading word"). A term or group of related terms that recurs in a given text, reflecting a prominent theme and thus aiding the interpreter to identify the text's meaning.

Metaphor. A figure of speech whereby a word uses an unexpressed comparison to indicate what it is similar to.

Metonymy. A figure of speech whereby a word is used in a sense other than, but associated with, its literal meaning.

Pericope. A selection from a book, especially a section chosen for liturgical reading. The term is used in biblical studies to indicate a discrete paragraph, especially in the Gospels, or a continuous section of the text on the same subject.

Proof-text. A verse or longer passage that is used to prove a point or a doctrine. Although this method is not objectionable in principle (assuming that it reflects careful exegesis), the term often implies an approach that isolates a passage from its context and thus functions arbitrarily.

Reader-response theory. An approach to the interpretation of texts that minimizes or even rejects authorial intention and emphasizes the role of the reader in discovering or constructing meaning.

Rhetoric. The study of principles of composition, especially the rules formulated in the ancient world for effective writing and speaking. The phrase *rhetorical criticism* refers to the modern study of literature in the light of such rules.

Sedes doctrinae (Latin for "a seat/chair of doctrine"). One of several large blocks of biblical text that give sustained presentations of specific doctrines.

Semantics. The study of meanings.

Sensus plenior (Latin for "fuller meaning"). The view that passages of Scripture contain a meaning (or meanings) intended by God, in addition to the historical meaning intended by the human author.

Structuralism. In linguistics, an approach that focuses on the character of language as a structured system (as opposed to the analysis of elements in isolation from one another). In the study of literature, a movement that focuses on recurring patterns of thought and behavior. (The term is also used in other disciplines, such as psychology and anthropology.)

Synecdoche. A figure of speech whereby the part is used for the whole, or vice versa.

Typological interpretation. Distinguished from allegorical interpretation, this approach affirms the historical meaning of the text but also notes that entities (people, objects, events) mentioned in the text prefigure subsequent and corresponding entities (for example, King David is viewed as a *type* of Christ).

[NOTE: This glossary does not include all technical literary terms, since most of them are defined in context and not used elsewhere.]

Annotated Bibliography

Many useful introductions to biblical interpretation have been published in the last
decade or so. One of the most successful is Gordon D. Fee and Douglas Stuart,
How to Read the Bible for All Its Worth: A Guide for Understanding the Bible, 2d
ed. (Grand Rapids: Zondervan, 1993), which uses a clear and interesting style
to help the Christian reader develop a method of Bible study. A work that was
especially popular during the 1950s and 1960s but can still be read with profit
is Bernard Ramm, *Protestant Biblical Interpretation,* 3d ed. (Grand Rapids:
Baker, 1970). For a valuable introduction that is not written from an
evangelical perspective, note Robert Morgan and John Barton, *Biblical
Interpretation* (New York: Oxford University Press, 1988).

Among more extensive works intended as textbooks for college or seminary, Milton S.
Terry, *Biblical Hermeneutics: A Treatise on the Interpretation of the Old and New
Testaments* (1885; reprint, Grand Rapids: Zondervan, 1974), served as a guide
for several generations of students; although it is now out of date, it contains a
gold mine of useful and interesting information. A generation ago, A. Berkeley
Mickelsen's *Interpreting the Bible* (Grand Rapids: Eerdmans, 1963) became a
widely used textbook. Most recently, two very detailed works aimed at
theological students have appeared: Grant R. Osborne, *The Hermeneutical
Spiral: A Comprehensive Introduction to Biblical Interpretation* (Downers Grove,
Ill.: InterVarsity, 1991), and William Klein et al., *Introduction to Biblical
Interpretation* (Dallas: Word, 1993). Either of these textbooks may be viewed
as essential reading for anyone who needs a thorough exposure to the whole
field of biblical hermeneutics. Two other recent additions are David S.
Dockery, *Biblical Interpretation Then and Now: Contemporary Hermeneutics in
the Light of the Early Church* (Grand Rapids: Baker, 1992), and Millard J.
Erickson, *Evangelical Interpretation: Perspectives on Hermeneutical Issues* (Grand
Rapids: Baker, 1993). More advanced and difficult, covering specialized
terrain, is Anthony C. Thiselton, *New Horizons in Hermeneutics: The Theory and
Practice of Transforming Biblical Reading* (Grand Rapids: Zondervan, 1992).

In addition, there are many books available that have a more specific focus. Readers
interested in developing a specific method that includes technical skills should
consider Douglas Stuart, *Old Testament Exegesis: A Primer for Students and
Pastors* (Philadelphia: Westminster, 1980), and Gordon D. Fee, *New Testament
Exegesis: A Handbook for Students and Pastors* (Philadelphia: Westminster,
1983). For a work that covers broader issues, note Walter C. Kaiser, Jr.,
Toward an Exegetical Theology: Biblical Principles for Preaching and Teaching
(Grand Rapids: Baker, 1981), in which he develops his "syntactical-theologi-
cal" method. Two books that focus on dangers to be avoided are D. A. Carson,
Exegetical Fallacies (Grand Rapids: Baker, 1984), and James W. Sire, *Scripture
Twisting: 20 Ways the Cults Misread the Bible* (Downers Grove, Ill.: InterVarsi-
ty, 1980).

The series Foundations of Contemporary Interpretation (Grand Rapids: Zondervan,
1987–94), which is aimed at beginning theological students and informed lay
Christians, focuses on interdisciplinary issues. The volumes include Moisés

Silva, *Has the Church Misread the Bible? The History of Interpretation in the Light of Current Issues* (vol. 1, 1987), which serves as an introduction to the series; Royce Gordon Gruenler, *Meaning and Understanding: The Philosophical Framework for Biblical Interpretation* (vol. 2, 1991); Tremper Longman III, *Literary Approaches to Biblical Interpretation* (vol. 3, 1987); Moisés Silva, *God, Language, and Scripture: Reading the Bible in the Light of General Linguistics* (vol. 4, 1990); V. Philips Long, *The Art of Biblical History* (vol. 5, 1994); Vern S. Poythress, *Science and Hermeneutics: Implications of Scientific Method for Biblical Interpretation* (vol. 6, 1988); and Richard A. Muller, *The Study of Theology: From Biblical Interpretation to Contemporary Formulation* (vol. 7, 1991).

Scripture Index

289

Name Index

Subject Index